The Community of Horodlo
(Horodło, Poland)

Translation of
Di Kehila Fon Horodlo

Original Book Edited by: Y. Ch. Zawidowitch, Former Residents of Horodlo in Israel

Originally published in Tel Aviv, 1966

JewishGen
מרכז עולמי לגנאלוגיה יהודית
The Global Home for Jewish Genealogy

A Publication of JewishGen
Edmond J. Safra Plaza, 36 Battery Place, New York, NY 10280
646.494.2972 | info@JewishGen.org | www.jewishgen.org

MUSEUM OF JEWISH HERITAGE
A LIVING MEMORIAL TO THE HOLOCAUST

The Community of Horodlo (Horodło, Poland)
Translation of *Di Kehila Fon Horodlo*

Copyright © 2025 by JewishGen. All rights reserved.
First Printing: January 2025, Tevet, 5785
Original Yizkor Book Edited By: Y. Ch. Zawidowitch, Former Residents of Horodlo in Israel
Project Coordinator: Susan and Shawn Dilles
Cover Design: Rachel Kolokoff Hopper
Layout and formatting: Jonathan Wind
Indexing: Laurence Broun

Library of Congress Control Number (LCCN): 2024947167

ISBN: 978-1-962054-11-9 (hard cover: 234 pages, alk. paper)

About JewishGen.org

JewishGen, is a Genealogical Research Division of the Museum of Jewish Heritage - A Living Memorial to the Holocaust, serves as the global home for Jewish genealogy.

Featuring unparalleled access to 30+ million records, it offers unique search tools, along with opportunities for researchers to connect with others who share similar interests. Award winning resources such as the Family Finder, Discussion Groups, and ViewMate, are relied upon by thousands each day.

In addition, JewishGen's extensive informational, educational and historical offerings, such as the Jewish Communities Database, Yizkor Book translations, InfoFiles, Family Tree of the Jewish People, and KehilaLinks, provide critical insights, first-hand accounts, and context about Jewish communal and familial life throughout the world.

Offered as a free resource, JewishGen.org has facilitated thousands of family connections and success stories, and is currently engaged in an intensive expansion effort that will bring many more records, tools, and resources to its collections.

Please visit https://www.jewishgen.org/ to learn more.

Vice President for JewishGen: Avraham Groll

About the JewishGen Yizkor Book Project

Yizkor Books (Memorial Books) were traditionally written to memorialize the names of departed family and martyrs during holiday services in the synagogue (a practice that still exists in many synagogues today).

Over the centuries, as a result of countless persecutions and horrific atrocities committed against the Jews, Yizkor Books (Sefer Zikaron in Hebrew) were expanded to include more historical information, such as biographical sketches of famous personalities and descriptions of daily town life.

Following the Holocaust, the idea of remembrance and learning took on an urgent and crucial importance. Survivors of the Holocaust sought out other surviving residents of their former towns to memorialize and document the names and way of life of those who were ruthlessly murdered by the Nazis. These remembrances were documented in Yizkor Books, hundreds of which were published in the first decades after the Holocaust.

Most of these books were published privately, or through *Landsmanshaftn* (social organizations comprised of members originating from the same European town or region) that still existed, and were often distributed free of charge. The languages used to document these crucial histories and links to our past were mostly Yiddish and Hebrew. JewishGen has undertaken the sacred responsibility of translating these books into English so that the culture and way of life of these communities will be preserved and transmitted to future generations.

In 1986, a group of farsighted JewishGenners started a project to pool their efforts together in groups based upon their ancestors' towns and donate funds to translate the Yizkor books of their ancestral towns into English. As the translated material became available, it was made accessible for free at https://www.JewishGen.org/Yizkor . Hardcover copies can be purchased by visiting https://www.jewishgen.org/Yizkor/ybip.html (see section below).

It is our hope that the translation of these books into English (and other languages) will assist the countless Jewish family researchers who are so desperately seeking to forge a connection with their heritage.

Director of JewishGen Yizkor Book Project: Lance Ackerfeld

About JewishGen Press

JewishGen Press (formerly the Yizkor Books-in-Print Project) is the publishing division of JewishGen.org, and provides a venue for the publication of non-fiction books pertaining to Jewish genealogy, history, culture, and heritage.

In addition to the Yizkor Book category, publications in the Other Non-Fiction category include Shoah memoirs and research, genealogical research, collections of genealogical and historical materials, biographies, diaries and letters, studies of Jewish experience and cultural life in the past, academic theses, and other books of interest to the Jewish community.

Please visit https://www.jewishgen.org/Yizkor/ybip.html to learn more.

Director of JewishGen Press: Joel Alpert
Managing Editor - Jessica Feinstein
Publications Manager - Susan Rosin

Notes to the Reader

The images in the original book were reproduced from photographs from the time of the first edition. These reproductions were already of poor quality, most being pre-war and others at least 60 or more years old. As a result, the images in the book are the best achievable.
A reader can view the original scans of the book on the websites listed below.

The original book can be seen online at the Yiddish Book Center website:

https://www.yiddishbookcenter.org/collections/yizkor-books/yzk-nybc314189/zavidovits-yosef-hayim-di-kehileh-fun-horodla-yizker-bukh-nokh-di-kdoyshim-fun-horodla

OR

at the New York Public Library Digital Collections website:

https://digitalcollections.nypl.org/items/76e863e0-9ad5-0134-e692-00505686a51c

To obtain a list of Shoah victims from **Horodlo (Horodło, Poland),** the reader should access the Yad Vashem web site listed below; one can also search for specific family names using family name option. These lists are continually updated by Yad Vashem, so it is worthwhile to periodically search them.

There is more valuable information (including the Pages of Testimony, etc.) available on this website: https://yvng.yadvashem.org/

A list of all books available from JewishGen Press along with prices is available at: https://www.jewishgen.org/Yizkor/ybip.html

Cover Photo Credits

Cover Design by: Rachel Kolokoff Hopper

Front and Back Cover:

Horodlo, illustrations by Rachel Kolokoff Hopper

Back Cover Photos:

>   Top Left: *Kalmen Nayman and his family,* [Page 261]
>   Top Right: *Miriam Stav (Moshe Stav's wife) and her son*, [Page 89]
>   Bottom Right: *Shloyme Blat and his family,* [Page 170]

Poem on Back Cover:

>   *Remember the Devastation of the Jews*, by Dr. M. Dvorzhetsky

Geopolitical Information

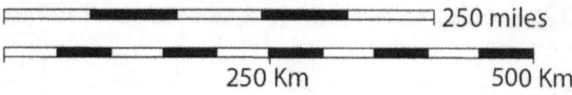

Map of Poland showing the location of **Horodło**

Horodło

Horodło, Poland is located at 50°53' N 24°02' E and 161 miles SE of Warszawa

	Town	District	Province	Country
Before WWI (c. 1900):	Horodło	Hrubieszów	Lublin	Russian Empire
Between the wars (c. 1930):	Horodło	Hrubieszów	Lublin	Poland
After WWII (c. 1950):	Horodło			Poland
Today (c. 2000):	Horodło			Poland

Alternate Names for the Town:
Horodło [Pol], Horodlo [Yid], Khorodlo [Rus], Gorodlo, Horodle

Nearby Jewish Communities:

Ustyluh, Ukraine 5 miles ESE
Hrubieszów 8 miles SW
Skryhiczyn 10 miles NNW
Dubienka 13 miles NNW
Volodymyr Volynskyy, Ukraine 13 miles E
Kryłów 14 miles S
Uchanie 17 miles W
Grabowiec 21 miles W
Wojsławice 21 miles W
Dolsk, Ukraine 22 miles NE
Tyszowce 23 miles SW
Lyuboml, Ukraine 24 miles N
Sielec 25 miles WNW

Varyazh, Ukraine 26 miles S
Turiysk, Ukraine 26 miles NE
Pavlivka, Ukraine 26 miles SE
Świerże 26 miles NNW
Lukov, Ukraine 26 miles NNE
Łaszczów 28 miles SSW
Milyanovichi, Ukraine 28 miles NE
Lokachi, Ukraine 29 miles ESE
Chełm 29 miles NW
Skierbieszów 29 miles W
Kraśniczyn 29 miles W
Sokal, Ukraine 30 miles SSE
Ozyutichi, Ukraine 30 miles E

JewishPoulation in 1900: 717

Project Coordinator Introduction

Why Horodlo?

It is our hope that this translation will help keep the memory of Jewish life in Horodlo alive, and perhaps it will add some context to your own family history.

I first heard of Horodlo almost 50 years ago as a young child listening to stories my mother's parents told us about their home back in the "old country". Both were born in the nearby town of Hrubieszow and they were fortunate to have come to America by 1920. My grandfather, Charles Pachter z"l immigrated to America with his parents and younger sister. My grandmother Celia Schneider Pachter z"l, the youngest of 9 children, came with her mother and 5 of the siblings. A few other relatives made it to Mexico and Israel, but many remained and perished during the Shoah. In 1987 I interviewed Celia and Charlie as part of an oral history project. Looking back, I wish we had taken more time to learn about their childhood and life in the Hrubieszow area.

We learned about the JewishGen Yizkor Book translation project in 2019, and jumped at the opportunity to support the effort. In 2020 we volunteered to coordinate translation of the Hrubieszow book. It was amazing to see the translators unlock the previously inaccessible chapters one by one. Each new chapter that was translated helped fill gaps in our family history and provided rich context about the people living in the area and the types of lives they led.

The Hrubieszow book provided an account of the many flavors of Jewish life in the area, and we decided to explore more by translating books from adjacent towns. A Yizkor Book had already been translated for the town of Ustilug, located about 15 miles north east of Hrubieszow on the Ukrainian side of the River Bug. In between Hrubieszow and Ustilug is the town of Horodlo, on the Polish side of the River Bug.

We started the Horodlo Yizkor Book project in 2023 and completed it in 2024. Although the town is a fraction of the size of Hrubieszow, the variety and intensity of Jewish communal and organizational life described there is remarkable. Several individuals make appearances in both the Horodlo and Hrubieszow books, and they also depict some of the same events from different perspectives as they unfold across the area.

The overlapping historical accounts show the value of taking a regional approach to translating Yizkor Books. As a result, we are now working toward translating Yizkor Books for the towns of Krasnystaw (NW of Horodlo), Dubienka (North of Horodlo), and Grabowiec (west of Horodlo between Hrubieszow and Zamosc). Our goal is to translate the Yizkor Books covering the region located south of Chelm and east of Zamosc to the River Bug, which forms the border between Poland and current day Ukraine. A Yizkor book from Chelm has already been translated through JewishGen.

Serving as the translation project coordinator has been rewarding beyond description. We expected to learn about the history and culture of the town, and about the lives and fates of many of its residents. We also hoped to learn new information about relatives that may have been mentioned in the book, and we were not disappointed. A few of the articles were even written by relatives, and others are mentioned in various accounts. These invaluable accounts have enriched our knowledge of our family, and their good deeds are an inspiration.

The translation projects have also brought us into contact with distant relatives and other descendants of town residents, each with their own remarkable stories. Along the way we discovered and joined groups of landsmen from the area that connect online, who have provided support and much appreciated encouragement throughout this project.

We conclude by quoting Max Fire who wrote "I bless the hands of those who, in poring over this book, are honoring the memory of those that we lost."

Susan and Shawn Dilles
January 2025

Acknowledgments

It has been a privilege to help unlock the story of Horodlo for new generations of readers. This project was made possible by JewishGen, an organization dedicated to (among other aims) translating more than 800 Yizkor Books from their native languages into English, and making the translations widely available over the internet and through print on demand editions like this one.

We thank Mr. Avraham Groll for his strategic vision, dedication, and oversight of the organization. Mr. Lance Ackerfeld provided expert support and advice for the entire translation effort. His professionalism and extraordinary patience is praiseworthy. We also thank Mr. Joel Alpert, director of JewishGen Press. Joel provided important guidance early in the project that saved significant effort later.

We owe the translation itself to Yael Chaver, who also translated the bulk of the Hrubieszow book, the entire Horodlo book, and is currently nearing completion of the Krasnystaw book. Yael is a uniquely skilled, exceptionally erudite and professional translator. Time and again we were impressed by the research she conducted to clarify obscure words, acronyms, and organization names. Yael 'rescued' the meaning of many words and idiomatic phrases, which may otherwise have been lost.

The JewishGen Press dedicated and hard-working team turned the JewishGen online version of the translation into the book you are holding. The team, led by Susan Rosin includes a graphic artist (to design the cover), layout and formatting specialist, an indexer, a photo extractor, a Library of Congress coordinator, a social media specialist and a publicity volunteer. They made the entire process seamless. We just had to review the text a final time.

Finally, we would like to extend our heartfelt appreciation to all of the volunteers that work behind the scenes at JewishGen to help preserve Jewish family history and heritage for future generations.

We were fortunate to have this entire motivated team helping make this translation possible. Their task included working on articles written by different authors with different writing styles and different levels of writing proficiency. As a result, readers may notice these natural stylistic differences.

Translation work is ongoing with dozens of other Yizkor books, and readers may support these ongoing efforts by contributing to the JewishGen general Yizkor Book fund or directly toward specific translation projects.

Susan and Shawn Dilles
January 2025

Dedication

This translation is dedicated to Selma Pachter Saltz (z''l) and Melvin Saltz (z''l), who instilled in us the importance of family and community.

Table of Contents

The Community of Horodlo
(Horodło, Poland)

50°53' / 24°02'

Translation of
Di Kehila Fon Horodlo

Editors: Y. Ch. Zawidowitch, Former Residents of Horodlo in Israel

Published in Tel Aviv, 1966

Acknowledgments:

Project Coordinator

Susan and Shawn Dilles

Our sincere appreciation to Yad Vashem
for the submission of the necrology for placement on the JewishGen web site.

This is a translation of: *Di Kehila Fon Horodlo* (The community of Horodlo), Editors: Y. Ch. Zawidowitch, Former Residents of Horodlo in Israel, Tel Aviv 1963 (Yiddish)

Note: The original book can be seen online at the NY Public Library site:

Horodlo (1966)

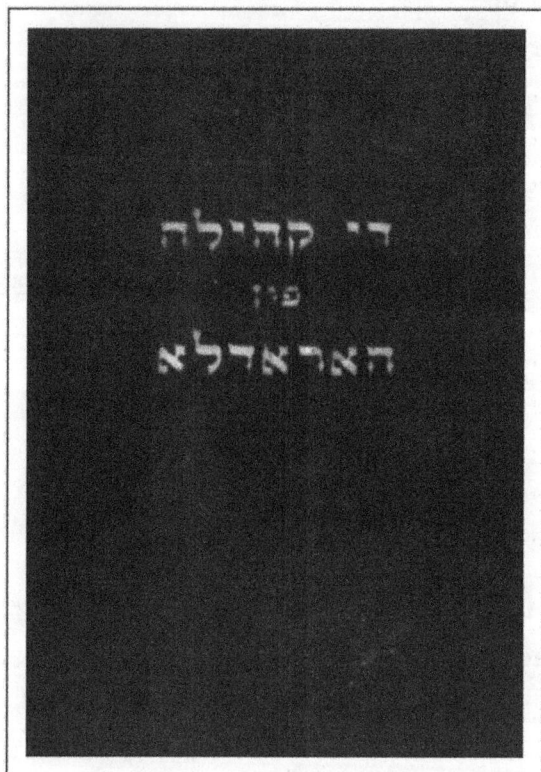

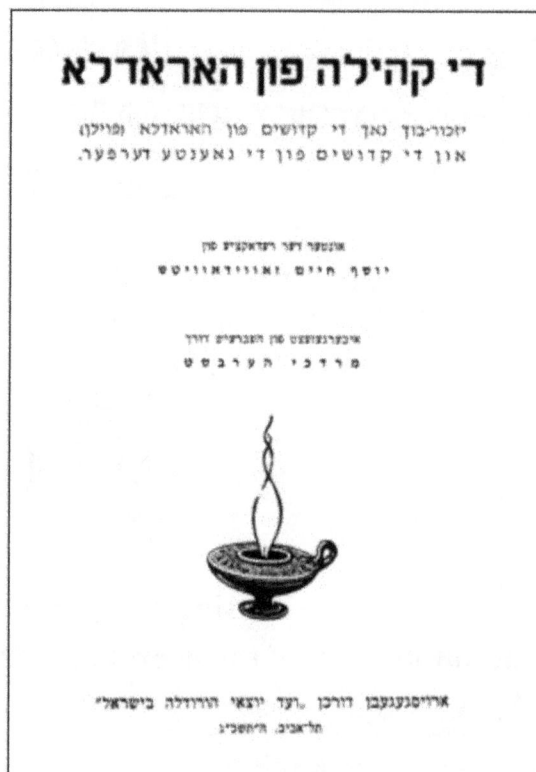

די קהילה פון האראדלא

די קהילה פון האראדלא

יזכור־בוך נאך די קדושים פון האראדלא (פוילן)
און די קדושים פון די נאענטע דערפער.

אונטער דער רעדאקציע פון
יוסף חיים זאוווידאוויטש

איבערגעזעצט פון העברעית דורך
מרדכי העלבֿשט

אַרויסגעגעבן דורכן „וועד יוצאי הורודלה בישראל"
תל־אבֿיב, ה'תשכ"ג

Translations by Yael Chaver except where noted otherwise.

[Page 1]

The Jewish Community of Horodlo

Yizkor Book for the Martyrs of Horodlo (Poland) and the Martyrs of the Nearby Villages[1]

Edited by Yoysef Khayim Zavidovich
Translated from Hebrew by Mordkhe Herbst

Published by the Committee of Horodlo Survivors in Israel
Tel Aviv, 1963

[Page 2]

Ha-Po'el Ha-Mizrachi Printers, Tel-Aviv

[Pages 3-4]

[Page 5]

Introduction

[Page 6]

[Blank]

[Page7]

A Word From the Publishers

After much work and efforts invested in collecting these materials and preparing them for publication, we present to all natives of Horodlo – wherever they may be – and anyone who is interested, this **Yizkor Book of the Jewish Community of Horodlo**, which was annihilated by the German Nazis (may their names be blotted out), together with all the Jews of Poland, during the great devastation of World War Two in Europe.

The Committee of Horodlo Natives, the Horodlo Association in the U.S., and the Horodlo Aid Association of Argentina resolved to publish this book, in order to erect an eternal monument to the martyrs of Horodlo who perished at the hands of the German murderers and their allies, those anonymous victims whose gravesites and the location of whose sacred bones are unknown.

It has been more than five years since we published our first letter to fellow natives of Horodlo, announcing our intention to publish a Yizkor Book and asking them to provide articles, memoirs, and images of the martyrs of Horodlo, as well as any other materials connected with the town. Materials slowly arrived, punctuated by long gaps. We adapted them and prepared them for publication.

No written documentation of the lives of the Jews of Horodlo has survived the devastation. We therefore had to make do with the memoirs and accounts written by Horodlo natives, long after they had left the town and even longer after the events described took place.

[Page 8]

This is also the case with the witness statements of the refugees from Horodlo and vicinity, who experienced the bitterness of war and were miraculously saved from the gruesome fate of the Horodlo community, while suffering unimaginable pain and torment in their hiding places. Their descriptions were also provided and written years after the great tragedy. Understandably, therefore, the writers and narrators could not avoid errors in dates and other technical details. The editorial committee decided to print their accounts as given, aware that these errors do not affect the actual facts and tragic events.

The editorial committee encountered great difficulties when compiling the list of martyrs. As there is no official and precise list of martyrs, and the list provided in this book was first provided by Ben-Tsiyon Bergman of Argentina, and checked by Horodlo survivors living in Israel and the United States; changes and corrections were introduced. Naturally, the committee took these into account, but was unable to decide cases of inconsistencies between the original writer and later revisers. The corrections made by the U.S. association were done after consulting a number of other people.

The editorial committee thanks all those who considered it their sacred duty to share in the creation of this memorial to the martyrs of Horodlo, and offered articles, photos, documents, and oral recollections. All this enabled the publication of this Yizkor Book.

The committee also wishes to thank the association in the U.S. for its significant contribution of important material and images, as well as for its financial help in covering a large part of the publication expenses.

[Page 9]

The Committee would also like to express its thanks to the Horodlo mutual aid society in Argentina for collecting materials, setting down recollections, and compiling the list of martyrs.

At this time, we wish to emphasize that we cannot claim the finished product to be accurate and free of errors. We have done our best to minimize the number of omissions and errors due to the conditions under which we worked: the lack of time, and the geographical distances. We have made efforts to provide an illustration of the way of life of this community, which suffered so greatly and was decimated by the ruthless hand of the bloodthirsty enemy.

Let this book be an eternal memorial and witness to the Jewish community of Horodlo!

Editorial Committee

Yoysef-Khayim Zavidovich
Yisro'el Barg
Shmu'el Froynd
Moyshe Zakai
Henekh Berman (U.S.A.)
Arn Flach
Avrom Kulish
Eliezer Shmidt
Ben-Tsiyon Bergman (Argentina)

June 1959, Israel

Translator's Footnote:

1. The Hebrew yizkor means "remember" and is the traditional term for commemorative books produced in Europe, used since at least the 13th century, to commemorate Jewish victims of persecution, and throughout the Middle Ages. After the devastation of 1933-1945, when six million Jews were killed by Nazi Germany and its collaborators, the genre re-emerged to commemorate the lives and communities lost. This translation uses the Hebrew term in transliteration.

[Page 10]

Blank

[Page11]

May Their Memory Live Forever
by Yosef Khayim Zavidovich

In recent years, a strange and gruesome literature has developed among Jews – the spiritually rich "People of the Book." This distressing, dark literature recounts the fate of millions of Jews – men, women, and children – who were cruelly annihilated during the years of World War II by savage, vile murderers produced by the German people, and whose bodies were turned to ash in the crematoria built by the same murderers. This literature describes sacred communities in the countries of Europe, which were uprooted from their homes and exterminated by the German foe.

This dreadful destruction did not spare the Jewish community of Horodlo (a small Polish town in the Hrubieszow region), located on the banks of the Bug river. For many generations, the Jews there lived a distinctive life, until they were annihilated (along with their brethren, the Jews of the nearby villages of Strzyzow, Kowel, and Kapilow) by the horrible enemy, for no fault or reason.[1]

The decent, innocent Jews of Horodlo! Why was their blood spilled in the streets? Blameless children of Horodlo! Schoolchildren and babies in cradles, why were you led like sheep to the slaughter by the flesh-eating monsters? Why were you taken to your destruction without pity, like lambs to the wolves?

Where are you, the community of Horodlo? Where are you, precious Jews of Horodlo? Where is your gifted rabbi, and the righteous ritual slaughterers? Where is your beautiful synagogue? Where are your houses of prayer?

Woe unto you, blind and deaf humanity! How could you stand and watch the destruction of the Jewish people!

[Page 12]

* * *

These pages are dedicated to you, the holy Jews of Horodlo, you holy community of Horodlo, a link in the great chain of millions of Polish Jews. They are written by Jews of Horodlo who are scattered all over the world. May they serve as a monument and eternal memorial to our dear martyrs, who were cut down by the Nazi killers! May they be an eternal flame honoring the holy martyrs of Horodlo!

Translator's Footnote:

1. I was unable to identify Kapilow.

[Page 13]

Eulogies and Appreciations

[Page 14]

Remember the National Catastrophe![1]

by Dr. M. Dvorzhetsky

Remember the catastrophe of the nation; remember the loss and the resistance, keep the memory for generations to come.

Let that memory be with you always, when you sit at home and when you walk along the road, when you lie down and when you arise.[2]

And you shall betroth yourself forever to the memory of brothers who are no more. And the memory shall become part of your flesh and your blood and your bones.

Gnash your teeth and remember; when you eat your bread, remember; when you drink your water, remember; when you hear music, remember; when the sun rises, remember; when night falls, remember; on holidays and at celebrations, remember.

When you build a house, leave a break in the wall, as a constant reminder of the destruction of the Jewish people.

When you plow a field, set up a pile of stones as a monument to those of your brethren who have not been buried in a Jewish cemetery.[3]

When you accompany your children to the marriage ceremony, let the memory of those children who will never be married be uppermost in your mind in the midst of your joy.

Let them be as one: the living and the dead, the fallen and the survivor, those who are gone and those who remain.

Hearken, people of Israel, to the voice that cries out to you from the depths; Do not remain silent, do not remain silent.

Translator's Footnotes:

1. This page is translated from the Hebrew, which is written in a biblical prophetic tone.

2. The latter part of the sentence is copied verbatim from Deuteronomy 6:7.

3. In the Bible, setting up a pile of stones is an act of commemorating an event or a person.

[Page 15]

Remember the Devastation of the Jews...[1]

by Dr. M. Dvorzhetsky

Remember the catastrophe that befell our people, remember the struggle and the revolt, and learn from them.

Let this memory be your constant companion, when you walk along the road, when you lie down and when you wake up.

Let the memory of the catastrophe be your bread and your salt, let it permeate you, your blood, your flesh, and your bones.

When you build a house, leave a break in a wall, so that you may always notice the destruction of the Jewish people.

When you plow a field, set up a pile of stones as a witness and a monument to those of your brethren who have not been buried in a Jewish cemetery.

When you accompany your child to the marriage ceremony, let the memory be uppermost in your mind of those children who will never be married, and will never even have anyone to say Kaddish for them.[2]

Let them be as one: the living and the dead, the fallen and the survivor, those who are gone and the remnant of the people of Israel.

Hearken, people of Israel, to the voice that cries out to you: do not remain silent! Do not forget!

Translator's Footnotes:

1. This Yiddish version of the text is more conversational.

2. The Kaddish prayer for the dead is usually said by a relative. This sentence implies that no relatives survived the devastation.

[Page 16]

[Blank]

[Page 17]

Remember What Was Done to Us!

by Rabbi Khayim HaLevy Berman, United States

Remember what Amalek did to you![1] Let us remember what Hitler (may his name be blotted out) did to us!

Our sacred Torah commands us not to forget, because it is human nature to forget; it is possible to forget even the savagery and the terrible slaughter perpetrated on the Jewish people in Poland and other European countries by the German murderers. The slaughtered included our mothers and fathers, our brothers and sisters, without respecting the weak and the ill, or even the children.

Our Torah commands us: "Write this for a memorial in a book"… because a book reminds us and prevents forgetfulness.[2]

Let us never forget, down all the future generations, that which the German Amalekites did to us!

Let us not be swayed by the friendship and goodwill that the Germans exhibit. Historical experience teaches us to remember, and never to forget.

The Jewish people have always written down their troubles and misfortunes. The prophet Jeremiah wrote the Book of Lamentations as a reminder of the great national disaster that was the destruction of the Temple.[3]

The Lament for the two holy communities of Mainz and Worms (which is included in the Lamentations said on the Ninth of Av) mourns: "Oh that my head were waters, and mine eyes a fountain of tears, that I might weep day and night."[4]

We commemorate the martyrs who died for their faith in 1096 - 1145 by chanting the Av ha-Rachamim prayer every Saturday before the afternoon service.[5]

[Page 18]

Rabbi Nosn Note Hannover (may his righteous memory be for a blessing) commemorated Jewish bravery, and the martyrs who were killed for their faith, in his book *Yeven Metsulah*.[6] Rabbi Shabtai HaKohen (author of *Siftei Kohen*, may his righteous memory be for a blessing and protect us), set down the sufferings of the Jews during the Khmel'nyts'kyi rebellion against Polish rule led by Bohdan Khmel'nyts'kyi in his *Megillah Afah*: the hideous murders and pogroms in the Jewish communities that were widespread during this period.[7]

Every period in our history has its notable events. The great devastation of our time must be written down, and must be memorialized.

"Write this for a memorial in a book." Natives of Horodlo in Israel, the United States, Canada, Argentina, and everywhere, let us remember the Horodlo community and its martyrs. Let us inscribe their names in a Yizkor book. Let us preserve for eternity their martyr's path, their suffering and terrible deaths in the gas chambers that the German barbarians established, as well as the other dreadful deaths that they underwent, along with the six million Jews, their brothers and sisters, who were cut down during the devastation of Europe.

Woe is us! The survivors are robbed and broken! Thus wails the mourner during the lamentations of the Ninth of Av. We do not even know the date when our martyrs were murdered, or their memorial day, or the locations of their graves.

May this Yizkor book serve as a monument to the Horodlo community, and forever preserve the sacred memory of the Horodlo martyrs, may God avenge their blood!

How desolate and forlorn lies the city of Horodlo![8] Where are the dearly beloved children; our parents; our brothers and sisters; our relatives and friends; the beloved, precious ones? Where is the rabbi who headed the rabbinical court of Horodlo, the old righteous rabbi, one of the greatest Hasids of Radzyn, the author of important books, our teacher and Rabbi Moshe Yehuda Leyb HaLevy (may his righteous memory be a blessing for the world to come! may God avenge his blood)? Where is his wife, my mother, the modest, righteous woman

[Page 19]

of great lineage, whose hand was always outstretched to the needy, the God-fearing Mrs. Rivka (may she rest in peace; may God avenge her blood), the grandchild of the renowned rabbi and righteous man, the leader of Kobrin Hasidism (may his righteous memory be a blessing for the world to come)?[9]

And where are the ritual slaughterers of our town, the righteous men who carried out their sacred function with complete faith? The martyred, innocent, honest Yankev Tshesner; and the other, who was like him, the martyred Mordekhai HaKohen Faygenboym, lesser in age but not in knowledge? May their memory be for a blessing, and may God avenge their blood.

Where are all the pious, innocent Hasids, religious students, and keepers of the commandments?! Where are the ordinary people and all the simple Jews, who were important in our town?! All were killed, and are gone from this world. May the bright memory of the Horodlo martyrs shine forever! We pray to the Almighty to grant rest under the wings of the Shechina to all the Jewish martyrs of Horodlo, along with the other martyrs; and all those who were killed, incinerated, drowned, and hunted down, the babies at their mothers' breasts. May they rest in the Garden of Eden; blessed is God, who restores the deceased to life and will add their souls to the bundle of life!

May the murderous nation be sentenced to eternal shame and disgrace! May the German Nazi people be cursed among the nations, and eternally mocked! May the land that absorbed the blood of our nearest and dearest be cursed above all lands! Woe to the nations with merciless hearts who knew very well what was happening to us, and were silent, when they could have saved tens and hundreds of thousands of lives – and did nothing. Moreover, they closed their doors to the numerous refugees who had barely managed to save themselves. Woe to anyone who did not support these refugees who confronted their exterminators! Woe to you, humanity, for being stubbornly silent and cruelly passive, and thus becoming a partner of the German Nazi Amalek, may his name be blotted out!

Woe to you, hard-hearted humanity, for looking on

[Page 20]

with arms folded as our nation was being annihilated.[10] You are no better than they! The God of vengeance will avenge the blood of His children, that was shed without cause!

* * *

"Comfort ye, comfort ye, my people" quoted the great Jew, the Chief Rabbi of the Land of Israel, the great scholar and righteous Avrom Yitzkhak HaKohen Kook (may his righteous memory be a blessing for the world to come), in a letter he wrote to an elderly member of the Jewish community in the holy city of Jaffa, after the events of 1921, when the blood of our brothers and sisters was shed in our holy land by cursed pogromists.[11] He ends his letter of the 7th day of Iyar, 5681, thus:[12] "Thank God, no Jews in the Land of Israel or elsewhere will be discouraged by this band of vile murderers. Our holy heroes have revived the sacred spirit of the nation, through the blood that they shed. May we soon have the merit of witnessing God's help to his people and his land, and revenge on his enemies. May the nation of Israel succeed soon, in our lifetime. Amen."

The writer of the foregoing passage, who signs with his tears, is Rabbi Khayim HaLevy Berman, a native of Horodlo, the son of the martyred Rabbi of Horodlo. I headed the rabbinical court of Sienkiewiczóka, Łuck region, Poland; and now am living in Monroe, New York.

Translator's Footnotes:

1. Amalek is a nation described in the Hebrew Bible as an age-old enemy of the Israelites, beginning in Exodus. The injunction to remember Amalek's deeds is biblical (Deuteronomy 25:17).

2. The quote is from Exodus 17:14.

3. The reference is to the First Temple, destroyed by the Babylonians in 586 BCE.

4. This lament treats the annihilation of the Jewish communities of Speyer, Mainz and Worms (Germany) among the larger communities that were destroyed at the very beginning of the Crusades, in 1096. The text is from Jeremiah, 9. Similar prayers have been incorporated in Jewish mourning rituals.

5. These were the years of the First Crusade and the massacres of Jews that accompanied it. The memorial prayer "Av ha-Rachamim" was written in the late eleventh or early twelfth century, after the destruction of the Ashkenazi communities around the Rhine River by Christian crusaders during the First Crusade.

6. Hannover (d. 1683) chronicled the Khmel'nyts'kyi uprising in Ukraine (1648), which was accompanied by widespread massacres of Jews. In Venice in 1653, he published a Hebrew chronicle, titled *Yeven metsulah* (Deep Swamp), that describes the sufferings of the Jews in the first years of that rebellion.

7. Shabtai HaKohen (1621–1662) was a noted scholar, known for his work Siftey Kohen (Lips of a Priest), a commentary on the *Shulchan Aruch* -- the most widely consulted of the various legal codes in Judaism (written by Yosef Karo in 1563. HaKohen's *Megillah Afah* (Flying Scroll)

8. Quoted from Lamentations 1:1.

9. This eulogy incorporates a phrase from the biblical Proverbs, 31:20: "She stretched out her hand to the needy."

10. The phrase "And you stand there looking on with folded arms" is from a well-known poem by the Yiddish poet Mordechai Gebirtig (1877-1942) that commemorated prewar pogroms in Poland and was sung (to music by Gebirtig) as a song of defiance during the Holocaust.

11. Rabbi Kook (1865-1935) was the first Ashkenazi Chief Rabbi of British Mandatory Palestine, a Zionist who is considered one of the great Jewish thinkers of the 20th century. The letter mentioned begins with a quote from Isaiah 40:1. The events in May 1921 were a series of violent riots that began in Jaffa and spread to other parts of the country, resulting in fatalities and injuries; the majority of the casualties were Jews.

12. Original note: The letter was printed in *Machanayim*, the Israel Defense Army's religious weekly, No. 41, Vol. 4, on 3 Elul 1957, in the tenth year of Israel's existence. [The Gregorian date was May 17, 1921.]

[Page 21]

A Yizkor Book

by Henekh Berman, United States

The historical fate that accompanies the Jewish people in exile – that of wandering – did not skip our town, Horodlo. Many Jews of the town took up their walking-sticks many years before the emergence of the Nazi beast in Germany and in the other European countries. Hoping for a brighter future, they traveled to the distant parts of America, Canada, Brazil, and other South American countries. Among the wanderers were those who had had enough of life in the exile of Poland and other countries, and preferred to go to the Land of Israel, our fatherland, and join the ranks of its builders and defenders. Thanks to them, there survives a remnant of the Horodlo community that was destroyed in the devastation of Europe. The small contingent that remains can, and must, establish a monument, in the form of these memorial pages, to the martyrs of the Horodlo community, our parents, brothers, and sisters, who were cruelly murdered together with the rest of the six million Jews by the German murderers (may their name and memory be blotted out) during World War Two.

These martyrs, whose bodies were burned in the crematoria of Auschwitz, Treblinka, Sobibor and other death camps, do not even have grave markers. No monuments have been set up over their final resting place. Their sacred ashes alone have been scattered over the soil of Poland and Germany, like dung over the field.

But, if no stone monument has as yet been erected, we must set up another type of monument, a spiritual one, in the form

[Page 22]

of commemorative pages and Yizkor books, which will recount for the ages the actions of the German murderers towards the Jewish people, and how millions of innocent, precious Jews were exterminated. These Yizkor books will detail the humble lives of these Jews and their customs every day as well as on holidays; the mundane and spiritual lives of this large and well-established Jewish population, which was obliterated so savagely.

Among the Yizkor books commemorating the Jewish communities, books written by survivors of cities and towns in Poland, Lithuania, Czechoslovakia, and other countries, the Horodlo Yizkor book will take its honored position. It will serve as a monument to our dear ones, the pure, innocent martyrs who were unjustly murdered by the barbaric Germans and their helpers, may their names be blotted out, in such a cruel, horrific manner.

[Page 23]

An Eternal Monument

by Shaul Kupershtok, United States

This Yizkor book has been composed and edited thanks to the initiative of community leaders in Israel, the United States, and Argentina, in order to commemorate the Horodlo community. It will become part of the tragic literature of the devastation, and will join the shelves of Yizkor books for the Jewish communities of Poland, Lithuania, Latvia, and other European lands – all of which were murdered by the German enemies and their allies.

Although the Horodlo Yizkor book may not attain the scope of the Yizkor books devoted to other, larger towns, it is nonetheless dear to us, as beloved as the Horodlo community itself. This small town enjoyed the advantage of being beloved and cherished by its residents, who knew each other, and were like one large family.

I remember the friendly relations and brotherly feelings in Horodlo. If someone celebrated a joyous occasion, all the Jews of the town joined in. If the reverse happened and someone suffered a misfortune – may God preserve us! – all the residents commiserated.

The kindness of the Horodlo residents and their mutual brotherly feelings were renowned; to this day, natives of Horodlo all over the world continue this attitude.

I remember my father, Leybish (may his memory be for a blessing), who died on July 10, 1951, who would devote days and weeks to the collection of Mo'es Khitin for the needy of Horodlo. He carried out this good deed

[Page 24]

for many years, even when he grew old. Though he was becoming weaker, he would make efforts to locate the poor of Horodlo and hand them the contributions.

The tragic events and the great devastation completely changed the Jewish map. The Horodlo community was obliterated, and the few who remained were scattered throughout the world. It is incumbent upon us to erect a monument to our dear Horodlo community. At the call to publish a Yizkor book, we, a few town natives in the United States, gathered: Henekh Berman, Rabbi Khayim Berman, Moyshe Biderman, Ester and Yankev Tish, Getsl Zis, Yisro'el Fuks, Arn Fuks, and the writer of this contribution. We decided to help accomplish the goal of the initiative, with written materials, pictures and documents, and financial aid. May this Yizkor book serve as an eternal monument to the martyrs of Horodlo, whose blood was shed by the barbarians!

[Page 25]

Kaddish for Our Home Town

by Mordkhe Herbst

A yortsayt candle, in whose flame the souls of the cruelly murdered martyrs flicker, is lit every 19th of Elul in the homes of Horodlo natives worldwide, natives whose souls are enveloped in mourning and sorrow.[1] These lives were not allowed to run their natural course but were extinguished in a storm of blood. The flames of these memorial candles evoke memories and images of the small Jewish town, so dear to us because of its way of life and the recent deaths of our nearest and dearest in it.

* * *

Horodlo was small, but it constituted a world of its own, a Jewish country in miniature. It was one of the Jewish towns in Poland where Jews lived a full Jewish life: the air, the river, the market – all were steeped in Jewishness. The charming, unaffected sound of Torah study could be heard from the kheyders. Scholarship sounded from the houses of study, the brilliance of the rabbi was evident, and the virtuous ritual slaughterers were enveloped in piety. Young people avid for knowledge read the books in the library, and sang in the Zionist organizations. A dream-like shine illuminated the members of the drama club, and those about to emigrate to the Land of Israel glowed with anticipation.

The sound of prayer resounded on Shabbat and weekdays alike from the

[Page 26]

house of study and the artisans' synagogue, and was transformed into ecstasy in the small synagogues of the Radzyn and Turisk Hasidim. Hasidic melodies were borne from one synagogue to the next, filling the air with the Jewish faith that nourished the community.

Shabbat, after a week of hard work, spread feelings of contentment and pleasure through Jews in shining coats and well-kept beards, modest little girls with newly washed braids, and charming boys in caps.

* * *

Now the town lies buried in two mass graves of people whose lives were cut short, and whose Torah study was choked off…

Here is where prayers are directed from all parts of the world, wherever Horodlo natives are found; pain-laden prayers shattered by sobs. Prayers resounding through the grass covering the graves: "Yisgadal ve-Yiskadash…"[2]

[Page 27]

[3] [4] The memorial monument established in 1957, in the Chamber of the Holocaust on Mount Zion, Jerusalem

[Page 28]

In Commemoration of the Horodlo Jewish Community
(Hrubieszow county, Poland)

May God remember
The Horodlo community
And its Jews; may He avenge the blood
Of our dear brothers and sisters
Who were murdered together with their Rabbi and leader
Author of *Tiferet-Banim* and *Khok Moshe*.
By the Germans and their accomplices, may their names be blotted out, during the destruction
Of the Jews of Europe during World War II.
Their dear, sacred memory will be with us
Forever.

The Horodlo natives in Israel and abroad.

Translator's Footnotes:

1. A memorial candle that burns for 24 hours is lit on the Jewish anniversary (Yiddish: yortsayt) of a death. I do not know why this date was chosen as a memorial day for the martyrs of Horodlo.

2. These are the opening words of the Kaddish mourner's prayer, translated as "Sanctified and extolled" [be the name of God].

3. The text in the image of this photo is translated into Yiddish on p. 28. This translation presents the figure caption below the photo on p. 27.

4. The Chamber of the Holocaust is a small museum, which was Israel's first museum (1957) dedicated to the devastation in Europe.

[Page 29]

The Town of Horodlo,
Its Residents, and Its Jewish Community

[Page 30]

[Blank]

[Page31]

The Town of Horodlo,
Its Residents, and Its Jewish Community (Overview)

by Yosef Khayim Zavidovich, Israel

The town of Horodlo lies between two solidly Jewish communities – Ustylúh in the east and Hrubieszow in the west – on the western bank of the Bug river. Surrounded on three sides by broad fields, between villages and agricultural settlements, it is crowned by ancient forests that stretch far into the distance east of the Bug.

The town is old, and is mentioned in Polish history as early as the 15th century. The Jewish community dates back to the same period. Though it was not large in number, it was significant in its quality. The Horodlo community included many who were learned and scholarly. It was headed by the Rabbi, who was renowned for his knowledge of Talmud and commentaries, and famous for his incisive intelligence. Even unlearned Jews joined his classes and were remarkable for their modesty, simplicity, and their Jewish decency.

The Horodlo community was also unusual in its economic makeup. Manufacturers and merchants headed the economic scale, followed by owners of notions shops and shoe stores, then by grocers and shopkeepers. Below them economically were artisans and craftsmen: tailors, shoemakers, carpenters, etc. These were simple Jews, who worked hard at their various trades to earn a living. This group also included the itinerant peddlers, who made the rounds of the villages, selling various goods to the Gentiles

[Page 32]

in return for agricultural products, which they then sold to businessmen who operated on a larger scale.

* * *

The town was divided into two sections. Its central part, which included the broad marketplace and adjoining streets, housed the Jewish neighborhood. The other parts, along the roads to Ustylúh, Hrubieszow, Dubienka and villages in the vicinity, were inhabited by Christians.

The fact that Jews occupied the town center gave it a Jewish character. Though Jews constituted only one-third of the population, Horodlo seemed to be a largely Jewish town. Its Jewish quality was especially noticeable on Shabbat and Jewish holidays, when the entire town seemed to be at rest.

Study and Prayer

The large synagogue in all its glory was visible in the middle of town, which was the center of the Jewish area. It was constructed like an ancient fortress: the walls were made of stone, the windows were tall and vaulted, and its towering, sloping roof was the highest in town. There were two additional halls in the building, which served as prayer venues: the Radzyn "small synagogue" and the artisans' synagogue. The congregation of the Radzyn Hasids was remarkable for its scholarship and sharp intellect. When you entered the synagogue, you'd see Jews bent over volumes of Talmud, Mishna, and religious laws, immediately marking them as Jewish scholars.

The artisans' synagogue was used on Saturdays and holidays by hard-working Jews. The house of study (beit ha-midrash) was not far from the synagogue. That was where

[Page 33]

The Great Synagogue

most of the town's Jews prayed on weekdays; it also served as the center of Jewish scholarship and prayer, and the focus of community life. Though they were very busy with daily affairs and making a living, the Jews of Horodlo found time to pray and study in community, in the house of study. They started streaming towards it early in the morning, for morning prayers; and returned at twilight for the afternoon and evening prayers. They would continue sitting there, at the long wooden tables, and studying a bit of Talmud,

Mishna, *Ein Ya'akov*, or the weekly Torah portion.[1] After studying, they would stay and talk about business or current affairs.

The Town on and Holidays

As noted earlier, Shabbat and holidays had a great effect on the town. One could sense the approach of Shabbat

[Page 34]

as early as Thursday, when Jewish housewives began preparing the Shabbat dishes. At that time, ready-made bread was not available in the bakeries; every household baked bread on the eve of Shabbat for the week to come. It was common to see Jewish women late on Thursdays kneading dough for bread and other baked goods, which were placed into the oven before dawn on Friday. One could easily sense the approach of Shabbat in the air.

In the late afternoons on Fridays, when the shops would close and the artisans stopped working and locked their workshops, the Jews of Horodlo shed all their cares. After washing, they would wear their festive Shabbat clothes and walk sedately to the great synagogue, one of the small synagogues, or the house of study. Now they looked like aristocrats and nobles, as they studied enthusiastically. After prayers, they strode joyously back to their homes. Indoors, all was neat, gleaming with cleanliness, with a festive light reaching into every corner. Each family sat at their table, celebrated the Shabbat meal, and seemed to have attained a higher plane of living, filled with light and joy.

Early on Shabbat morning, they would wake and go to the synagogue for several hours of study before prayers. After prayers they went home to eat the rich Shabbat meal, and then returned to the synagogue for further study.

This was the Shabbat routine of the Horodlo Jews, suffused with study and prayer, pleasure in the special dishes, and release from all weekday cares.

Before a Jewish holiday, the city was enveloped in the same atmosphere, though two or more weeks earlier.

The approach of Passover could be sensed long before the actual date.

[Page 35]

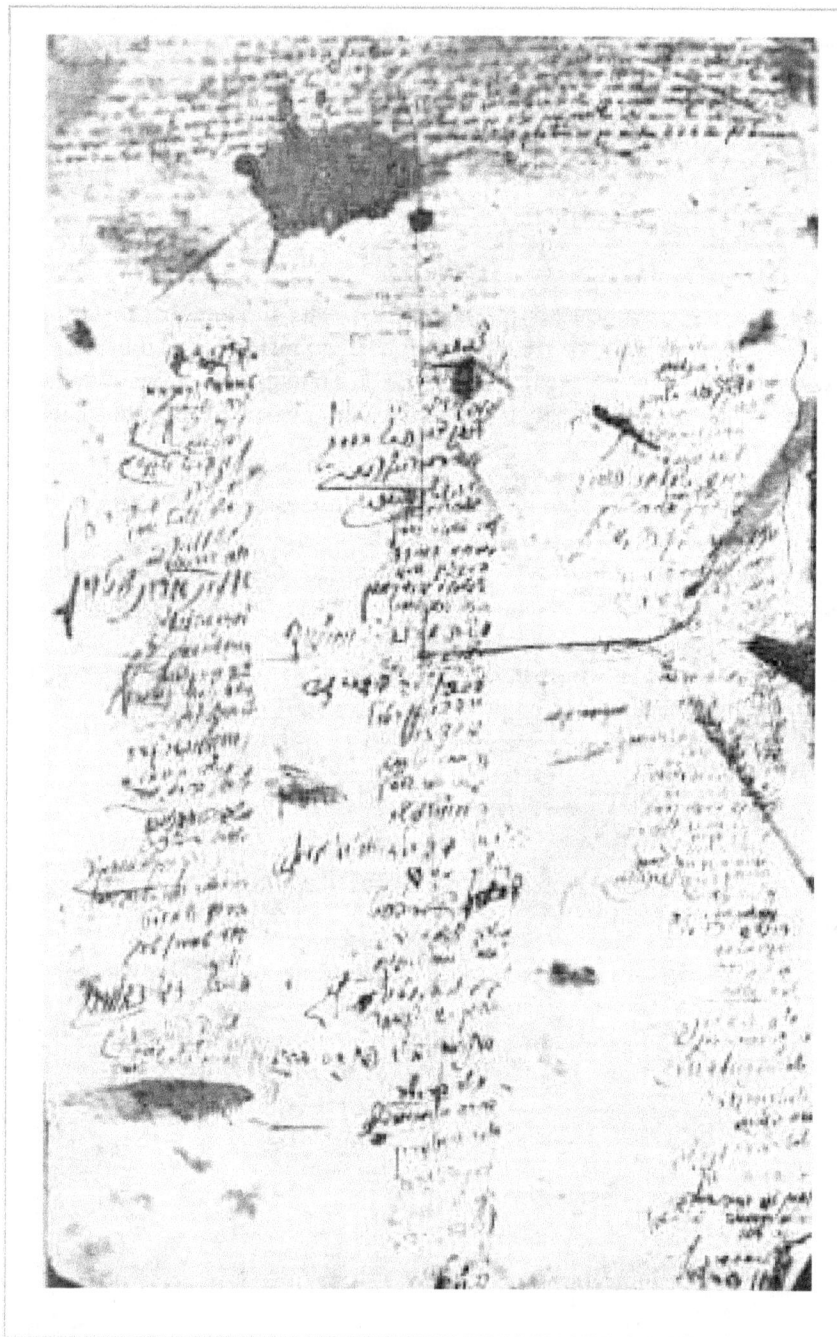

A page from the community's chametz-selling record-book[2]

Horodlo natives will surely recognize the signatures of local Jews who signed in the presence of the Rabbi (may his righteous memory be for a blessing) while selling the chametz. (Received from Rabbi Khayim Berman, son of the Horodlo rabbi.)

[Page 36]

Preparations for Passover began immediately after the fifteenth day of Shevat; these included scouring the flour mill for remnants of any leavening, and baking kosher matza.[3] In those days, people in the Polish towns had not heard of ready-made matza made in kosher matza plants, as is the case today. The matza was baked in a bakery that had been specially prepared for Passover. Two bakeries in Horodlo were prepared to bake matza for each Jewish family in turn. The impending holiday could be felt a few weeks earlier, by way of the following indications: the bakeries were made kosher, and the matza-carrier placed the long matza-basket on his shoulder in order to walk from the bakery to their homes one by one.

As the matzas were being baked, the housewives started to scour, clean, whitewash their walls, and clean out their kitchens thoroughly for the holiday. All the Jews in town were busy preparing. When it was time for the Seder on the eve of Passover, all the Jewish homes cast off their weekday took on a special aura of sanctity, and the holiday's atmosphere spread through the entire town. The Jews then looked as though they were liberated, the houses were bright and joyous, the synagogues were scoured and lit up, and full of congregants and students, and the entire Jewish community seemed to be glowing with delight. On holidays and Shabbat, the Jews of Horodlo observed the old rule set by the sages: "Devote half to God and keep half for yourselves." They spent most of the day studying, praying, and conversing; the rest of the day was spent enjoying the delicious holiday meals.

The Individual and the Jewish Community

The Horodlo community had few wealthy Jews. Most of its members made their living by commerce and

[Page 37]

small shop-keeping; a few were artisans. Yet their hearts and hands were always open towards those in need. The town leaders and activists helped a family known to suffer from hunger by raising enough money to support them. If a Jew was harassed by the authorities, the town's notables worked tirelessly to relieve the pressure. All the Jews in the town joined family celebrations, as it did at times of sorrow. The Jewish residents had a strong sense of mutual responsibility and brotherliness.

Most of the Jewish families were long-time residents, with histories going back many years, possibly for generations. No one knew when they had come to Horodlo. This was why there were no lonely Jews in the town; the families were branched out and interconnected, and everyone had many relatives thanks to their parents, who usually lived in Horodlo or nearby, as well as in distant towns. All the classes of Jews lived in the same town and created a unified community, part of the organic fabric of the Jewish community of Poland.

Relations between Gentiles and Jews in the Town

Relations between Gentiles and the town's Jews were not always bad. The old-timers would talk about times of peace and quiet, when the Gentiles treated the local Jews with respect, as befits old-time residents.

The creation of a new Polish state in 1918 swept the Polish population with a wave of nationalism saturated with anti-Semitism. The Poles in Horodlo were infected by this fanaticism, and began to exhibit hatred towards the

[Page 38]

town's Jews, who were as deeply rooted as the ancient trees in the municipal park. The Jews were told on various occasions that they were considered low-status citizens and strangers in the revived Polish state.

At first, this animosity towards Jews was limited in scope and was felt in narrow circles; however, it later began to spread to the majority of the town's Poles. Jews felt physically endangered if they walked at night on streets where Poles and Ukrainians lived.

From right: Henekh Zuberman, Ben-Tziyon Bergman, Binyomin Berger, Tzvi Zaltzman, Eliezer Lerner, Moyshe-Khayim Bergman, Yekutie'el Zavidovitsh, Dovid Lerner, Fishl Gertel, Shimen Zuberman

Jew-beating became became a common event, especially on Christian holidays. The air seemed ever more suffocating. The Jews of Horodlo were beginning to understand that they could not rely on the friendliness of the Poles in times of trouble.

As anti-Semitism grew in Poland in general and in

[Page 39]

Horodlo in particular, Jewish young people began to become more self-aware, the Zionist movement became the main social trend, and the idea of returning to Palestine swept the majority of Poland's young Jews. Zionist groups were formed in Horodlo as well, and included most of the young Jews; these Zionist groups took up substantial action to rebuild the Land of Israel. They collected money for the Jewish National

Fund as well as for Keren HaYesod, started Hebrew classes, and carried out various cultural activities.[4] Organizations of young pioneers were formed, such as He-Halutz and Beitar. Community activity was dynamic and vigorous.

As animosity towards Jews increased as well as economic pressure on the part of the Polish government, the young people began thinking seriously about other safe places. Members of the pioneering youth organizations went to training farms and prepared to emigrate to the Land of Israel. A different segment of the Jewish population, who were not enthusiastic about the notion of a Jewish renaissance, also realized that the changed conditions in Poland offered no prospect of a decent existence for Jews; they, too, began to dream of emigrating to other, safe countries, such as the United States, Canada, and South America.

The Rise of Hitler (may his name be blotted out) to Power in Germany

In 1933, the most malevolent person in human history, the bloodthirsty murderer Hitler (may his name be blotted out), came to power in Germany, and brandished his sword against the entire Jewish people and the Jews of Poland in particular. His rise to power, along with that of his party–the savage Nazis–encouraged the dark forces in Poland. The anti-Semitic political parties, always vociferous Jew-haters, intensified

[Page 40]

their persecution of Polish Jews. Waves of malice increased, providing such a focal point for the Poles that they were unaware of the coming war their great historical enemy was planning.

Polish animosity towards Jews escalated and became ever more dangerous. The general atmosphere grew more and more oppressive and unbearable. The Poles began to vilify Jews and refer to them as an alien element in the country, especially as concerned the local economy. The head and members of the government constantly talked of "the Jewish problem that must be solved." Economic pressure on the Jews intensified, anti-Jewish regulations were promulgated from time to time, and the Jews of Poland found it increasingly difficult to continue their economic life. Many Jews were dumbstruck at this new situation, and asked themselves whether they could consider Poland – where they had lived for centuries – as a secure home in the future.

Increasing Jew-hatred also led to heightened Zionist and community activity, which encompassed more and more members of the Polish Jewish population. The impulse to emigrate to the Land of Israel, as well as to other safe countries, spread further, and engulfed almost all the young people of Horodlo. Even those who believed that the new conditions were temporary began to doubt their conviction and began to think about emigration, or moving from their small hometown to larger Jewish communities. The number of Jews emigrating to the Land of Israel and to North and South America rose.

[Page 41]

The End of the Horodlo Jewish Community

Despite the pressure to emigrate, most of the town's Jews remained in place, and the Jewish community continued its traditional way of life. After all, not everyone could leave their established home in Horodlo and take to the roads. Most Jews lacked the means to emigrate or move to other locations.

The Horodlo Jews continued their humble lives, making no great demands. They could not imagine the possibility of a general extermination, nor could they sense the impending genocide of the Jews of Europe and Poland. Like many Polish Jews, those living in Horodlo believed that the crisis of malice and evil would pass with no serious consequences.

Alas! In 1939, Hitler's army stormed through Poland and took the entire country in a few months. The Nazis began executing their plan to murder and exterminate the large community of Jews in the country. Once they had occupied Poland, they turned their attention to other European countries that had been conquered by their armies. After occupying these countries, the Nazi military immediately began to slaughter their Jewish communities mercilessly. Millions of Jews were killed by various horrendous methods. Men, women, and children were burned in the crematoria built by the savage murderers. The Horodlo community was not spared from this cruel fate; all the men, women, and children were massacred.

* * *

The few survivors have borne witness to the bitter end of the Horodlo community

[Page 42]

and the end of the Jews, accompanied by suffering and pain. The survivors successfully saved themselves from the hands of the murderers by staying in various hideouts through many difficulties and dangers. The remaining sections of this book present their accounts.

Translator's Footnotes:

1. *Ein Yaakov* is a 16th-century compilation of all the Aggadic material in the Talmud together with commentaries.

2. Chametz is the term for foods with leavening agents that are forbidden on Passover. According to Jewish law, Jews may not own, eat, or benefit from chametz during Passover. A person or a community may sell or give the chametz to a non-Jew, and is released from responsibility.

3. The fifteenth day of the month of Shevat was set by the post-biblical sages as a holiday celebrating trees. It usually falls in January or February. Passover usually occurs in March or April.

4. The Jewish National Fund (JNF) was founded in 1901 to buy and develop land in Ottoman Syria for Jewish settlement. Keren HaYesod was established in 1920 to provide the Zionist movement with resources needed to establish a Jewish homeland in Palestine. Both organizations continue their activities to this day.

[Page 43]

The Jews of Horodlo and their Spiritual, Social, and Community Life

[Page 44]

[Blank]

[Page45]

The Town Rabbi of Horodlo (may his righteous memory be for a blessing), his Life and Family

by Rabbi Khayim Berman

Among the martyrs of the holy community of Horodlo, who sanctified the name of God by their death, was the town's rabbi, my father, the great teacher, rabbi and martyr Moyshe Yehuda-Leyb HaLevy Berman (may his righteous memory be for a blessing). Most of his children and grandchildren were murdered in the same way.

The town rabbi of Horodlo (may his righteous memory be
for a blessing, may God avenge his blood) and his son,
Rabbi Khayim (may he live long)

[Page 46]

My father (may his righteous memory be for a blessing) was appointed Rabbi of Horodlo at age 23. He succeeded to the rabbinate after the death of his father-in-law, the great rabbi Yekuti'el Gelernter (may his righteous memory be for a blessing), himself the brother-in-law of the Rebbe of Radzyn, the great rabbi Gershon Khanokh-Henekh (may his righteous memory be for a blessing).[1]

My father (may his righteous memory be for a blessing) was born in 1866, in the town of Łomazy. His father – my grandfather–was Rabbi Dovid, known among the Hasidim of Radzyn as Reb Dovidl of Łomaz; he was both a scholar and a tradesman. His adherence to Hasidism and great piety spread his fame far and wide. My father's mother, my grandmother Rokhl (peace be upon her), was renowned for her piety and fine qualities.

At the age of 15, my father became the son-in-law of the rabbi of Horodlo, the great Rabbi Yekuti'el Gelernter. He spent eight years in the Radzyn rabbi's house of study, where he sat for long hours studying religious texts. He quickly became famous for his incisive intelligence and vast knowledge of every aspect of the Torah, including its mystical secrets. He assisted the Hasidic leader of Radzyn, Rabbi Gershon-Henekh, in organizing his works.

After the death of his father-in-law, my father was elected as his replacement: the rabbi and head of the religious court of Horodlo. He took up this position with the agreement of the rabbi of Radzyn and a certificate issued by him; he also became certified, by the great Rabbi Yehoshue'le Kutner (may his righteous memory be for a blessing) as a decider on practical questions of Jewish law. This was in 1889.

Seventeen years after the wedding, his righteous wife, Madam Brokhe-Gitl, gave birth to a son – my older brother, Gershon-Henekh Berman (long may he thrive). He studied as a youth with the great Chofetz-Chayim (may his righteous memory be for a blessing) in Raduń, and now lives in Minneapolis in the United States.[2] He is well known for his activities for the State of Israel.

After his first wife died, my father married his second wife – my mother, the righteous Madam Rivka (peace be upon her; may God avenge her blood). She was the daughter of Rabbi Mordechai Chayim Palevsky of Kobrin (may his righteous memory be for a blessing). This grandfather was the brother of

[Page 47]

ספר

שו״ת

חק משה

והיא חלק ראשון מחאו״ח מעשרה חלקים
שיבואו אי״ה בדפוס :

כולל ביאור יפה בכמה סוגיות בש״ס, ותחובר
לזה, חידושי ברכותי הוספה על חק משה
שכבר נדפס בשנת תרס״ד, מבערמ״ח ספר, תפארת
כנים על מסכת אבות, וספר, חק משה׳ על הש״ס :
חברו הקטן והצעיר שבישראל משה ליב בלאאמו״ר
דוד הלוי בערמאן האבד״ק הוראדלא פלך לובלין.

נדפק פעדער וצרשא, וזאמענהוזן, 41

תרפ״ז

CHOK MOSZE.

t. j. Komentarz na Talmud

od Rab. M. BERMAN Horodla z. Lub.

Druk. Feder W-wa, Zamenhofa 44.

Printed in Poland

Title page of *Chok Moshe,* comprising collected responsa and
commentary on the Talmud, by Rabbi Moshe Yehuda Berman of
Horodlo. Printed in Warsaw, 1927[3]

[Page 48]

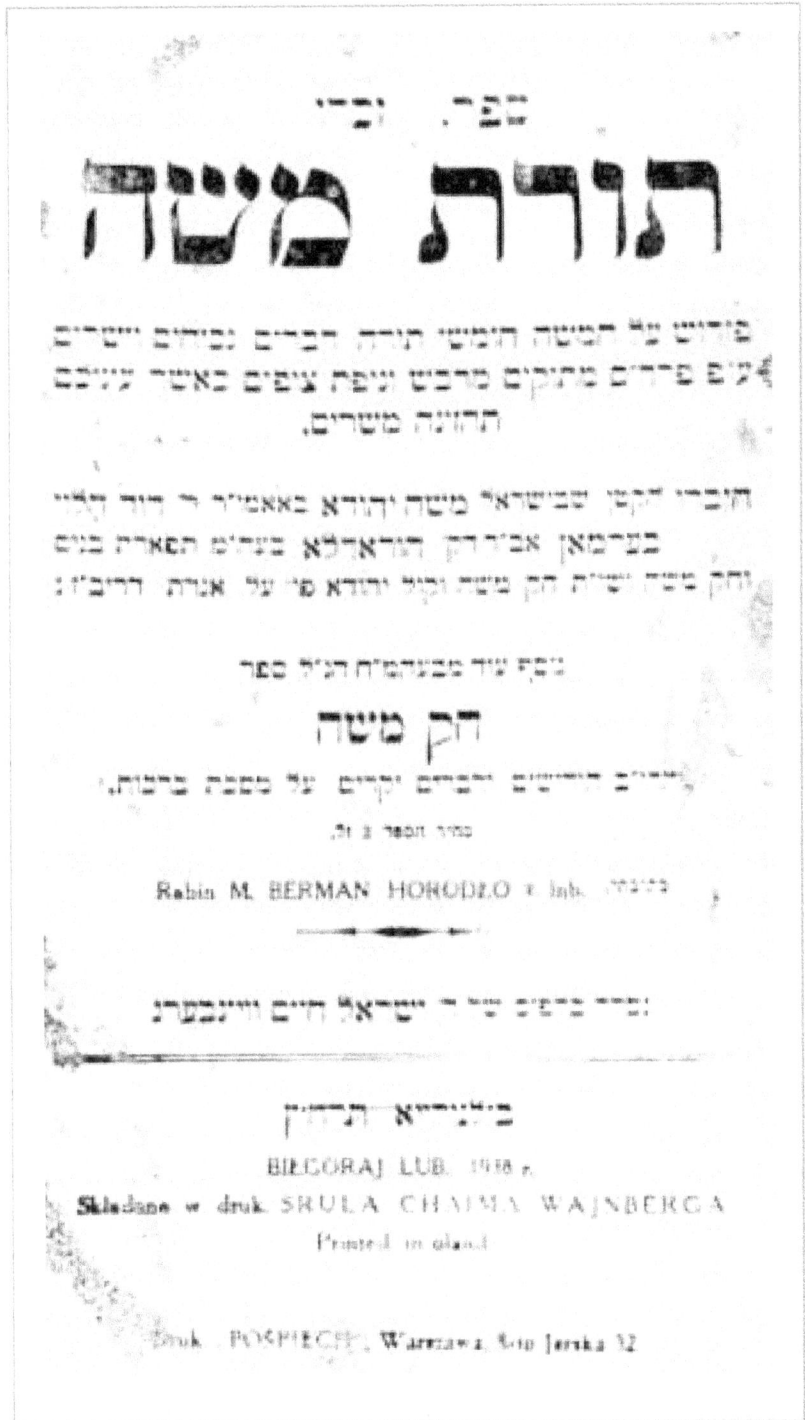

Title page of *Zikhru Torat Moshe*, commentaries on the Torah, by
Rabbi Moshe Yehuda Berman of Horodlo; also comprising *Chok
Moshe*. Printed in Bilgoraj, 1938

[Page 49]

the great scholar and righteous Rabbi of Kobrin, Noyekh-Naftali (may his righteous memory be for a blessing) and the grandson of Rabbi Moyshe of Kobrin (may his righteous memory be for a blessing).

Any small town in Poland could become a center of Torah learning, if the town rabbi was a remarkable scholar, and influenced the members of his community with his knowledge and piety. This was the case in Horodlo, where my father (may his righteous memory be for a blessing) constantly devoted himself to community affairs and to the cause of increasing Torah scholarship in the community.

During his time as Rabbi of Horodlo, my father wrote many sacred books, but was able to publish only four in his lifetime: *Tiferet Banim* (a commentary to the Mishna tractate *Avot*), *Chok Moshe* (responsa about Part 1 of *Orach Chayim*).[4] The latter work comprises 34 of the 250 responsa that were in manuscript form and were lost during the years of destruction wreaked by World War II. *Zikhru Torat Moshe* is a commentary on the Five Books of the Torah, according to the Pardes system.[5] *Kol Yehuda* provides a commentary on the letter of Rabbi Yochanan Ben-Zakkai.[6] Of the lost manuscripts (most of which were written in Rashi script), the following were found: *Lekhem Mishneh* (on the Mishna); *Yalkut shel nevi'im u-khetuvim* selected from the *Zohar*, *Tikunei Zohar*, and selected sections of the *Zohar*; *Chok Moshe*; *Darosh Darash Moshe* –new interpretations of Midrash.[7]

My mother (peace be upon her) gave birth to five children, as follows: my sister Esther (peace be upon her) was remarkably talented, but died in the bloom of youth, at age 19, on June 15, 1920 (she was engaged to the son of Yitzchok Meir Kahn of Zamość, the brother-in-law of the rabbi of Radzyn, the great scholar Mordechai Yoysef Layner – may his righteous memory be for a blessing) and buried in Hrubieszow.

My dear brother, Rabbi Shmuel HaLevi Berman (may God avenge his blood, and may his memory be for a blessing), born on 18 Cheshvan 1907[8], murdered by the German

[Page 50]

Nazis (may their name be blotted out), in our town of Horodlo, together with his wife and his three children: Mordechai Yosef Elazar (may God avenge his blood), David (May God avenge his blood), and Zvi Hirsh (may God avenge his blood).

I, Chaim Halevy Berman, witness to the great disaster that overtook our nation, was born on March 14, 1910. I was ordained as a rabbi by eminent Polish rabbis and scholars, and was certified by my father as a legal authority. At age 22, I married my dear gentle wife, the gifted, intelligent and God-fearing Brokhe (may God avenge her blood, and may she rest in peace), who was killed by the Nazi murderers (may their name be blotted out), in the city of Lwów.[9] Her father was the great Rabbi Yehuda Gordon, the Rabbi of Malyniv (Volhynia), who was murdered in that town by the Nazi killers (may their names be blotted out).

My exceptional, virtuous sister, Freydl (may she rest in peace, and may God avenge her blood), born in 1922, was murdered by the Nazis along with with her husband, the great, pious God-fearing rabbi, the scholar Rabbi Dov Ber Maliniak (may God avenge his blood) from Praga, Warsaw, along with their two dear, gifted children (may God avenge their blood).[10] My brother-in-law, Rabbi Dov-Ber Maliniak, wrote the book *Mishmeret Mitzvah* (Warsaw, 1932) when he was only 16. In this book, he manifested his profound knowledge and incisive thought concerning the precept of doubtful (safek) mitzvah[11]. His teachers were two famous Talmudic scholars, Rabbi Shimen Shkop (may his righteous memory be for a blessing), head of the Grodno yeshiva, and Rabbi Menachem Zemba (may God avenge his blood, and may his righteous memory be for a blessing) of Praga, Warsaw.

My exceptional sister, my parents' youngest daughter, Chave-Chane Rochl (Rokhele) (may God avenge her blood), was murdered with her husband, the great rabbi and descendant of Rabbi Naftali (may God avenge his blood), the son of the righteous Rabbi Chaim (may God avenge his blood, may his righteous memory be for a blessing), head of the rabbinical court and legal authority of the Jewish community of Boryslaw (Galitzia), and the son-in-law of the great Rabbi of Komarno (may his righteous memory be for a blessing). Their only daughter Feygele (may God avenge her blood) was also murdered, along with her sanctified parents (may their memory be bound up in the bond of life).

* * *

[Page 51]

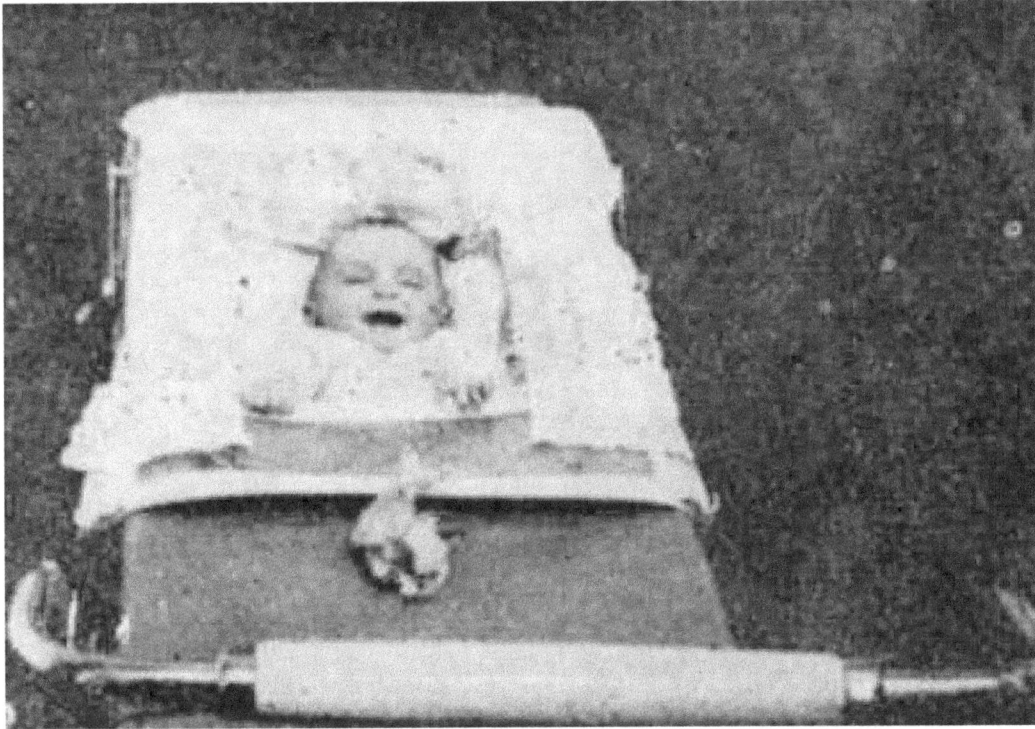

The Rabbi's Grandchild
(may God avenge her blood)

We mourn our nearest and dearest, killed by the evil kingdom. They suffered the same fate as the burned Torah scrolls – the scrolls are burning but the letters fly free.[12]

Let the collective Kaddish[13] prayer that the survivors of Horodlo say every year to commemorate the martyrs of their town be an eternal memorial, and a call for revenge on the unspeakable murderers of our martyrs, who were killed for no reason or sin and died the death of martyrs.

[Page 52]

פרוש לשי"ת

בע"ה

Opening page of Responsa written by the town Rabbi Moshe Yehuda
Berman (may his sacred memory be for a blessing)

[Page 53]

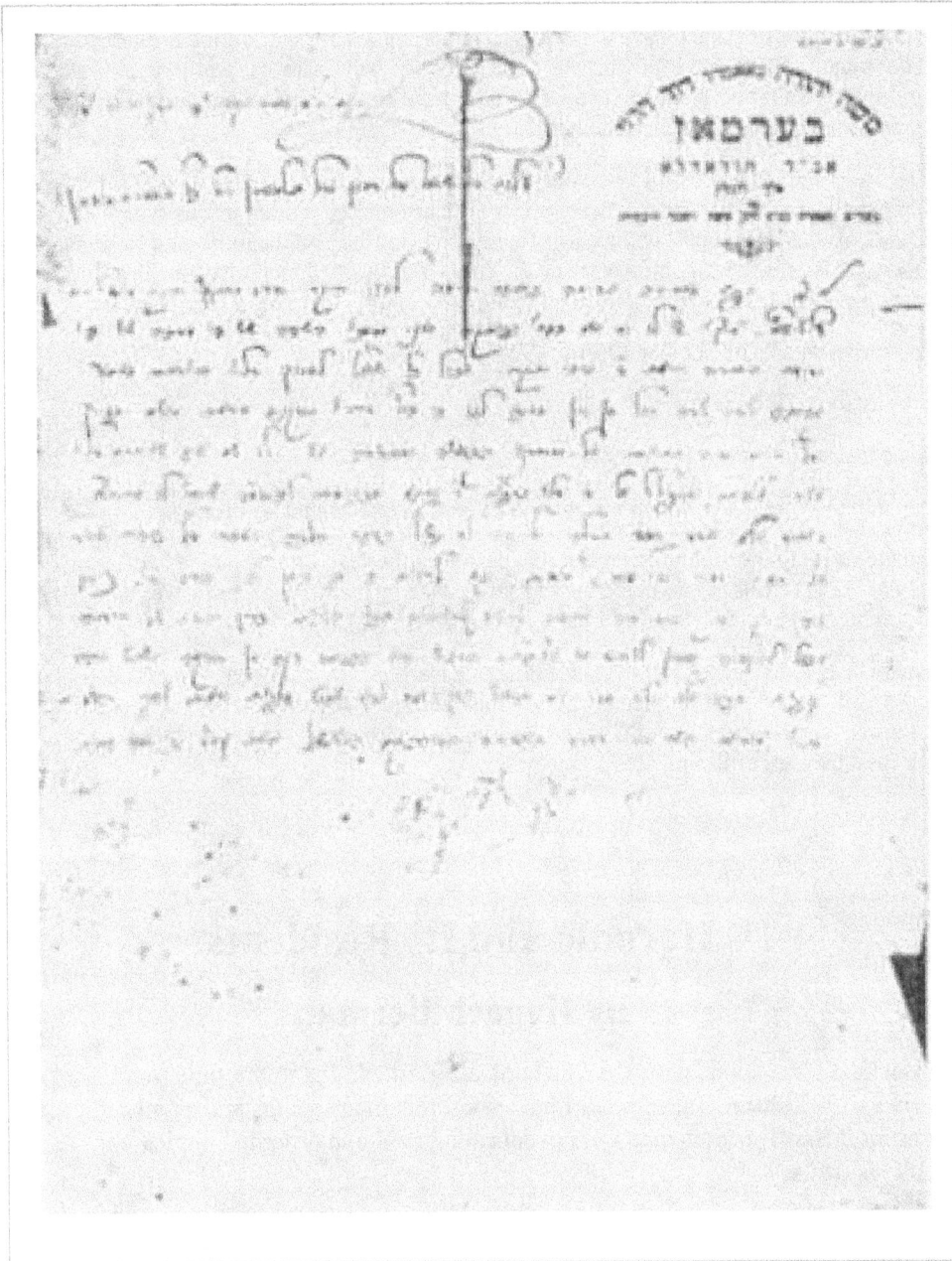

A letter written by the Rabbi (may his sacred memory be for a blessing)

Translator's Footnotes:

1. Radzyń-Podlaski was the home of a Hasidic dynasty, founded in the mid-19th century.

2. Rabbi Yisra'el Me'ir Ha-Kohen Kagan (1838-1933) is known popularly as the *Chofetz Chaim* after his book on slander and other works of Jewish law. His works continue to be influential in Orthodox Jewish life.

3. Responsa are the body of written decisions and rulings given by deciders of Jewish law.

4. *Orach Chayim* is a section of Rabbi Jacob ben Asher's compilation of Halakha, Arba'ah Turim. The section addresses aspects of Jewish law pertinent to the Hebrew calendar.

5. Pardes is a Kabbalistic theory of Biblical exegesis that comprises four approaches: the literal meaning of the text, its allegorical meaning, metaphorical meaning, and hidden meaning.

6. Rabbi Yochanan Ben Zakkai (30-90 C.E.) was an important Jewish sage during the late Second Temple period and in the transformative era following the destruction of 70 C.E. He was a primary contributor to the Misha, the core text of Rabbinic Judaism. The letter, addressed to the Jewish community of Rome, is dated to 53 C.E. and is a polemic against Christianity.

7. Rashi Hebrew script is based on 15th-century Sephardic semi-cursive handwriting. It is named for the rabbinic commentator Rashi (1040-1105), whose works are customarily printed in this typeface. *Tikunei Zohar* is a main text of the Kabbalah which was composed in the 14th century and a separate appendix to the *Zohar*; *Chok Moshe* is a commentary on the entire *Tikunei HaZohar*, also known as the *Tikunim*, is a main text of the Kabbalah, which was composed in the 14th century, and a separate appendix to the Zohar.

8. The Gregorian date is 26 October 1907.

9. Present-day Lviv, Ukraine.

10. Praga is a district of Warsaw.

11. Thereby demonstrating significant insight and a nuanced understanding of Jewish Law.

12. This image refers to the Talmudic legend that describes the sage Rabbi Hanina ben Teradyon, who wrapped his body in Torah scrolls before being burned at the stake by the Romans; as he was dying, he called out "The scrolls are burning but the letters fly free" (*Avodah Zara* 18:2).

13. The Kaddish is a 13th century prayer. Kaddish means 'sanctification' in Aramaic and it is related to the Hebrew word Kadosh, which means 'holy.' The Mourner's Kaddish never mentions death or dying, but instead proclaims the greatness of God. By reciting it, mourners show that even as their faith is being tested by their loss, they are affirming God's greatness.

[Page 54]

Horodlo and Its Residents

by Henech Berman

The reminiscences I am contributing to this book are limited, due to the time that has elapsed. As I left Horodlo as early as 1923, during those years I have forgotten many things and events concerning the town. I will try to present memories connected with events and people, in order to supplement the descriptions of the town and its residents.

* * *

The small town of Horodlo, on the western bank of the Bug River – the natural boundary line between Poland and Volhynia Province (the easternmost part of Poland) – was no different in its character and substance from other Polish towns. Like every other Jewish community in Poland, that of Horodlo consisted mostly of Orthodox Jews.

Most of the Horodlo Jews, headed by the town rabbi, my father (may his righteous memory be for a blessing), Rabbi Moshe Yehuda Leyb Berman, and the two ritual slaughterers, were adherents of the Hasidic leader of Radzin (may his righteous memory be for a blessing). However, some Jews were considered members of other Hasidic dynasties, such as those of Ger, Belz, etc.[1]

Although the Jewish community of Horodlo was small, it was renowned throughout the towns in Poland, thanks to its great rabbi, my father (may his righteous memory be for a blessing), who was famous for his piety and his knowledge of the Torah. He instructed his community devotedly for many years, accompanied his community constantly up to their final journey, and was murdered together with the community and his family, in the crematoriums of Sobibor.[2] I survived, as did my brother

[Page 55]

Chaim, who had by a miracle gone to the United States shortly before the war and thus escaped the fate of the Horodlo Jews and the destiny of murder that decimated our family.

We set the 25th of Sivan as the date for memorializing our martyred family members.[3] They are the following:

The Rabbi's wife Rivka – the second wife of my father (may his righteous memory be for a blessing)– who was descended from pious people, including her grandfather Moshe Kobrin (may his righteous memory be for a blessing).

The Rabbi of Horodlo
(may his righteous memory be for a blessing),
with his grandson Mordechai (Motele), and a friend

My brother Shmuel and his family, may their memory be for a blessing. My sister Freydl and her husband, Rabbi Mordechai, descended from martyrs (may his memory be for a blessing), son of the Rabbi of Yaroslavl. My brother-in-law, Rabbi Naftali, studied with my father (may his righteous memory be for a blessing), and was de facto Rabbi of Horodlo during the last years before the catastrophe. My sister-in-law, Bracha, the wife of my brother Chaim, was the daughter of the Rabbi of Malyniv.

My father (may his righteous memory be for a blessing), the Rabbi of Horodlo – as he was known throughout the Polish rabbinical world – was recognized as one of the most

[Page 56]

eminent scholars in Poland. He wrote important books of Jewish religious law; great rabbis turned to him with questions and responsa, and trusted his religious decisions as they would a final authority.

His first book, *Tiferet Banim*, was printed in 1905. I possess a trove of his manuscripts, which he sent me through my brother Chaim (now a ritual slaughterer in New York).[4]

My father (may his righteous memory be for a blessing) obtained his first rabbinical position at the young age of 19. He did not come from a family of rabbis. He inherited the position from his father-in-law – my grandfather – Rabbi Yosef Gelernter (may his righteous memory be for a blessing), who was the rabbi and head of the rabbinical court in Hrubieszow. He was the father-in-law of the Hasidic leader of Radzin, the author of *Orchot Chaim*, Rabbi Gershon Henech Leiner (may his righteous memory be for a blessing), who discovered the source of the *tekhelet*.[5] He was a great scholar, and the author of significant works of scholarship that were renowned throughout the world of religious learning.

My mother (may her memory be for a blessing), Sarah-Gitl the Rabbi's wife, died in full bloom, at age 38, when I was 3 years old. She was a respected woman, famous for her acts of charity as well as for her friendly relationships with people beyond Horodlo.

After I had studied several years with my father, he sent me to the yeshiva of the great sage, the Chofets Chaim, in Radin.[6] As a yeshiva student, I dressed like Lithuanian Jews, in shorter garments (unlike the long clothing of Polish Jews). They wore fedora-style hats rather than the caps usually worn by Polish Jews. Many of them also trimmed their beards. When I was in Radin, I, too, trimmed my beard, and exchanged my clothes for those worn by Lithuanian Jews – European style. When I returned home in 1915, wearing my Lithuanian outfit, the residents of Horodlo were shocked and looked at me angrily. I think I was the only Jewish young man in the town with short clothing and a non-Hasidic appearance.

[Page 57]

Incidentally, I wore Hasidic garb on Shabbat and holidays; I was afraid I'd be thrown out of the synagogue because of my Lithuanian appearance.

Most of my father's livelihood derived from litigation in the rabbinical court. Besides the Horodlo Jews, who addressed him with their problems, Jews from the entire area brought him their issues. More than once, representatives of the surrounding Jewish communities came asking him to hear their cases and issue rabbinical rulings. Jewish communities would also invite him to arbitrate some important matter and issue a rabbinical ruling. More than once, property-owners protested against the Rabbi's acceptance of such invitations, which required him to be absent from Horodlo, albeit for brief periods.

Rabbi Chaim Berman
(long may he live),
his wife Bracha
(may God avenge her blood),
and his brother Shmuel
(may God avenge his blood)

Shmuel Berman, the Rabbi's son,
with his children

[Page 58]

The rulings of my father (may his righteous memory be for a blessing) became famous throughout the region, and even secular judges took them into account. I would like to recount an episode in this connection:

At that time, Jews did not file suits in the government courts, but brought their disputes before the town rabbi. Only rarely did the losing party seek "justice" in the official courts.

Once, a Jew was found guilty by my father's religious tribunal, and demanded a new trial in the district court of Hrubieszow. The judge there was a Russian named Lashkevitch. During the trial, the judge wanted to know the verdict of the rabbi of Horodlo, and asked to have it translated. When he received the Russian translation of the verdict, he first came to his feet and read it with reverence. Than he turned to the Jew standing before him and scolded him for rejecting the verdict of the Horodlo rabbi "whose common sense transcended all the civil written laws." This judge, of course, confirmed the verdict handed down by my father (may his righteous memory be for a blessing). The judge's words made a great impression on the Jews in the area. But when my father, the rabbi, heard the judge's words, he laughed the matter off: "A Gentile, even if he is a judge, considers every rabbi a scholar…"

At the time, Czarist Russia controlled large parts of Poland, including Horodlo. Russian law required the town rabbi to know Russian. If a local rabbi did not know Russian, the authorities would appoint a supplementary rabbi who knew Russian. Such a rabbi would be termed "Official Rabbi" – in other words, government-appointed. The residents gave him the title of "Rabbiner." Naturally, the government was none too particular concerning the spiritual qualities and scholarly knowledge of the rabbi it had appointed.

In Horodlo, too, the authorities appointed an "Official Rabbi,"

[Page 59]

"Rabbiner Mandel," from the nearby town of Dubienka. The influential people of Horodlo wanted my father (may his righteous memory be for a blessing) to learn Russian, so that he might be appointed "Official Rabbi" in addition to being the legally acknowledged rabbi of the Horodlo community. A meeting of the town's homeowners was convened at our house on this matter. The participants were Shmuel Biderman, Aharon-Chaim Feder, Yisro'el Safir, Hershl Grosburd, Dovid Bergman, Moyshe Mendl Vallach, Fishl Stav, Dovid Yosef Zuberman, Elazar Halperin, Aharon Leyb, Moyshe Fraynd (the last two were members of the city council), and other homeowners. My father (may his righteous memory be for a blessing) agreed that learning Russian was necessary, and he sent me to Lashkevitch the teacher (who was later appointed a district judge in Hrubieszow) to set a schedule. Shortly after he began these studies, my father sent me to Lashkevich to announce that the lessons would be discontinued. At one of the weekly Saturday night gatherings at our house, where town matters would be discussed, the rabbi was asked about his chances of becoming the Rabbiner, and whether he was studying Russian in preparation. The rabbi's response was that he had decided to stop his Russian studies, because "if I would put as much effort into studying Torah (not to mention them in the same breath) as into studying Russian, I would be a world-renowned genius. I therefore renounce my position and resign as 'Official Rabbi.'"

I would also like to mention the wife of the previous rabbi – my maternal grandmother, Fradl (may her memory be for a blessing). She came from Slavuta, and was a descendant of the renowned Shapiro family and a grandchild of Rabbi Pinkhes Koretser (may his righteous memory be for a blessing). People in the town said that my grandmother Fradl had a document tracing her family's lineage back to King David. When my father (may his righteous memory be for a blessing) inherited the rabbinical position from my grandfather, Rabbi Yekutiel (may his righteous memory be for a blessing), my father's father-in-law (incidentally, he was the thirty-sixth rabbi in

[Page 60]

the chain of fathers and sons in this role) undertook the support of Grandmother Fradl (may her memory be for a blessing) in the weekly sum of two rubles.

Grandmother Fradl, the rabbi's wife, later lived with her daughter Zissele (my aunt), the wife of Leybl Zavidovich (who was nicknamed "the Rabbi's Leybl"), and died before the beginning of World War I, at age 84.

My Aunt Zissele (may her memory be for a blessing)

My Aunt Zissele was a righteous, highly respected woman. She never failed to pray three times a day, and knew the prayers by heart. She was well versed in religious law, and famous for her refinement. He appearance was elegant and respectable; the town residents held her in high regard.

When World War II broke out, she was able to cross the Bug River (the temporary border between Germany and Russia) and

Zissele Zavidovich (Zissele the Rabbi's daughter), her son Yosef Zavidovich,
with wife and children, and her sons Fishl and Mordechai Zavidovich (may God avenge
their blood)

[Page 61]

was reunited with the families of her son Yosef Zavidovich and her daughter Malke, who lived in Ludmir. She was also joined by her daughter Khane, son-in-law Moyshe Tenenboym, and children, as well as by her son-in-law Note Perlmuter (currently in Montreal, Canada, with his daughter Fradl and her family). But the bitter fate of the Jews of Poland followed her to Ludmir, where she was captured by the Germans (may their name be blotted out). It was her terrible fate to witness the murder of her sons and daughters, as well as her numerous grandchildren by the German killers (may their name be blotted out). She was eventually slaughtered along with the Jews of Ludmir.

The Great Synagogue, the House of Study, the Prayer Houses

The Great Synagogue, with its massive walls and high, vaulted windows, was strong and solidly built. Its foundations were thick and its walls were constructed of large stones. It was the tallest building in town, and was located on a central square in front of the marketplace. The congregation of the Great Synagogue consisted mostly of ordinary Jews, laborers and artisans, headed by the town rabbi. The regular cantor for holidays was Kalmen Nayman (may his memory be for a blessing), whose sweet voice made the hearts of the listeners tremble. The synagogue's manager was Zelik, known as Avrom-Aharon's son (may his memory be for a blessing) Adjoining the prayer hall, a small synagogue existed in the anteroom, where some artisans prayed; this was managed by Fayvl Sher. A similar small synagogue (shtibl) was active in one of the synagogue's rooms; the congregation consisted of the Radzin Hasids[7] and its members were scholars, Hasids, and homeowners. It was also used by the House of Study 'regulars'. During the afternoon service of the High Holidays, my uncle Leybl Zavidovich (may his memory be for a blessing) led the prayers, and his son Levi-Yitzchak performed the Torah readings. The House of Study was nearby, not far from the synagogue. Those who used it came from all the town's circles: homeowners, scholars, artisans, etc.

[Page 62]

Standing: Rabbi Chaim Berman (long may he live)
Seated, from right: Mordechai Zavidovich (may God avenge his blood), Hershl Groysbord (may God avenge his blood)

There were two regular sextons in Horodlo: Mordechai (known as Moti), and Moshe Vortsl. Besides his community duties, Moshe Vortsl was occupied with his trade: laying shingles on roofs. Yet he was very poor, and barely made a living.

Horodlo also had a town elder, appointed by the authorities (the town magistrate); this was Chaim Hersh Vayntroyb, who was also the town's watchman. None could compare with Chaim Hersh, when he wore his official government chain with its image of the Polish eagle at the edge, as a symbol of his "elevated position"…

Miriam, Chaim-Hersh's wife, also had a public position as the supervisor of the ritual bath. Yet, with all these positions, Chaim-Hersh was poor, and always sought money to celebrate Shabbat. He was an ordinary, God-fearing Jew. In his favor, I can say that

[Page 63]

throughout the years when I rose very early in order to go to the House of Study, Chaim-Hersh was the only person who preceded me. I would see him in a corner, chanting Psalms with all his heart.[8]

Three Jews were notable among the Jews of Horodlo. They were characteristic types. They made a living by drawing water from the town well and carrying it in two buckets to people's homes. These were Volf (or, as he was known, "Volvenyu") Kapel, who was also the town's gravedigger (may God preserve us), and Dvoyre, who also earned a living for a time as a water-carrier.

It's important to remember that at that time, the small towns

Kapele the water-carrier; left, Fishl Shek

[Page 64]

of Poland had never heard of water pipes and faucets. Water had to be carried in buckets from the city wells. In the early morning hours of summer and winter alike, we could hear the confident strides of the water carriers echo throughout the marketplace, the yoke across their shoulders bearing two full buckets of water. The carriers would empty these into the water barrels in the Jewish households. They would then return to the well and fill their buckets once again. It was an arduous occupation that required hard physical labor, and they carried it out with responsibility and devotion.

There were also two well-known woodchoppers in the town. These were the brothers Zalmen and Berl Holts.[9] In addition to chopping wood, they worked and did various menial tasks for the Jewish households of Horodlo.

Most of the Jews in town were either tradesmen or storekeepers. They could be divided into two general classes: artisans, and middle-class. There were no rich Jews in Horodlo, except for two who were considered relatively wealthy. These were Hershl Grosburd (a family friend) and Aharon Berger. The latter had two sons, Pinkhes and Nokhem. As a rich person, Aharon made efforts to marry them to brides from important families. His son Nokhem was married to Sarah Gitl, the daughter of the Rabbi of Ciechocinek (may her memory be for a blessing). Yisroel Shafir also married into the family of the Rabbi of Ciechocinek (may his memory be for a blessing).

Rabbi Ya'akov Chesner, the Shochet (Ritual Slaughterer)

The ritual slaughterer, Rabbi Ya'akov Chesner, was a holy, first-rate person. He was naive and cautious, not involved in life's events, and famous for his piety and Hasidism. He would spend long hours, day and night, studying Torah and following God's precepts. It was common to find him sitting late at night in the Radzin synagogue, as well as in the pre-dawn hours.

[Page 65]

Looking through a window of the illuminated Radzin synagogue, you'd see him bent over a copy of the Talmud and studying a chapter.

His piety and diligent observance of all commandments were unprecedented. I am personally acquainted with the following episode. Once, his wife – whom he never referred to by name because of modesty, following the custom of old-time Hasids, but by a nickname such as "the wife" or simply "she" – bought a new kitchen utensil. Rabbi Ya'akov believed it had not been properly purified in natural water. As he wasn't sure which utensil was the new one, he brought all the kitchen utensils to the well, placed them in a bucket, and lowered them into the water for ritual purification.[10]

Rabbi Ya'akov believed every Jew to be as modest and naive as himself, and could not imagine that some Jews were not as devout but, on the contrary, frivolous. I remember one wintry Friday night. After the Shabbat-eve meal, some friends and I went for a short walk. My companions were Leyb Zuberman, Moshe Grosburd, Muni Halperin, Aharon Vallach, and Avrom Shek. As we walked, a thick snow began falling, and we decided to go into the small Radzin synagogue. Rabbi Ya'akov the shochet also came in, and began chanting the Shema with his typical enthusiasm.[11] We listened to his chanting with reverence, trembling with awe as we stood there. "Happy is the man who is so devout!!" we said. When he had finished chanting the prayer, he came up to us and rubbed his hands together in his usual manner. Smiling with satisfaction almost childishly, he began a conversation: "I hear you are becoming more devout," etc. etc. When the conversation became a discussion, Rabbi Ya'akov said, "Why argue? I'll show you a well known, compelling rabbinical quotation, and I'm sure you'll agree that it's true: when the Torah was given to the Israelites,

[Page 66]

God brought in all the unborn souls, down to the last generation." All, together with the Israelites who were present, called out, "All that God has said, we will do, and we will obey!"[12]"Nothing more needs to be discussed!" he called out triumphantly. Smiling victoriously, he added, "I thank God for having supplied me with the right quotation. Thanks to it, I could fulfill the sage's phrase, 'Know how to answer a doubter.'"[13] He made his farewell, saying "Shabbat Shalom!" and resumed his studies.[14]

In 1915, Poland was occupied by the German-Austrian armies. Horodlo was held by the German army during the first two weeks of the war. (The behavior of the German army during World War I was different from their behavior during World War II.) The military authorities ordered us to leave the town, as it was on the front line, and would be gravely affected by the horrors of war. Almost all the town's residents did leave, and moved to the farming village of Teptiuków, near Hrubieszow.

When we were settled in our new place, the German commander (with the rank of General) demanded that we select a mayor. I happened to be standing next to my father (may his righteous memory be for a blessing); the General saw me and asked who I was. I told him that I was the rabbi's son. He then ordered that I be "selected" as Mayor, and lead the residents. I never found out why he selected me, out of all the people. I believe it was thanks to my modern, European-style clothing; I was almost the only one not wearing the traditional long Hasidic garb common to the Horodlo Jews.

I held that august position for only three months. The Christians were not happy to have a Jew as mayor, and they did their best to replace me with a Christian. When the Austrian authorities took over, they were strongly influenced by Polish intellectuals, and managed to have me dismissed

[Page 67]

from my mayoral post. I was replaced by Prince "Padebinski of Rybna village."[15]

I left Horodlo in 1918, for Kiev.[16] After about four years in Russia, where I sampled the miseries of the Russian revolution, I returned to Horodlo in 1922. Some of the young people had abandoned the House of Study, and most had exchanged their Hasidic clothes for European dress. Anti-Semitism had increased, and the enemies of the Jews grew bolder. The economic regime of the new Poland (under Grabowski) impoverished most Jews.[17] Most young people began to think of leaving the country to go abroad. I, too, considered the situation, and decided to leave for a country where the future was more secure.

After a long journey, I arrived in the United States. I had had to travel to Kishinev and stay there for some time, in order to obtain permission to come to America.[18] While I was there, I was able to work and sustain myself. I also became acquainted with my future wife. In 1925, I left Kishinev and came to the United States.

Translator's Footnotes:

1. Ger is the Yiddish name for the town of Góra Kalwaria.

2. I could not find any reference to crematoriums at Sobibor extermination camp.

3. The Jewish month of Sivan usually falls in May-June.

4. A ritual slaughterer, or Shochet, is a person certified to prepare kosher meat.

5. Tekhelet was a blue-colored dye that held great significance in ancient Mediterranean cultures. In the Hebrew Bible and Jewish tradition, tekhelet was used to color the clothing of the High Priest, the tapestries in the Tabernacle, and the fringes attached to the corners of ritual garments, including the tallis. Its precise source is not known, but it seems to be derived from a creature in the Mediterranean.

6. Rabbi Israel Meir ha-Kohen Kagan (1838-1933), known as the Chofetz Chaim (after the title of his book on malicious gossip), was an influential Lithuanian Jewish rabbi and legal authority whose works continue to be widely influential in Orthodox Jewish life.

7. A small space used for prayer by Hasids was often termed a shtibl (literally "small room").

8. Saying Psalms is considered a vehicle for gaining God's favor, regardless of the circumstances.

9. The last name of these brothers, Holts, is Yiddish for wood or lumber.

10. Jewish law requires new pots and pans to be ritually purified in natural water (in a spring, well, or ritual bath) before they can be used.

11. The Shema prayer forms the centerpiece of the morning and evening prayers.

12. The response of the Israelites when God's covenant was read out (Exodus 24:7).

13. Sayings of the Fathers, 2:14.

14. Literally "Gut Shabbes" in Yiddish. Have a good Sabbath!

15. Possibly a nobleman by birth, but his exact position in Rybna is unclear.

16. Present-day Kyiv.

17. The text here has "Grabowski" apparently in error. Władysław Grabski was the political economist and prime minister of Poland (1920, 1923–25), who reorganized the country's monetary and financial system, often to the detriment of the Jews.

18. Present-day Chisinau.

[Page 68]

The Jews of Horodlo and their Scholarship

by Moshe Biderman, New York, United States

Horodlo was a small town, with a small population. The Jewish population was not large, either, but Jewish Horodlo was nonetheless considered important qualitatively. Every Jew of Horodlo was an entire world in his own right.

Let me start with the town rabbi, the great scholar Moshe-Leyb (may his righteous memory be for a blessing), the son-in-law of Rabbi Yekutiel (may his righteous memory be for a blessing), and his wife Fradl (may she rest in peace). This rabbinical dynasty was unbroken for twenty-four generations. He himself was a disciple of the Rabbi of Radzin (may his righteous memory be for a blessing), the author of *Orchot Chaim*.[1]

Rabbi Moshe-Leyb had modest requirements, and did not seek – or demand – comfort. He spent countless hours studying and praying. He studied at home, in the House of Study, and in the small Radzin synagogue. Besides caring for the religious needs of the community, he constantly studied. He was a Torah expert, and his knowledge of Mishna (with commentaries) and religious law was famous. He wrote important legal and interpretative works. He led his community faithfully, and accompanied his flock with devotion and love, to the bitter and horrible devastation wrought by Hitler and his accomplices (may their names be blotted out).

Horodlo was known for its students and scholars. Anyone entering the House of Study or the Radzin synagogue on a weekday, let alone on Shabbat, found Jews sitting and studying. The site in the synagogues was impressive, especially on Shabbat and holidays: Jews sat at long tables, dressed in their best, setting aside all

[Page 69]

their mundane worries, and studied. The topics of study were varied: the weekly Torah portion, the Talmud with commentaries, the Mishna, Ein Ya'akov or a book of Hasidism.[2] On Saturdays and holidays, a Jew of Horodlo spent most of his time praying and studying in the synagogue, the House of Study, or the small Hasidic synagogue.

As one of those who studied in the Hasidic synagogue, I would like to mention the Horodlo Jews who studied there, whom I can remember. I'd like to emphasize that most of these men could study on their own very well, but they preferred to study in pairs or in groups, which helped to clarify the issues, especially of topics that required special attention and thought.

One of these faithful students was Moshe (son of Yisroel Fishl) Stav, who usually studied together with his friend Yerachmiel (son of Aharon Yehuda) Fraynd. Another group consisted of Shimon Vizenberg, Moshe Vizenberg, Ya'akov Vizenberg, and Yehoshua Vizenberg with his son Getsl.

The same small synagogue was the scholarly home of Levi-Yitzchak Zavidovich and his sons (two of whom, Yosef and Yehoshua, now live in Israel) and of Yosef Zavidovich, Levi-Yitzchak's brother (whose daughter lives in Israel and whose son lives in the United States), as well as Ya'akov Goldman, the son of Motl (may he rest in peace).

Another renowned scholar was Yitzchak Blum (known in town as Yitzchak, Melech's son). He taught Talmud, commentaries by the students of Rashi, and by other scholars, to the youths of Horodlo.[3] I too was his student, together with my friend Moshe ("Munye") Halperin (son of Elazar Halperin, who was a devoted Hasid and studied in the same small synagogue).

During the period that I studied there, I knew some young men who were remarkable for their incisive thought. These included Aharon Valach (now in Israel, the son of Moshe Mendl – may he rest in peace), Moshe Grosburd (son of Tzvi Grozburd), Pinkhes Ayzen, Aharon Zuberman (the son of

[Page 70]

The Hasidic leader Rabbi Shmuel Shlomo Layner (may his righteous memory be for a blessing; may God avenge his blood), the Rabbi of the Radzin Hasidism, during a visit to Ludmir. Also present are Moshe Mendl Buxenboym, Chaim Dovid Tsuker, Gershon Henech Buxenbaum, and Chaim Berman

Yoel Yitzchak of Strzyżów village, Henech Zuberman (Tzvi Zuberman's son), Aryeh Herbst (Shmuel's son, now in Argentina), Moshe Halperin, Aryeh Leybl Herbst (Shimshon's son), Henech Goldman, the son of Motl the melamed, Gershon Henech (now in the United States), the Rabbi's son.[4]

This group of young men was remarkably devoted. Scholars of the House of Study would rise at 4 a.m. and study all day, until midnight, breaking only for food.

[Page 71]

Others in the House of Study group were Yekutiel Zavidovich and his brother, Fishl Zavidovich. I remember one holiday walk that we (Aharon Valach and I, with his father Moshe Valach) took on Shavuot after the midday meal, walking the length of the marketplace. As we walked, Moshe Mendl quizzed us on our knowledge of, and familiarity with, the texts we were studying. Aharon recited from memory about twenty pages of the *Chidushei Ha-Rim* commentary on the Tosfot "They do not study it for its own sake."[5]

Many homeowners, excellent scholars, were important participants in the study at the small synagogue. Among them were Shmuel Zisberg (who was called Shmuel Kay), Leybl Zavidovich, David Bergman, Elazar Halperin, Aharon Chaim Feder, Shimon Biterman, Tzvi Shek, Hillel Shek (Rabbi of Gyavitz), Mendl Lerner (a great scholar and expert), Shmuel Yehuda (who studied at night, and died suddenly while studying, during the week of Pesach).[6] The first people in the synagogue early the next morning found his body sitting at the Talmud volume, his glasses resting on the open page. Petachya Blat, who made a living thanks to the oil press that he owned, would come in after a hard day's work and devote long hours immersing himself in the text. This was also the habit of Yaakov Zuberman. He owned a bakery, and would come to the synagogue after work, for in-depth Talmud study. Last but not least among the scholars were the pious slaughterers Yaakov Chesner and Mordechai Faygenboym.[7]

The House of Study offered a similar scene peopled by devoted students and scholars. Those who studied there came from various backgrounds, and consisted of ordinary people, homeowners from different classes, some who had trouble making a living, and artisans and craftsmen. They considered it their duty to spend time studying sacred texts, after long hours of work. One table was used by people studying Talmud, while another was occupied by people studying the Torah with Rashi's commentary. The tables near the large oven were used by people studying the Mishna and *Ein Yaakov*.[8]

I remember the following dedicated students at the House of Study:

[Page 72]

Moshe-Mendl Valach was a great scholar, sharp-minded and very knowledgeable. As a lumber merchant, he was occupied in the forest all day, as the representative of a large lumber company. In the evening, on his way back from work, he would stop at the House of Study and spend hours studying eagerly. On Fridays, he would devote almost the entire night to studies. He usually studied standing upright, one foot resting on a bench, discussing fine Talmudic points, with which he was familiar. Another was Shimon Moshe Goldberg and his sons Henech and Shmuel, and his son-in-law Yitzchak Lerner. With them were Aharon Yehuda Ha-Levi Fraynd and sons Yosef, Avrom, and Dovid. Leybish Goldberg, Pinches Berger, David Yosef Zuberman and his sons Leybl Zuberman, Ben-Tziyon Zuberman, and Tzvi Zuberman.

Ya'akov Zuberman and his family: sons, daughters, and grandchildren

All these pure souls and martyrs were murdered because they were Jews.

The devotion to study exhibited by the Jews of Horodlo is illustrated by the following episode, which I heard from Shimon Vizenberg. The incident had happened to him more than fifty years earlier.

When Rabbi Moshe Leyb was still living with his father-in-law Rabbi Yekutiel (may his righteous memory be for a blessing), Rabbi of Horodlo at the time, he would study at the small synagogue

[Page 73]

until 2 a.m.[9] Shimon Vizenberg would also conclude his studies at that time, and the two would walk home together.

Once, Rabbi Moshe Leyb forgot to call Shimon when it was time to go home. Shimon was so immersed in his studies that he did not notice Moshe-Leyb's departure. When he realized that he had been left alone, he decided to spend the entire night in the synagogue hall, as he was afraid of walking through the corridor. It was where the plank for preparing bodies for burial was stored. Sometimes a gravestone would be left there before being installed at the cemetery.

That same night, Elazar Dovid's wife was undergoing a difficult childbirth. Her husband and family members went to the small synagogue to tie a thread from the Ark of the Torah to the hand of the woman, as a talisman that would ease childbirth. When Shimon heard the door opening, he remembered the folk tradition that the dead come at midnight to pray in the synagogue. He sprang to the window, broke the pane, and fled. Elazar Dovid's wife gave birth to a daughter that night. When people began coming for morning prayers, they were surprised by the intense cold, and noticed the broken pane. After investigation and attempts to understand the situation, they realized what had happened to Shimon that night, and understood that he had fled through the window.

There was so much beauty in the lives of the Jews of Horodlo who prayed in the great synagogue as well as in the smaller ones.

I will close with a wish: He who told the world that it was finished will tell our troubles the same. Let us witness consolation for those who mourn for Zion![10]

Translator's Footnotes:

1. This was Rabbi Gershon Chanoch Henech Leiner of Radzyn (1839 - December 15, 1890), the first Rabbi of Radzin.

2. *Ein Ya'akov* is a 16th-century compilation of Aggadic material in the Talmud, with commentaries.

3. Rashi (the acronym for Rabbi Shlomo Yitzchaki, 1040-1105) was a French rabbi, who is widely considered the greatest commentator on the Talmud and Hebrew Bible to this day.

4. A Melamed is a religious instructor, usually for children.

5. The Rim (the acronym of Rabbi Yitzchak Meir Rothenburg, 1799-1866) was the founder and first leader of the Ger Hasidic dynasty. The Tosfot are medieval commentaries on the Talmud. The reference is to an item in the Mishna section on bills of divorce (Gittin).

6. I was unable to find any town with the name of Gyavitz.

7. The 'slaughterers' were ritual butchers that prepared kosher meat. The Hebrew term for this role is shochet.

8. Large brick ovens are traditionally used in Europe to heat sizeable buildings. *Ein Yaakov* is a 16th-century compilation of all the Aggadic material in the Talmud together with commentaries.

9. It was customary for fathers of brides to provide room and board for the young family for the first few years of marriage. The term would be set in the marriage contract (Ketubah).

10. This is a common phrase of response to a disaster.

[Page 74]

Horodlo, Our Town
(Reminiscences)

Ben-Tziyon Bergman, Argentina

The heart floods with blood, and tears choke the throat, when one sits down to write about the town of Horodlo. You are writing about your home town, where you were born, where you enjoyed the springtime of your life, and had so many dreams, wove so many plans…

You left behind your nearest and dearest, your childhood and your youth. You parted from a living Jewish town, with all its Jewish charms, stored deep in your heart, so longed for, and now you are setting down your memories of it… True, memories are the only thing that remains of a life that was, and of those who lived…

It gnaws at your heart, pulls at your soul. You're dipping your pen not only in ink but also in blood and tears that suffuse your very being, as you try to set down at least a partial memorial to the home town that was Horodlo.

* * *

Horodlo was a historic town, and for a short time – even the capital of a bygone Poland, during the reign of King Jagiełło.[1] The old city park, on the road to Uściług, contained a remnant of the royal palace, and, in fact, the park bore the name of the king.

The Jewish population of Horodlo consisted of 150 families, which included about 1250 individuals.

[Page 75]

Synagogues

The Great Synagogue in the center of town was the tallest structure in town, and remarkable for its height and beauty. Its thick walls were built of stone, the windows were vaulted and very impressive, and it had the general appearance of an ancient fortress. The Ark of the Torah was magnificent, and its decorations reached to the heights. The large bimah and its ornamentation were also striking. A sense of majesty suffused the structure.

This was where the town rabbi prayed, and an honored seat was set aside for him, at the eastern wall, near the Ark of the Torah.

The small synagogue of the Radzin Hasids and the small synagogue of the artisans were inside the building. There was also a House of Study in the town, a synagogue of Turiisk (Trisk) Hasids, and a small synagogue where Zionist youth prayed. Both the small synagogue and House of Study were used by young men and homeowners who studied Torah until late at night. The study chant could be heard outside, in the nearby streets.[2]

Cemeteries

There were three Jewish cemeteries in Horodlo. One was on the road to Strzyżów, and the other two were very old, one on the road to Uściług, and another near the Bug River. The one near the river (not far from the market) was the oldest of the three, and its ancient gravestones attested to the antiquity of the Horodlo Jewish community. The cemetery on the road to Uściług was termed "the old cemetery," and the gravestones there dated to a remote, bygone past.

My father (may his memory be for a blessing) told us that the landowner – whose properties included the "old cemetery" – once wanted to repurpose the area, plow it up, and use it for planting. But

[Page 76]

an extraordinary thing happened: the horses yoked to the plow died before they could begin their task.

As I recall, in 1935 the landowner Wieszwicki sold his property, including the cemetery (for use as a field to plant grain). The town rabbi, Rabbi Moshe Leyb Berman (may his righteous memory be for a blessing) and my father, Yosef Bergman (may his memory be for a blessing) visited him and requested that the cemetery not be sold. They told him what had happened to the previous landowner's horses when he wanted to desecrate the cemetery. The current landowner burst out laughing.

A few days later, he called for my father (may his memory be for a blessing) and informed him that he was giving the cemetery to the Jewish community, as he feared a disaster would happen there. He added that a few days earlier he had suddenly become ill and had had to stay in bed.

Every time we strolled down the Uściług road, we would visit the cemetery and study the inscriptions on the partially sunken gravestones. The inscriptions on some stones were 150 years old.

The Hill near the House of Study

A low earthen mound not far from the House of Study was fenced and had an aura of mystery. The Jews of Horodlo said that the mound was the resting place of a newly wed couple who had died on one and the same night. They also said that the author Ansky had visited the site before he wrote *The Dybbuk*, and had wanted to hear all about the mysterious mound.[3]

The Town Rabbi and the Ritual Slaughterers

In my time, the town rabbi was Moshe-Leyb Berman (may his righteous memory be for a blessing). He was renowned throughout Poland for his knowledge and standing, and the Horodlo community was proud to have such a great and venerated spiritual leader at its head.

[Page 77]

Our town also had two ritual slaughterers (shochets) who were pious and scholarly, and of exemplary character: Yaakov Chesner and Mordechai Faygenboym (may their memory be for a blessing). The rabbi and the slaughterers were eminent Radzin Hasids.

Educational Institutions

There were five cheders in Horodlo, where Jewish boys aged 5-13 received their first Jewish education, typically comprising Hebrew, Torah, and Mishna[4]. They entered the system gradually. A boy who reached cheder age began in the youngest age group, and started learning

Children near the home of Mates the Melamed
Zelig Zeyf is visible on the terrace

[Page 78]

Hebrew, staying there until they were old enough to study Talmud. They would then transfer to a higher-level cheder, where they studied Talmud for several years. When judged to be prepared, they would begin studying with Rabbi Yosef Shmuel – a learned and knowledgeable scholar, who taught the boys Talmud with commentaries and *Yoreh De'ah*.[5] Another option was study with Rabbi Yitzchak (Melech's son), another great scholar who taught Talmud with medieval commentaries.

A Jewish boy who had gone through the various cheders, and studied with Yosef Shmuel or Yitzchak (Melech's son), was considered a scholar and could study on his own, in the House of Study or a small synagogue.

Horodlo did not have a Jewish school that offered general studies, except for a short time. Anyone who wanted to acquire general knowledge had to study with private tutors who were brought to Horodlo by those who were interested; they changed often. Local Hebrew teachers were Fishl Blay and Mordechai Fraynd, in addition to others who were brought into the town.[6]

The Hasids of Horodlo

The vast majority of the Jews in town were Hasids, and most of them belonged to the Radzin group; they were usually in charge of religious affairs in town. Others belonged to the Trisk, Ger, and Belz groups.

The Radzin Rabbis Mordechai Yosef Elazar Layner (may his righteous memory be for a blessing, may God avenge his blood) occasionally visited Horodlo. Others who visited were the Trisk Rabbis Velvele (may his righteous memory be for a blessing) and Nunyele (may his righteous memory be for a blessing). When the Hasidic leaders visited, the town took on a festive air.

Other visitors in the town were emissaries from the Land of Israel, from the Rabbi Meir Ba'al HaNess (may his merit protect us) organization.[7] The organization's representatives in Horodlo were

[Page 79]

Shimon Biterman (may his memory be for a blessing) and Mordechai Faygenboym (may his memory be for a blessing). Naturally, the visit of such an emissary was an important occurrence and aroused much interest.

Community Institutions

Similarly to every Polish town, Horodlo had an organized Jewish community that ran Jewish affairs, and supervised religious needs. The community was recognized by the Polish authorities as the body responsible for the town's religious institutions.

During my time, the community heads were Petachya Blatt and Aharon Chaim Feder, both belonging to the Radzin Hasidic group.

The community also had the municipal bathhouse, with the Jewish ritual bath alongside. Moshe Vortsl and Beryl Holts were in charge of the ritual bath. There was also a hostel for wayfarers (personally supported by Yaakov Boymeyl) for indigent travelers. The community was in charge of the chevra kadisha (burial society), which was managed by Yizchak Blum.

Jewish Delegates in the Town Council

The council consisted of 24 members: twelve Poles, six Ukrainians, and six Jews. The last Jewish representatives were Pinkhes Berger, Yosef Bergman (my father, may his memory be for a blessing), Aharon-Leyb Fraynd, Shimon Biterman, Yehoshua Ayzen, and Mendl Lerner.

The Tarbut Library[8]

The town had a Tarbut library, and comprised Hebrew and Yiddish books. It was the focal point of Zionist activities, and fund-raising for Zionist institutions such as Keren Kayemet, Keren Ha-Yesod, and Keren Tel-Chai.[9] The library functioned within the framework

[Page 80]

of the Zionist youth organizations He-Chalutz, Beitar, and the Union of Artisans. The Library management offered various study courses such as Hebrew, Bible, talks about literature and politics, dramatic readings and other cultural activities. An amateur drama group connected with the library presented historical and social performances.

After branches had been established of the Zionist Organization and the Zionist Keren-Kayemet and Keren Ha-Yesod, emissaries from the Land of Israel would occasionally come to raise funds on their behalf.[10] The arrival of such an emissary aroused much interest among young people and excitement among Zionist activists. I remember the visit of the Keren Kayemet delegate, Yaakov Melamed (may his memory be for a blessing), and his meetings concerning Zionism with members of the synagogue, as well as the lecture he gave in Hebrew to young Zionists. His visit and the meetings aroused national feelings among the Jews of Horodlo.

General Institutions

There were many committees and institutions for charitable, social, and Zionist activities. Among them was a women's association whose mission was to provide light breakfasts and milk for cheder students and poor children in general. During the years of World War I, an aid committee was set up by the "Joint," to supply food and clothing to the needy.[11] They also ran a food kitchen. Shabtai Shek, Aharon Zuberman, Ben-Tziyon Zuberman, and Aharon Valach were members of the committee.

The first library was founded by Nokhem Berger, Henech Berman, Ben-Tziyon Zuberman, Aharon Zuberman, Shlomo Zuberman,

[Page 81]

Tzvi Zuberman, Henech Zuberman, Fishl Davidovitsh, Aharon Stav, Dovid Fraynd, and Aharon Valach (now living in Israel).

The *Tarbut* library was founded by Henech Zuberman, Tzvi Zuberman, Shlomo Zuberman, Binyomin Berger, Dovid Fraynd, Yitzchak Fraynd, Ben-Tziyon Bergman, Bluma Zuberman, Gitl Berger, Malka Valach, Rokhl Zuberman, Hinda-Rivka Stav (now living in Uruguay), Perl Biderman (now living in Brazil).

A local branch of HeChalutz was established by Ben-Tziyon Bergman (now living in Argentina), Moshe Zuberman (now living in Israel), Rokhl Zuberman (now living in Argentina), Michael Berger, Avrom Kulish (now living in Israel).[12] Among its members were Efrayim Ayzen, Aryeh Shtayn, Yehoshua Zisberg, Yehoshua Berger, Moshe Zavidovich, Pinches Varman, Shmuel Harfin, and Shmuel Vagshal.

Members of HeChalutz had to undergo physical and agricultural training before their emigration to Palestine. Horodlo members who took this training course were: Ben-Tziyon Bergman, Moshe Zuberman (in Bilgoray), Shmuel Vagshal (in Baranavichy), Yehoshua Zisberg, Shmuel Harfin, Aryeh Shtayn, and Avrom Kulish (in Skryhiczyn).

The candidates for emigration had to pass an examination at the end of their training course. These were held at various sites, including Zamość. Candidates from Horodlo who took that examination (in which Mr. Dobkin, the director of the HeChalutz took part) included Moshe Zuberman, Avrom Kulish, and Ben-Tziyon Bergman.

The Beitar youth movement: A branch of Beitar was formed in Horodlo in 1929, after a Beitar convention in which delegates from the following nearby towns participated: Hrubieszow, Ludmir, Uściług, and Uchańe.[13] Its founders were Eliezer Lerner, Shimon Zuberman, Tzvi Zaltzman, Yosef Zavidovich (now living in Israel), Fishl Gertl (now living in Canada), Shimon Goldberg, Michael Bergman (now living in Argentina), Tzvi

[Page 82]

Members of the Beitar Youth Movement in Horodlo

Zuberman (now living in the U.S.), Eliezer Shmidt (now living in Israel). Tzvi Zaltzman was elected branch leader, and Eliezer Lerner was elected treasurer.

After some Beitar members joined HeChalutz Ha-Mizrachi, and others moved away from Horodlo, the branch was led by younger members: Moshe Zuberman, Moshe Chaim Bergman, Eliyahu Grosburd, Yitzchak Shruver, Fishl Fraynd, Shmuel Fraynd, Yekutiel Zavidovich, Rokhl Grosburd, Etel Sherer, Moshe Harfin, Shmuel Link, Moshe Zisberg, Shimshon Fraynd, Libe Bernshteyn, Yaakov Shruver, Moshe Shruver, and Fishl Rozenblum.[14]

The branch was very active and organized sports and cultural events. The 11th day of Adar – the anniversary of the death of Yosef Trumpeldor, the hero of Galilee – was celebrated with great ceremony.[15] The branch members would hold a military march, which concluded in the Great Synagogue with a memorial service for Trumpeldor and his fallen comrades. These Beitar activities made a tremendous impression on the town's residents.

Revisionist Zionism: Some time afterwards, a branch of Revisionist Zionism was established in town, by

[Page 83]

Ben-Tziyon Bergman (chairman), Shmuel Zuberman, Binyomin Berger, and Aryeh Herbst (secretary).[16]

The Artisans' Association: The wave of social organization included the artisans, who had traditionally not been organized. They created

A Beitar group in Horodlo

[Page 84]

the artisans' association. The leaders of the association were Yechiel Sherer (chairman), Efrayim Ayzen, Ya'akov Mederdrut (now living in Argentina), and Mordechai Sofer (now living in Canada).

Keren Kayemet, Keren HaYesod: A local branch was established by Tzvi Zuberman, Aryeh Herbst, Yitzchak Fraynd, Mordechai Zuberman, Ben-Tziyon Bergman (chairman of HeChalutz), and Yechiel Sherer (chairman of the artisans' association). The first meeting of the Keren Kayemet activists was held in the home of Shmuel Goldberg. The following members were elected to the first local committee:

Yehoshua Kupershtoko

Tzvi Zuberman, Aryeh Herbst, Yitzchak Fraynd, Ben-Tziyon Bergman, Binyomin Berger, Mechl Berger, Rokhl Zuberman.

The Tel Chai Fund[17]: Members and sympathizers of the Revisionist movement created the Tel Chai Fund. The authorized leader was Ben Tziyon Bergman, Aryeh Herbst was secretary, and Binyomin Berger the treasurer. Shmuel Zuberman was also a member of the branch management.

Before I left for Argentina, the central committee of the Fund in London sent us an honorary certificate signed by Jabotinsky (may his memory be for a blessing), recognizing my devoted work for the fund.

Horodlo was surrounded by farming villages, which had Jewish residents. These families, whose livelihood forced

[Page 85]

Efrayim and Eliyahu Kupershtok,
the sons of Yehoshua Kupershtok

them to live among many Gentiles, isolated from Jewish culture, maintained religious and social ties with the Jewish community of Horodlo. They would leave their villages before the solemn High Holidays as well as other holidays, and celebrate with the Horodlo Jewish community, which considered the village Jews part of themselves.

After Keren Kayemet and Keren HeYesod were established in the town, we included them in our fund-raising activities. We supplied them with Keren Kayemet and Keren HaYesod collection boxes, and would send our members to empty the boxes. Thus, we all shared in Zionist activities.

Jewish families lived in the villages of Strzyżów, Rybne, Kowal, Kopyłów, Łysek, Mącice, Łuszków, Usiniv, and Janki.

There was a large sugar factory in Strzyżów,

[Page 86]

owned by a Polish company that employed many Poles. Before Pesach, the owners would invite our rabbi to render the factory Kosher for the holiday. The rabbi would appoint the following supervisors: Shmuel Herbst, Yosef Bergman, and Yehuda Biterman.

Once World War I was over, a social and national revival began among the young people of Horodlo. News that a Jewish Legion had been established at the initiative of Jabotinsky (may his memory be for a blessing) spread through the town.[18] This word of an armed Jewish force, which fought the Germans and the Turks alongside the British army, sparked nationalist excitement among the young people of Horodlo. Local youth groups organized in the town, practiced military exercises, and taught them to others in the town. On one occasion, we were arrested by the authorities because of these activities, and were released thanks to the efforts of my father (may his memory be for a blessing).

When the new Polish state was created in 1918, nationalistic feelings increased among the Poles, accompanied by animosity towards Jews. The authorities attacked the library and arrested us on the pretext that we were carrying out Communist activities in the space. One again, we were freed thanks to my father's efforts.

Memories of Hanukah; the Synagogue Caretakers

As I recall, all the synagogue caretakers spoke nasally, walked with a limp, or stammered. I remember our joy as children and teenagers when a mocking version of a Hanukah song began, "He walks, he lights, he burns, the caretaker burns."[19] I conducted this "choir" when the blessings were said; the caretaker always made mistakes in the blessings. So he was always annoyed with me – though secretly pleased, because the "choir" concealed his mistakes

[Page 87]

from the congregation.

Whenever there was a Sholem-Zachar or Sheva-Brachot celebration in town, or calling on a bridegroom to read from the Torah, the caretaker would rap on the lectern on Friday evening when prayers were concluded, and announce that so-and-so was inviting the congregation to a sholem-zachar or a circumcision ceremony.[20] He would confuse the topics and the announcement came out topsy-turvy.

I would get him going, and it was very lively in town afterwards. The caretakers were Moshe Vortsl (he was also in charge of the ritual bath), Yaakov Matsher, Mordechai Shammes, and Alter Shek.

* * *

Oh, how can one forget the town and its Jews, when it lives on with you and in you?

Even though so many years have passed, and so many events separate you from your youth, your town accompanies you wherever you go. It lies deep within your heart and mind, and will never leave you for the rest of your life.

Translator's Footnotes:

1. Wladyslaw II Jagiello (14th-15th centuries) was an important king of Poland.

2. The Trisk Hasidic Dynasty originated in the city of Turiisk, located today in the Ukraine.

3. Shloyme Zanvl Rapoport (1820-1920), known by his pseudonym S. Ansky, was a Jewish author, playwright, researcher of Jewish folklore, and cultural and political activist. He wrote the play *The Dybbuk, or Between Two Worlds* between 1913 and 1916. The play, which depicts the possession of a young woman by the malicious spirit – known as a *Dybbuk* in Jewish folklore – of her dead beloved, became a canonical work of both Hebrew and Yiddish theater, and was translated and performed around the world. Much of the action is set in a Jewish cemetery.

4. A cheder is a religious school for Jewish children. The Mishna is the first major compilation of rabbinic literature.

5. A 16th-century compilation of Jewish law.

6. Traditional Jewish education did not offer Hebrew as a subject of study.

7. Rabbi Meir was a Jewish sage who lived in the Land of Israel in the second century C.E. and according to tradition was buried in Tiberias. He is considered to have been a miracle-worker, and requests for help are placed at his tomb. Charities also bear his name. Emissaries from these charities often visit Jewish communities to collect donations.

8. Tarbut was a network of secular Zionist educational institutions that functioned in Poland in the interwar period; the language of instruction was Hebrew.

9. These are charitable organizations dedicated

10. Keren Kayemet LeIsrael is better known as the Jewish National Fund. It was established in 1901, is a non-profit organization that buys and develops land for Jewish settlement in the Land of Israel. Keren Ha-Yesod, (established in 1920 and now known as United Israel Appeal) supports programs and projects that meet the challenges facing the State of Israel and Jews throughout the world.

11. The JDC (Joint Distribution Committee, familiarly known as the "Joint"), is a Jewish relief organization founded in New York City in 1914, and providing support to Jews throughout the world.

12. HeChalutz ("the pioneer") Jewish youth movement (founded 1918) trained young people for agricultural settlement in British Mandate Palestine. The training courses were held in various agricultural locations.

13. Beitar is the acronym of a right-wing Revisionist Zionist Jewish youth movement founded in Riga, Latvia in 1923 by Vladimir (Zev) Jabotinsky.

14. HeChalutz Ha-Mizrachi was a youth movement of religiously observant Zionists.

15. Yosef Trumpeldor (1880-1920) was an early Zionist activist who helped to organize the Zion Mule Corps in the British army, and bring Jewish immigrants to Palestine. Trumpeldor died defending the Galilee settlement of Tel Chai in 1920 and subsequently became a Jewish national hero.

16. Revisionist Zionism is a form of Zionist characterized by territorial maximalism, such as on both sides of the Jordan River.

17. This monetary fund was originally established in the wake of the 1929 riots in Palestine. It was initially dedicated to training young Jews in self-defense and took its name from a former Jewish settlement in northern Israel that was the site of an early battle in which the founder of Zionist Revisionism, Joseph Trumpeldor, had been killed.

18. The Jewish Legion was a military formation of Jewish volunteers in World War I who fought in the British Army (1915-1918) for the liberation of the Land of Israel from Turkish rule.

19. I could not find a source for this song.

20. A Sholem-Zachar celebration is held on the first Friday night after the birth of a baby boy. Sheva-Brachot are seven special blessings that complete the wedding ceremony and can extend to the festive meals during the week after the wedding.

[Page 88]

Reminiscences

by Rokhl Bergman, Argentina

Horodlo was a small town, with only a few hundred Jewish families. Spiritually however, in bygone times its Jewish community had considerable significance, thanks to the numerous Jews who were outstanding in their scholarship and vast knowledge. The young people also strove to broaden their knowledge, and were remarkable for their familiarity with Jewish tradition as well as with general areas.

Jewish young people were educated in cheders, which supplied religious education exclusively. They could acquire a general education at the Polish school; but many of the teachers there were extremely anti-Semitic. Jewish parents allowed themselves to send only their daughters to the Polish school, as the attitude towards them was more or less appropriate. Young boys studied in cheders; when they grew older, they transferred to the House of Study or the Hasidic synagogues.

The spirit of general [i.e. secular] education had also spread through our town. Those Jewish young people who spent their time in the House of Study or the Hasidic synagogues were affected by the same atmosphere as in the large cities of Poland, and expressed the desire to gain a general education. The possibilities for that in Horodlo were very limited, but the economic conditions of those Jews who wanted to send their children to school elsewhere was just as constrained. This situation was augmented by the contempt of the pious Jews of Horodlo for a general education. These circumstances forced the young people of Horodlo to try and develop cultural activities on their own.

One of the first activities initiated in this way

[Page 89]

was the establishment of a library by young women.

This took place in 1916. We gathered a group of women and several girls at the house of Fradl Stav, with the sisters Hinde and Rivke Stav (Hinde lives in Montevideo, and Rivke in Argentina), and discussed the creation of a library of Yiddish books.[1] My young cousin Mirl Zuberman (may her memory be for a blessing) and I were the youngest in the group. We decided to collect donations and buy books. We ordered

Miriam Stav (Moshe Stav's wife) and her son

books by mail from book dealers in Warsaw. Once the books arrived, the library was opened for lending.

Apparently, the library activists were motivated by left-wing ideals: the *Marseilleise* was dispensed together with books, and we were taught to sing it.[2] At that time, I was not aware of the song's meaning and its political significance, and sang it with great enthusiasm. But

[Page 90]

my brother Henech (may his memory be for a blessing) was very familiar with these aspects – he was highly educated by then – and knew about the various political movements. He explained the political importance of the song (I think he forbade me to sing it). He was also aware of the left-wing leanings of the group that gathered around the library. Henech considered this group a danger to young people, from a national point of view. He called a meeting of the best young people and the existing library group, in order to establish a large general library.

The major difficulty they faced in this mission was the lack of a suitable space. The older generation was pious, and its members made sure that no Jew rented us an apartment or a room for our activities. At that time, gathering boys and girls together at meetings and activities was considered a major sin. Parents often used to show up at a meeting and force their daughters to return home. However, we continued the work and even made progress.

We were eventually able to rent a room from Rokhl Berger. I remember well the first general assembly of our small club, and our excitement when preparing for it! The general interest among the public was great as well. The mood was celebratory on the evening that the assembly elected a committee to manage the library and its cultural activities.

The committee members were my brother Henech, chairman (may his memory be for a blessing), one of the Stav sisters (vice-chairman), Mordechai Zuberman (secretary), and Shlomo Zuberman (treasurer).

The library was open twice a week to borrow books. People gathered almost every evening to talk and read. On Friday nights and Saturday afternoons, readings and talks took place about various issues. These community

[Page 91]

Moshe Grosburd, his wife Chave, and their children, in the company of friends and relatives

activities excited the town's young people, and the club offered them a place to meet.

Some time later, the library moved to a different location, rented in the home of Zlate Stav (now living in Israel). Now we were able to increase the range of our activities. There were memorial meetings for Dr. Theodor Herzl, Joseph Trumpeldor, and other Zionist leaders. We held literary evenings and gatherings on various topics. The speakers and masters of ceremony at these meetings were Henech Zuberman – my unforgettable brother – Ben-Tziyon Zuberman, Mordechai Zuberman, Binyomin Berger, and others well versed in culture. All the cultural events we organized were of high standards, and were well-organized and interesting. The non-local guests expressed their admiration for our young people and for the town.

Most of the young folks were already well-informed, and strove to broaden their wisdom and knowledge. Most could

[Page 92]

study Talmud, and quite a few of them knew Hebrew well.

My brother Henech was one of the most respected of the younger generation. He had vast knowledge, and was an expert on Hebrew. He had gained his entire education by studying on his own.

I mentioned earlier that there was no Jewish school in Horodlo. We girls received our general education in

Henech Zuberman with his wife Chana and their two children, Henech's mother and brother

a Polish school. We studied Jewish subjects and religious topics with tutors, who were poor in cultural expertise. I studied with Shlomo Todros (may his memory be for a blessing), who might have been considered an expert in religious topics, but had little general knowledge and poor pedagogical practices. Naturally, we could not demand too much of such teachers. It was then decided to create a Hebrew school that would be headed by gifted teachers.

[Page 93]

That is when the Tarbut school was established, which was led by Ya'akov Brik, a teacher from Uściług. He had extensive knowledge and was an excellent teacher, who was able to elevate the school to an advanced level. Children from all social classes attended with great enthusiasm, paid attention to the teacher during classes, and did their homework in good time. The girls who attended the Polish school also went to the Hebrew school, in spite of the difficulties: we went to the Polish school in the morning, rushed home for our Hebrew books and notebooks, and ran to the Tarbut school to be there punctually. It was quite an effort. But our desire to learn Hebrew overcame all the problems. It is worth bearing in mind that our pious parents were displeased at the creation of a Hebrew school; they believed that the cheder should be the only educational framework for Jewish children. Their opposition caused the Tarbut students many problems, and interfered with the school's operation.

The library's development and increased number of readers led to the need for a larger space. We rented a large house outside the Jewish neighborhood, which comprised several large rooms; the house was surrounded by a fruit tree orchard. The house had once belonged to a priest, who had let it run down severely. But we repaired it and adapted it for our activities. On these new premises, we created a room for drama and events, and were able to expand our cultural activities. A drama club was organized, which occasionally gave performances. It was headed and directed by the artist Mittelpunkt, from the nearby village of Dubienka. Among the plays we performed were "Bar-Kochba", "The Yeshiva-Student" and others.[3] The performances were

[Page 94]

very well done, and attracted many viewers; the actors were excellent. I remember the wonderful acting of the beautiful Chana Chesner and my cousin Bluma Goldberg, as well as other girls and boys.

The original founders and activists of the library and the Zionist club gradually left their positions. Some of the older ones moved to other towns, while the majority began to raise families and left their community roles to younger people. One of the younger Zubermans was elected library chairman, and I was elected secretary. Yehoshua Zisberg (Aharon-Osher's son) was selected treasurer, and other positions were given to young people. As a result of the numerous activities, the office responsibilities increased: the minutes and all office documents had to be in Polish (in addition to the local Yiddish), in accordance with the laws of community activities. After every general meeting, we had to send the minutes to Hrubieszow, the regional capital, for confirmation. Yet our work continued, and we made progress.

At the time, anti-Semitism in Poland grew stronger. Ruffians attacked Jews at night, and we were often pelted with stones on the way home from the club. We were therefore forced to move the club from the Christian neighborhood to the Jewish neighborhood. A women's association to feed poor children was created. Those activists were Yocheved Zuberman (Chesner), Chana Zuberman (Zisberg, my sister-in-law), Beyle Fraynd (living in Israel), Tehila Grosburd, Chaya Katzhendler, and

[Page 95]

others. I was secretary of the managing committee, and Tehila Grosburd was the treasurer.

We often gathered at Berl (Dov) Grosburd's for tea, and discuss our activities and plans. The most active member of the association was Beyle Fraynd, who hardly missed any activity or party. She was always among those who handed out food to the children.

Beitar was the most prominent of the youth organizations of those years; it included most of the young people. The administrators of the local branch would often assemble at our house; my younger brother Moshe was then the branch secretary, and the branch commander was Tzvi Zaltzman.[4] Some of the activists now live in Israel and Argentina.

My extraordinary brother Henech was in charge of local Keren Kayemet activities for many years. When I left Horodlo to go to Argentina, I told him to follow in my tracks; he responded, "I've represented Keren Kayemet for eighteen years, and deserve a certificate to immigrate to the Land of Israel. I hope to receive it."[5] Alas! He was not lucky enough to have this wish come true. He endured the same fate as all the Polish Jews, who were murdered by the German Nazis (may their name be blotted out). All that is left is profound pain and longing for our dear ones who were alive and are no more.

Translator's Footnotes:

1. The Yiddish word "yidish" can refer to the Yiddish language as well as serve as the adjective "Jewish." The meaning here is unclear.

2. "La Marseillaise" is the national anthem of France. It was the rallying call to the French Revolution and during the nineteenth and early twentieth centuries, was recognized as the anthem of the international revolutionary movement.

3. "Bar Kochba" was a popular play by Avrom Goldfaden, considered the "father" of Yiddish theater.

4. *Beitar* branches were organized along military lines.

5. The British Mandate authorities severely restricted Jewish immigration to Palestine in the 1930s.

[Page 96]

The Young People
and their Social and Cultural Activity

by Moshe Zuberman, Israel

As a child, when I was still studying in the cheder with Motl, Fishl's son, World War I came to an end. A new era began for the Jews of Poland, one of lively political and cultural activity. Our town was affected by the new direction that the Jewish population was taking.

The young people of Horodlo continued to use the House of Study and be devoted to religious studies, and were completely separated from everyday life. But new ways of thought percolated into the Jewish population, and attracted a significant number of the young folks. They abandoned the benches in the House of Study, and began to partake in community cultural affairs. That was when the general library was established, began to exert its influence in the community, and shape its interests. The parents' generation was not pleased at this direction. They considered the library a departure from the moral ways that had been followed until then, and attempted to obstruct our activity in various ways. The young people ignored these attempts and continued their activity.

A significant milestone that occurred at that time was the foundation of a Hebrew school. The founders were Nokhem Berger (may his memory be for a blessing), Moshe (Alter's son, may his memory be for a blessing), and Tzvi Zuberman (may his memory be for a blessing), who brought Ya'akov Brik, one of the best Hebrew teachers, to our town. The young students were very excited at the chance to acquire a Hebrew education in a Hebrew school.

[Page 97]

The library's founders themselves could not foresee how important the library and the activities around it would be in forming the identity of the young people and their relationship to the Zionist movement as well as tor Zionist work. At that time, the Zionist way of thinking of mind was not widespread in the Horodlo public, and the Zionist ideal had not yet captivated the young people of the community. Community and cultural work was carried out by the library, which attracted the young folks and pointed them towards Zionist work and activities that supported the Zionist settlers in the Land of Israel.

Public Zionist activity, which was first organized in the Zionist club, took the form of a Hanukah event at the house of Dovid Berger. I remember the good impression the event made on the young people. The program was rich and full of variety, with Hanukah songs and recitations. The hall was decorated with Zionist flags and embellished in blue and white. The elevated, festive mood of the town was even more pronounced in the performance space; it was packed with young men and women.

At this point, I would like to mention the original initiators of Zionist activity in Horodlo; they were Ben-Tziyon Zuberman (may his memory be for a blessing), Fishl Zavidovich (may his memory be for a blessing), and Dovid Fraynd (may his memory be for a blessing).

Zionist activity as well as community cultural work were well organized and orderly. The leaders organized the memorial event on the first anniversary of Dr. Herzl's death (the founder of political Zionism).[1] Zionist speeches were given by Fishl Zavidovich (may his memory be for a blessing) and Henech Zuberman (may his memory be for a blessing. The speeches made a strong impression on the attendees, thanks to their rich content and excellent form.

Some time later, work began for the Zionist funds Keren Kayemet and Keren HaYesod. This marked the beginning of a

[Page 98]

From right: Henye Berger, Khaye Zuberman, Broche Zavidovich, Tzvi Zuberman, Mekhl Zuberman, Ben-Tziyon Zuberman

period of ambitious fund-raising. The first representative of these funds was Hirsh Zuberman (may his memory be for a blessing).

Several years later, Zionist and community activity was taken up by the young people, as a considerable proportion of the founding generation members had left Horodlo and moved elsewhere. Yet these activities grew more intense, as though to convince the adults of the available possibilities. A youth library called "Flowers" was established, at the initiative of Ya'akov Gruber (may his memory be for a blessing), Eliezer Goldberg (may his memory be for a blessing), and their friends. This library had a positive effect on Jewish education as well as on the development of Zionist activity among the young people.

[Page 99]

Our specific Zionist activity continued for a period of time, during which both libraries operated separately, until a local Tarbut association was established, and recognized officially by the authorities as a community cultural association. This association combined both libraries – the old one and the newer "Flowers" one – as a single Hebrew-Yiddish library. The local Tarbut association was headed by Dovid Fraynd (may his memory be for a blessing), my brother Mordechai Zuberman (may his memory be for a blessing), and Ben-Tziyon Bergman (may he be designated for a long life).

The formation of the new Tarbut association provided new impetus for Zionist cultural work. Various activities, such as events, celebrations, and dramatic performances were organized by the young people.

From right: Moshe Zuberman, Shmulik Zuberman, Eliezer
Goldberg, Meir Zis, Yehoshua Zisbergn

[Page 100]

General community activity then intensified, with most of the activities centered on Tarbut. Over time, Zionist activities became oriented toward practical matters. The young people, who until then were occupied with cultural work and debates on issues of Zionism, began to think of realizing their Zionist ideals. A local branch of HeChalutz was established by a group of young people who wanted to carry this out and emigrate to the Land of Israel.

The HeChalutz pioneers were Yehuda-Leyb Shteyn (may his memory be for a blessing), Mechle Berger (may his memory be for a blessing), Rokhl (Zuberman) Bergman (living in Argentina), Avrom Kulish (living in Israel), Shnuel Vagshal (living in Birobidjan), Moshe Zavidovich (may his memory be for a blessing).

Some time later, a local branch of Beitar was established, and attracted most of the young people. It offered mostly educational and scouting activities, as well as military drills; its effect on the young people of Horodlo was considerable.

When I left Horodlo and emigrated to the Land of Israel, Beitar was the largest youth organization in town. Others who stayed in Horodlo for a longer time I can describe the continuation of its activities. The local branch was founded by Michael Bergman (living in Australia), Shimen Zuberman (may his memory be for a blessing), Eliezer Shmid (living in Israel), Dovid Gruber (may his memory be for a blessing), Fishl Hecht (living in Israel), Fishl Shek (may his memory be for a blessing), Fishl Gartl (living in Canada).

Translator's Footnote:

1. Theodore Herzl died in July 1904.

[Page 101]

Reminiscences of Life in the Horodlo Area

by Tzvi Plat, Haifa, Israel

Horodlo! The small, intimate town that is engraved on my heart, and where I took my first steps toward personal and economic independence.

Horodlo, the town that arouses good memories of youth and young people, of love, suffering, and struggle, as well as achievements.

Horodlo, with its beloved, lively young people, who yearned for knowledge and aspired to education. Horodlo, the town that never disappointed its visitors, and always pleased them. Horodlo, where I found my life partner Rokhl Zisberg (the daughter of Shloyme and Mirl Zisberg). We will set before you, my dear town and my beloved townspeople, a respectful and dedicated document, pages of reminiscences, that will revive the time beginning in when I came to the town, the years I lived there, and events during that period.

I was born in Hrubieszow, about 14 kilometers from Horodlo. My parents, who were murdered by the Hitlerite soldiers (may their names be blotted out), were Mendl Plat and his wife. He was known in town as 'Mendl the gaiter-maker,' as that was his craft. Everyone, including me, helped him with his work. At the same time, I was active in the Po'aley Tziyon organization, where I helped to organize cultural and communal activities for the young people of the town.[1]

[Page 102]

I was 20 years old at the time, full of energy and youth, and enthusiasm for the Zionist ideal; I strove to immigrate to the Land of Israel and join those who were rebuilding there. This idea had captivated the majority of young people in the town. In fact, all our Zionist activity was geared toward immigration to the Land of Israel and realizing the dream of generations of Jews.

Along with this work, I realized that I had to become my own man and live independently, without relying on my father. I gathered up my courage and told my father about my thoughts and efforts, and my plan to move to another town and try to live independently. We agreed that if I was to "go into the world," in other words move to a different town I should move to Horodlo, as we had relatives there: Matl Sofer's family.

One wintry morning, I got up and traveled to Horodlo, and talked to my relatives about my intention to settle there. That same evening, I met with Meir Zis, my future work-partner. Several days later, on Tuesday (the day of which God said, during the Creation "it was good" twice over), my father gave me a new machine, food for the road, and I left Hrubieszow to try my luck in the world.[2] I went to Horodlo, that small, sweet town.

On my first Shabbat in Horodlo, my partner, Meir Zis, took me to the club at the Tarbut library. I made the acquaintance of several of the young people of Horodlo. That Friday evening, I met three dear young women: Rokhele Zisberg (now my wife), Bluma Goldberg, and Broche Tchesner. I also became acquainted with Eliezer Goldberg (may his memory be for a blessing) and my good friend Moshe Zuberman (living in Israel).

That first evening was fascinating.

[Page 103]

By the light of a small kerosene lamp (Horodlo hadn't been electrified yet), we talked about various topics: politics, literature, and ordinary friendly conversation, seasoned with sincere humor;

From right: Rokhl Zisberg, Yehoshua Berger, Chayke Lerner,
Moshe Zavidovitch, Meir Zis, Masha Berger

[Page 104]

everyone joined in, especially the girls. I was very impressed by the sincerity of their powerful drive towards education and knowledge. The next day, Shabbat, I was able to meet some other comrades, mainly older teens. They were serious, idealistic young men, who yearned for knowledge. I wondered at this concentration of distinguished young folks in such a small town.

I was filled with a good feeling and great hopes. I began hoping that I'd be able to prepare here for emigration to the Land of Israel.

Life in Horodlo was quiet and flowed slowly. I continued working at my trade, and made good wages. But material advancement did not satisfy me, as I wanted to devote myself to cultural work, and fill my life with spiritual content.

It was not long in coming. Once I became acquainted with more young people, and especially with a group of friends (those whom I met on that first Friday evening), we would often meet at the home of Rokhl Zisberg during the long winter evenings to read literature. Sitting close to the warm oven, we would read together, chat, and discuss various problems and topics linked with the rebuilding of the Land of Israel. I remember Rokhl's father, Shloyme Yasha (later my father-in-law), leaning back against the oven, listening to our conversation and discussions, and smiling with pleasure.

These shared conversations eventually gave rise to the idea of a "workers' Land of Israel," after some of the young people drifted away due to the influence of the leftist teacher Kalotnitski, with his anti-Zionist views.

The actual organization of a local Po'aley-Tziyon branch began with the establishment of the "Avant-garde" circle

[Page 105]

by a youth group. This circle mounted a strong information campaign, which led to the local foundation of Po'aley Tziyon in Horodlo. With the assistance of the Hrubieszow branch of the movement, we rented an apartment for a club. We set up a library, and the club served as a meeting place for many of Horodlo's young people.

Once the club opened, we began carrying out wide-ranging cultural projects. These included literary readings, political talks, conversations on topics linked with the Land of Israel, and hora-dancing (these were new in Horodlo, and aroused much enthusiasm for the Zionist project).

Establishing a branch of the party in Horodlo and the young people's activities caused considerable friction between parents and children. The adults (mainly the mothers) complained about the "new calamity" that had overtaken the town. Mothers said, "Who knows what they do in that party of theirs?" "Sons and daughters neglect family affairs and are occupied only with party business," the mothers would say. We often noticed mothers standing behind the club's windows, looking in silently, to find out what was happening inside. However, our organizing work only intensified our feeling of independence; we young people were not ready to reject our course.

Actually, I did not spend a long time in Horodlo – eighteen months in all. Yet it was one of the most interesting periods in my personal life: I met my life partner. When I received my immigration certificate for Palestine in the Spring of 1930, together with my partner Rokhl Zisberg, I considered it the conclusion and realization of all the time and work during my period in Horodlo.

[Page 106]

* * *

Beloved Jews of Horodlo! It pains me to think that I now must recount my memories of Horodlo and its dear residents, for the pages of a Yizkor Book. A book about a town and a community that existed, and was annihilated by the barbarians. A book whose mission is to memorialize the Horodlo Jewish community and the beloved Jews of the town, who were murdered by the arch-enemy of the Jews, together with millions of European Jews.

* * *

Dear martyrs of Horodlo! I will remember you all my life. I will weave your precious memory together with the memory of all the heroes and martyrs who gave their lives because of persecution as Jews, and their efforts to revive the Jewish nation in the Land of Israel.

Translator's Footnotes:

1. Po'aley Tziyon, founded at the turn of the 20th century, was a popular, widespread socialist Zionist organization.

2. In Jewish tradition, this detail of the Creation story renders Tuesday ("the third day") auspicious for new projects.

[Page 107]

The Young People of Horodlo

by Rokhl Plat (Zisberg), Haifa, Israel

I'd like to describe, to the best of my ability, the activities of the young people of Horodlo, their cultural life, and their efforts to study and make progress to achieve a cultural education.

Though Horodlo was a small town, and the possibilities for acquiring an education were limited, the town's youth was outstanding and knowledge. They were remarkable for their drive to gain an education and broaden their knowledge, and to make continual progress in all domains. They achieved this despite difficult conditions, mainly by studying on their own. One could find a great many Talmudic scholars, as well as older and younger youths who studied independently and became experts in spite of degraded, inconvenient conditions. Yet in spite of all the difficulties, they attained marvelous achievements.

Cultural activity in the town centered on the Tarbut library. We used the library's club for meetings, parties, and ordinary gatherings. Serious literary discussions were held in the club twice a week; the speakers were young adults who were knowledgeable about literature, and donated their time to lead the discussions. Our cultural activity was nourished by our own cultural experts. Each member made efforts to share their knowledge in order to advance our cultural development.

Searching for activists from beyond the town, we believed that

[Page 108]

the teacher Fishl Blay was a new cultural resource who would enhance study and general education. However, it became evident over time that his pedagogical abilities were poor, and his influence on students was limited. He lived in the house of his father-in-law, who was a carpenter, and studied in the workshop, in spite of the noise of hammers and saws, and being surrounded by woodworkers.

A group of Horodlo Jews attending the wedding of Yosef Rozenblum. The bride and groom are visible, together with their family

Obviously, under these odd circumstances we could not devote ourselves to studies, but preferred mischief and pranks. The peak of our mischief making was once when we flung all the sawdust up to the ceiling, and it completely covered our study space. Our Fishl was scared and became very upset, but soon

[Page 109]

calmed down. He removed our chairs and positioned us on the floor. We felt he was justified, as we realized that we had gone too far. We often resolved to change our behavior and treat our teacher properly, but under our current study conditions and the mood in the workshop we could not do it. Sarah, Fishl Blay's wife, was a quiet, unassuming woman, so quiet that she seemed to have trouble uttering a sound. During class, she did not intervene and was inaudible. We thought that she was uninterested in our studies, and that our presence in the house did not bother her. But when we came to delicate verses in the Torah, she would suddenly appear from some corner and tell her husband quietly, "Fishl, stop! Feh, that's not nice."[1]

* * *

The first theatrical performance by the young people of Horodlo agitated all the residents, young and old. It developed into an intense fight between young people and their elders.

The events unfolded approximately as follows:

One fine morning, Mittelpunkt, the theater director from nearby Dubienka, appeared in town, and proposed a performance of the play titled "The Yeshiva Student," under his direction. This proposal was greeted enthusiastically. We gave our consent, and the director chose suitable actors. We began to work, learned how to perform our roles, practiced a few times, and the project progressed. By the time we were ready for the stage, we realized that our group included artistically talented people, as well as those who yearned for the theater. Once we had learned our parts, it was decided to perform the play on a certain Saturday night, and we made preparations accordingly.

[Page 110]

Our parents, however, thought otherwise. They considered a theatrical performance highly inappropriate and prohibited, and resolved to prevent it from taking place.

We found out, on the evening set for the performance, that our parents, headed by the town's rabbi, would be coming to the performance space to disrupt our preparations. Naturally, we decided to defend our project and prevent them from carrying out their plans, and to hold the performance regardless of the situation. We placed a strong watch on the entrance to the hall, and kept the demonstrators out. This conflict was challenging and awkward; it is hard for children to fight against their parents and grandparents. But we were resolved to carry out our project.

I can never forget this clash. I remember, as I was on my way to the show with a friend, we heard clamor and shouts far away. The sound of the opposing camps was audible in the nearby villages. Incidentally, the peasants – who were unaware of the reason for the clash – thought that it was caused by a pogrom against the Jews. The peasants approved of the idea, and began running in that direction armed with sticks, scythes, and spades. However, when they saw the strange, highly unusual scene, they turned back.

The clash ended without physical blows, and was confined to shouts and threats. The young people were adamant, and the performance took place without disturbance. However, the conflict led to prolonged ill feelings between many parents and children, until the sides reconciled.

I would like to emphasize that the adult fighters did not consist only of men,

[Page 111]

but many women also joined in the demand that we abandon the idea of a performance. Even women who had approved earlier now switched to the opposition

Even Beyle Fraynd (she was known as Chaya's Beyle), who had baked a large challah for the show, changed her mind during the demonstration and joined our opponents. True, she did not take up a stick or other weapon, but kept demanding that her brother Avrom Yehoshua, who had the leading role, "do her a favor and not perform this time." A modest request!

Following the success of the first show, we practiced intensively for a second one. This time, we planned to mount "The Two Kuni Lemels."[2] Once my family heard of my plans to participate, I was disparagingly branded an "actress," and met with severe disapproval. I was forbidden to take part.

One day, we heard that a young Hebrew teacher, Mordechai Fraynd (living in Israel) had come to town, and wanted to teach the language. This marked the beginning of a new phase for those young people who wanted to learn Hebrew. There were new possibilities for those who wanted to be educated in Hebrew. Thanks to Mordechai Fraynd, we began to study Hebrew literature as we became more proficient in the language. Some of us became experts in Hebrew. Zionism became more widespread at the time.

I remember national activities and events that were held with great pomp.[3] Especially memorable was a celebration held to mark the opening of the

[Page 112]

Hebrew University in Jerusalem.[4] The entire town was impressed by the wonderful event, and our longing for the Land of Israel increased.

Mordechai Fraynd encouraged us to try our hand at writing poems and articles, which we recited during social gatherings. I remember a poem by our dear friend Ya'akov (Yankele) Gruber (may his memory be for a blessing), titled "These Candles" ("Ha-neros Halalu"), which he recited at one of our Chanukah events.[5] He recited very passionately, but the group wasn't too enthusiastic and began making remarks. Yankele, however, was not bothered. He broke off the recitation briefly, saying ingenuously, "What? You don't like it? Never mind, but let me finish reciting, and we'll have our discussion then." His words were naïve, yet with a streak of humor, and the hall was suddenly filled with peals of laughter.

Mordechai Fraynd left Horodlo after a very active period, and was replaced by Kolodnitsky, a teacher from Bialystok. Officially, he was in Horodlo to teach Hebrew, but it soon became quite clear that he was on a different mission altogether. His views were Communist, and instead of teaching Hebrew he inculcated his students with Communist ideas. Without realizing it, some of his students became infected with his own views.

When we discovered his real intentions, many of his students left; only a few stayed on. Eventually, none at all remained, and he left Horodlo.

Quite soon afterwards, a guest from Hrubieszow arrived – Tzvi Plat. He stayed with us for longer.

[Page 113]

An activist member of Po'aley Tziyon, he was not idle. Plat held meetings with a select group of young people, organized conversations with members on political and social themes, and so gathered enough members to establish a local branch of Po'aley Tziyon.

The group, which was initially small in number, worked to disseminate the idea of a "Workers' Land of Israel" among the youth of Horodlo.[6] Eventually, a segment of Horodlo's young people joined the new party, and became very active.

With all this political and community activity, a "romance" unfolded between me and Tzvi Plat – my husband – a romance that has brought us to this point.

* * *

We left Horodlo in 1930, leaving behind all our acquaintances and dear ones. We had no idea at all that the merciless murderer, Hitler (may his name be blotted out), would appear and would bring the Jews of Europe (including the Jews of Horodlo) to such a tragic end.

May their memories be blessed!

Translator's Footnotes:

1. The exact meaning of "delicate" is unclear; it may refer to words interpreted as immodest.

2. This 19th century comedy of errors, by Avrom Goldfadn (the "father of Yiddish theater"), was extremely successful throughout Europe.

3. "National" was a common synonym for Zionist at the time.

4. The event took place in 1925

5. This is also the title of a traditional prayer that is chanted immediately after lighting the Hanukah candles.

6. This type of Zionism is usually referred to in English as Labor Zionism, combining Zionism and Socialism.

[Page 114]

[Blank]

[Page 115]

Horodlo During the First Months of the War

[Page 116]

[Blank]

[Page 117]

Horodlo During the First Days of the War

by Shmuel Fraynd, Tel Aviv, Israel

A year before the outbreak of World War II, the mood in Poland was oppressive and stifling – a mood of impending war. Horodlo lived in fear of what was to come.

1939 saw heavy German pressure on the Polish government to vote to abandon all claims and demands concerning Danzig and other territories. Germany's threats of war led to a gloomy mood in Poland, as well as suspicion and fear, especially among the Jews, as Hitler (may his name be blotted out) threatened all the Jews of Europe (including those in Poland) with total extermination.

It is easy to imagine the terrible panic that seized our town, along with all the towns of Poland, with the appearance of the large posters bearing the word "Mobilization" in red ink.

I remember the day the war broke out, when the first bits of information came to Horodlo, over the radio and in newspapers, that German airplanes had carried out heavy bombing of Poland's large cities. People were overcome by a dull sadness. The Jews of Horodlo began seeking advice, and ways to avoid the oncoming storm.

Horodlo, on the western bank of the Bug River, was acutely aware of the terror that would envelop the city if it became a prolonged battlefront, with the Polish forces retreating to the eastern bank of the river and the river itself becoming the front line, as in previous Polish wars.[1]

[Page 118]

Before long, the forebodings became concrete fears. When the Polish forces retreated from the advancing Germans and began digging large trenches along the eastern bank of the Bug, the Polish soldiers were visible digging defensive trenches between the village of Czerniawka and Uściług. It was clear that the Polish army was preparing for a prolonged defensive campaign at the Bug, and that Horodlo would become a German-held front line.

The town's Jews feared falling into the hand of the Germans, as they were already aware of the horrific deeds the Germans had done to the Jews of the Czechoslovakian and Austrian territories.

Chaya Kulish

Several days later, the sounds of the approaching front became audible: the echoes of shooting and explosions were evidence of the nearing Germans. The Polish army hastily pulled back to the eastern bank of the Bug, and the German army – which had not yet entered the town – was shooting in the forest along the Bug as well as at Uściług; the latter had a large Jewish population. For several days,

[Page 119]

there was no authority in Horodlo.[2] The Poles had left town and retreated to the eastern bank of the river, and the Germans were still somewhere to the west but had not yet entered town. Cannons shelled the town steadily across the Bug.

It was just before Rosh Hashanah, and I decided to procure some fruit and vegetables for the holiday. I went to Pilsudski Street, which was populated by people who owned vegetable gardens and fruit orchards. I was walking to the Polish school, when the noise of powerful engines resounded. Suddenly many German tanks appeared. A "Halt!" command rang out, and I instinctively ran for cover. After some time, I crept back home through the vegetable gardens to the north of Pilsudski Street. I witnessed the German army marching into the large marketplace of Horodlo.

Tzipi Fayl and her husband

[Page 120]

As the front drew closer, the Jews of Horodlo sought refuge in hideouts and in the few basement apartments that could serve as shelters against cannon fire. My family, and a number of other families, hid in Mendl Lerner's home; it was on a side street and suitable for hiding. You can easily imagine how terrified we were when I came in and heard the report that the Germans had entered the city.

The day after their entry, a few German soldiers came into a room of Mendl Lerner's home; they looked at the trenches that we had dug as protection against bombs. They called us to them and informed us that we had dug the trenches as firing positions against German aircraft. They ordered us to stand against the wall with our hands in the air. We realized that they wanted to shoot us, and began begging and explaining that the trenches were meant as shelters. Suddenly a German officer burst in and ordered us to go to the marketplace immediately. We had been a hair's breadth from being murdered, and were saved by a miracle.

That same evening, the Germans made their presence felt in Horodlo. They broke into Moyshe Tenenboym's shoe store, and flung all the merchandise out on the street for the Poles who ran up with sacks to pick up the property of the Jews. It was not long before Moyshe Tenenboym's wealth, for which he had worked for years, was gone.

The next day, they broke into other Jewish shops and dumped the merchandise into the street for the Polish mob to gather. A few shops were more protected, and the Poles made every effort to force entry.

Two days later, on Yom Kippur, we sensed that the German army was drawing back. We saw them coiling their telephone wires and packing up their tents. We did not understand

[Page 121]

the reason for these preparations. This became clear later, when a Russian military contingent arrived. It was clearly the first wave of the Russian army's arrival in Horodlo.

It is easy to imagine the joy that overtook the town's Jews, at the thought that they were freed from the Germans. The day after Yom Kippur, the Jews opened their shops (those that had not been sacked), and the mood lifted. A large Russian army force arrived; however, it moved off in the direction of Hrubieszow and Chelm.

Moyshe Tenenboym

The lighter spirits, however, did not last for long. Only a few days later (during the week of Sukkot), it became clear that the Russians and the Germans had struck a deal concerning the border: it would be the Bug River, and Horodlo would be on the German side. The Jews were overcome by confusion and dread as the Germans returned to the town, and its future was unclear; there was a sense of indecision about the best course of action. Some Jews maintained that the opportunity to cross the river to the Russian side should be seized; others argued that it was foolish to leave without their property and to arrive penniless. It should be emphasized that the Russians

[Page 122]

announced that people could cross the Bug freely for a few days, before it became the official border of Russia.

My brother Fishl and I decided not to spend a single day under the Germans. Before Hoshana Rabbah, we crossed the river to Ustylúh, and continued to Ludmir.[3]

Chaim Druker

My father (may his memory be for a blessing) and mother refused to leave their property, and stayed in Horodlo with my sister. Once in Ludmir, we went to my uncle, who was overjoyed to welcome us. He insisted that we write our parents and urge them to join us in Ludmir. I returned to Ustylúh and sent a letter to my

[Page 123]

parents, at my uncle's demand. I stayed in Ustylúh for several days, going to the riverbank every day to watch for my parents and family. They finally arrived, only minutes before the bridge was blown up.

It is worth noting that the Jews were greatly affected by absence of clarity concerning the final disposition of the border and the general lack of security. Quite a few families had already crossed over to the Russian side, but could not endure their nomadic existence and life as fugitives among strangers. They returned to their previous homes, which were now controlled by the Germans. Among them were Dovid Katzhendler and his family, who had spent time with us in Ludmir. Dovid himself survived, after having escaped somehow from German-occupied Horodlo.

Even after the border was sealed, a few people managed to flee from Horodlo. These included Mordechai Shochet, Avrom Shek, Note Perlmuter, and Dovid Katzhendler. However, generally speaking, the border was blocked, and crossing was impossible.

While we were in Ludmir, we heard of the harsh new edicts against the Jewish population. This news arrived by way of Gentiles who had come from Horodlo; it was easier for them to cross the river.

Our hearts were full of dread, as we awaited news of the fate of those who remained in the town.

The Jewish Refugees in Ludmir

We thought that Ludmir would give us respite from the troubles of warfare. At first, we enjoyed a degree of freedom: Jews traded in various goods, and we were generally able to make a living. This continued for about one year.

[Page 124]

Overnight, the local Russian authorities announced that all the refugees, Jews and non-Jews, had to move 100 km away from the border. We refugees were immediately loaded onto train cars that carried us to Siberia. Following a long, exhausting journey, we arrived at the final stop: a labor camp 120 km from the city of Tomsk. It later became clear (after Germany attacked Russia) that this had been done for reasons of security, and proved to our benefit in the long run. I should also emphasize the positive attitude of the Russian authorities towards us; they took care to supply us with necessities, despite the difficult wartime conditions and a general food shortage.

Initially, our situation seemed hopeless, and the community of refugees was overtaken by despair. But God's ways are mysterious; the forced move to Russia was our salvation. Most of those who were not transferred, or who evaded the order, were later murdered by the Germans when they attacked Russia and took Ludmir.

Once in Siberia, we were put to work in the forests, felling large trees and milling them into lumber for various purposes: railroad ties, poles for telephone and telegraph wires, construction boards, etc. We had trouble grasping our new reality in the endless, snow-covered steppes of Siberia, and struggled to understand our new life in this strange, alien land.

We were in Siberia for eighteen months, until we were released by an agreement between Russia and Poland to release refugees of Polish origin. The freed refugees headed to Russian Central Asia, where most of the Jewish refugees gathered. We spent the rest of the war years there, and returned to Poland after the Germans were defeated.

Once back in Poland, we were able to see the total catastrophe that the German murderers brought upon the Jewish population of the country.

[Page 125]

We shuddered as we passed through the cities and the towns of Poland, in which Jewish life had thrived for centuries and which were now emptied of Jews. The old Jewish communities had been uprooted and destroyed. We realized that this was the end of the magnificent Jewish community of Poland.

We did not want to stay in Poland any longer – the land that was soaked with the blood of millions of Jews – and began our journey westward, hoping to join the Jewish displaced-person camps and wait for the chance to emigrate to the Land of Israel, the old-new Jewish homeland.

Translator's Footnotes:

1. The Bug River is a natural border between Poland, Belarus, and Ukraine.

2. Civil order was replaced by a situation where one being in charge.

3. Hoshana Rabbah is the last day of Sukkot.

[Page 126]

Horodlo in the First Months of the War
The Account of Ze'ev Frucht

by Ze'ev Frucht, Israel

I learned about conditions during the German occupation of Horodlo, and the destruction of the town's Jewish community at the end of World War II and afterwards. I was not an eyewitness to the tragic events; I was able to slip out of the grasp of the Germans at the beginning of the war and settle, together with a number of families from our town, in Czerniawka, a small settlement on the east bank of the Bug. The Horodlo families in Czerniawka were Ya'akov Zuberman and his family; Aharon Asher and his family; Aharon Chayim and his wife; Mordechai the Shochet (ritual slaughterer) and his family; Berl Stav; Chayim Mastenboym; Zelik's son-in-law Chayim; Moyshele Miler (the bricklayer), and his son. We all lived near the tar-works.

Conditions in Czerniawka were extremely harsh, and one needed profound patience as well as a strong will to adjust to the abnormal situation. However, Moyshele Miler and his son, Chayim Mastboym, and the ritual slaughterer's wife with her four children all abruptly returned to our town. (Her husband, Mordechai, and his grown son stayed with us.) Those who turned back maintained that life under such difficult conditions in Czerniawka was impossible, and they would not suffer as much in their own homes in Horodlo.

We heard that the Poles informed the Germans immediately, and the returning Jews were ordered to report in a nearby town the next day. The next morning, as they were on their way to the assembly place,

[Page 127]

two Germans appeared and killed them on the spot. When word of the murder reached Horodlo, Chayim Mastboym's daughter raised the alarm in the marketplace. The area was full of Germans, who murdered her on the spot.

The tragic fate of Petachya Blat's son-in-law, and of Shloymele, the son of Mordechai the Shochet (ritual slaughterer):

When we were staying in Czerniawka, Gentiles would come to buy salt from us (salt was a rare commodity at the time), carry it to Horodlo, and resell it at a profit. One day, we received a letter from Petachya Blat, informing us that he had leased a boat from a Gentile to bring his son-in-law (who had been in Ludmir the whole time) back to Horodlo. The letter contained information about the location of the waiting boat (not far from our lodgings), and the trip's schedule.

The day before the trip, Petachya Blat's son-in-law and Shloymele, the ritual slaughterer's son, visited us and let us know that they would be crossing the Bug and returning to Horodlo. We tried to change their minds, but Shloymele said that he had heard of the famine in Horodlo, and wanted to bring his mother some food. As I knew that the Russian guard at the border points had changed that day, I advised them not to try and cross the river. However, they thought differently, decided to keep to their original plan and to cross at the prearranged time. As soon as they approached the boat that was waiting as planned, the Russian guard discovered them. Thinking that they had just come from Horodlo, they ordered the Jews to swim back over the river. Shloymele, who could swim, crossed successfully, but Petachya's son-in-law, together with a Gentile (a former Polish official who had joined them), drowned in the river.

When Shloymele arrived in the town, he immediately went to

[Page 128]

his mother's house. However, it was too late. His mother and brothers were no longer there. They had been replaced by the Polish barber, who had proved to be a fervent Nazi during the German occupation. The barber handed Shloymele over to the Germans, who arrested him and tortured him to death. We heard this from the Gentile Stasz.

One evening, a Gentile from the village came to tell us that the young rabbi of Horodlo (the Rabbi's son-in-law), who had just arrived from Horodlo, was staying at his house. I immediately went to the Gentile's house, and found the young rabbi, who told me that he had fled from Horodlo, that many Jews had been killed in the town, and that the Germans had ordered him to bury the Jews near the river. The next morning, he and I approached the river. While still at a distance, we could see the old Rabbi surrounded by Germans who were forcing him to bury the dead. When the Germans spotted us, they began shooting. We quickly slipped away. The next morning, the captain of the Russian guard came over, holding the shtrayml of the young rabbi, which he had lost as he fled.[1]

These events took place in 1940. Not long afterwards, the Soviet security forces forbade people to live close to the border, and ordered us to go to Russia. We left our new, temporary home, and travelled to distant parts of Russia.

Translator's Footnote:

1.   A Shtrayml is a fur-trimmed hat worn by Hassidic men on Shabbat and Holidays.

[Page 129]

The Destruction of Horodlo
Accounts by Survivors

[Page 130]

[Blank]

[Page131]

The Jews of Horodlo during
the German Occupation, and Their Bitter End

by Fradl Shiffer (Perlmuter), Canada

Poland had been conquered.

When news spread that the Germans were coming, the Jews of the small towns west of the Bug – the Russo-German border – began to flee in panic, trying to escape to Russia.

The first to leave were those who were already acquainted with the Germans and their horrendous behavior in the towns they occupied. Of course, no one imagined that they would exterminate six million precious, fine Jews in such a terrible manner – people who had committed no crime and were not guilty of anything.

German soldiers arrived in Horodlo in September 1939. Those Jews who had not gone were still living in the town.

Immediately after their arrival, the Germans ordered all the Jewish shops to be opened, and all the merchandise to be flung out on the street, to the Gentiles' glee. They came from all parts of the city carrying sacks for their loot – the result of Jewish efforts. They were busy pillaging the shops all that day. However, they retreated that same night, and were replaced by the Russians, who held the town for two weeks. The Russians then returned to the eastern bank of the Bug River, which had been designated the political border between Germans and Russians.

Our town was on the western bank of the river, and thus became a border town occupied by the Germans.

[Page 132]

As the Russians fell back from Horodlo, a number of the town's Jews fled, including my aunt Chana Tenenboym (my father's sister) with her husband and their three children, my aunt Perl Zavidovich and her three sons, as well as my grandmother Zisl Zavidovich.

My parents hesitated and could not decide to leave. It was hard to leave behind whatever possessions they had, the result of years of hard work. In short, we stayed in Horodlo. Only my brother Moyshe joined Grandmother and escaped to Ludmir.

Moyshe Perlmuter, Dovid Zaydel

Among those who stayed behind were the town rabbi and his family.

It was not long before the Jews of Horodlo began to suffer many hardships. German soldiers burst into Jewish homes and took whatever they could. The Ukrainian mayor and the Polish policemen shared the Jewish property.

Jews began to be snatched up for forced labor. They were beaten and tortured en route to the labor site, and the work itself was accompanied by humiliation and abuse. They were bullied, and their beards were torn out

[Page 133]

along with the flesh. The Jews of Horodlo were observant, and protected their beards with zeal and devotion, in spite of being mistreated by the Germans.

Bullied and denigrated as we were, we were ashamed to show our faces; we could not bear the sight of the Gentiles, who mocked us and rejoiced at our misfortune.

Four weeks later, we received the first word of the death march of the Jews of Hrubieszow and Chelm. Using cunning and trickery, the German murderers removed several thousand Jews (including Leybl Zuberman) from their homes, gathered them in the marketplace, and marched them to Belzec, while the murderers rode alongside them.[1]Thousands of exhausted and dejected Jews stumbled on, beaten and tormented by the Germans. Laggards were shot on the road, while people helped and supported others along the dreadful way. Only a few arrived in Belzec, after a two-week-long march with no food or drink.

From right: Chaya Zisberg, Broche Zavidovich (Tchesner), Perl Zavidovich, Chana Tenenboym, Bluma Goldberg, Moyshe Zisberg, Fradl Perlmuter, the daughters of Chayim Tsuker, Yekutiel Zavidovich

[Page 134]

The savage Germans took no pity on these few survivors. When they came to Belzec, the Germans announced that they could drink from the town's well; when the miserable souls crowded around the well to quench their thirst, the killers opened fire, murdering them all.

This mass murder caused intense sorrow, and everyone was overcome by profound misery. Jews from all the surrounding towns observed Shiva for the dead, and mourned the devastation caused by the Germans.[2]

Panic and Flight

The German rampage caused a terrible panic among the Jews of our town. Everyone realized that staying under the Germans would lead to mass death. The Jews of Horodlo wanted to flee to the Russian side, and sought ways to do so. However, it was already too late.

A small number of Jews, my father Note Perlmuter among them, were able to cross the Bug. Gentiles ferried them across in boats, for a large sum of money.

The Mercy of Gentiles

This act of rescue also ended in terrible tragedy. Many Jews sought various means by which to cross the border, and paid Gentiles large sums to row them across. The Gentiles exploited the plight of these unfortunate Jews. Once they were in mid-river, the Gentiles capsized the boats carrying the refugees. Some drowned, and their bodies floated on the river.

After that escape, most of the remaining residents stayed in Horodlo with the Germans.

[Page 135]

Among these were my mother, me, my two brothers (Mordechai Yoysef Elazar and Yekutiel) and my little sister Broche Tsirele.

Forced Labor, Torture, and Abuse

The Germans ordered women to report to forced labor as well, and instructed the Judenrat[3], the body that carried out their orders, to round up the men for work.

I declared myself in charge of our home, and reported for work in my mother's stead.

At the height of winter, when the days were coldest and iciest, we – the town women – worked at washing floors and toilet stalls, as well as doors and windows. We had to work quickly in order to avoid the terrible blows that landed on the weak workers.

One of those killed by these blows was Shmuel Rozenblum (known in the town as Shmuel, Beyle's son). At that time

Girls from Horodlo at forced labor

1) Sarah, Mindl's daughter. 2) The daughter of Yitzchok Meylekh. 3) Mirele, the daughter of
Fishl's son Yisroel

[Page 136]

the Germans ordered us to wear a white patch with a blue Star of David. Anyone who was caught without
the Jewish patch was severely punished.

Curfew for Jews

At seven p.m., Jews were forbidden to be on the street. This was hard to bear, especially in summer, as
it was still full daylight at that time. We had to close the shutters, lock the doors, and endure stifling air in
rooms lit only by small kerosene lamps. There was no chance of fresh air.

Hunger and Disease

Hunger and shortages led to the outbreak of typhus, which rampaged through the community, leaving
hardly any Jewish home untouched. The town physician was forbidden to care for Jewish patients. It was
also dangerous to warn Jews about typhus, for fear that the Germans would find out. The lack of medical

treatment caused the death of Sarah Itte's husband and son. The Germans would raid Jewish homes and search for sick men.

I, too, was sick with typhus during one of these raids. When my mother noticed that the Germans were near the house home, she dressed me quickly and stood me up holding a book, leaning against the oven, so as to appear healthy. The act was successful, and we survived the search. But the fear of searches had an effect on me, and I became even sicker.

These were our conditions for two years, until the beginning of 1941.

The Destruction of the Great Synagogue

That year, during the High Holidays, the Germans ordered the demolition of the synagogue, which had been constructed of large, sturdy stones,

[Page 137]

and forced the Jews do the demolition work, under the direction of Polish builders. They also removed the gravestones from the Jewish cemetery, dismantled the fence around it, and turned it into pastureland. The brick-built Jewish shops were also destroyed.

It is worth noting that the first assault on the synagogue was carried out earlier, by the Poles. Gentile boys threw stones and shattered the synagogue's tall, vaulted windows. Then the adults began to rip out the wooden frames of the doors and windows.

As we watched the demolition of our synagogue, which was sacred to the entire town, the heartache was indescribable. We considered it symbolic of the destruction of the small, long-established Jewish community of Horodlo.

In addition to our spiritual suffering, we underwent terrible physical torture. As we were loading wagons with loose bricks, "Polish architects felt like pestering us" and flung shards of brick at our heads. The Polish and German policemen guffawed, and encouraged us to work by horrific blows.

The Attack on Russia

In June 1941, the Germans attacked Russia: they crossed the Bug, and took Ludmir within a few hours.

Ludmir was a large, beautiful city. Its Jewish community, long considered one of the most important communities of Poland, was enlarged during the course of the war thanks to Jews who had fled there to escape oppression by the German enemy. It is hard to imagine the terror of the Ludmir Jews when they realized that they were once again in the hands of the Germans.

[Page 138]

As soon as they came in, the Germans perpetrated a horrific murder in our family. A soldier buried my aunt Malke (my mother's sister) alive, together with her little seven-year-old daughter Broche-Gitl. It happened when Broche-Gitl ran outdoors after the curfew order, and Aunt Malke ran after her in order to bring her back home. At that moment a German soldier appeared, shot, and wounded Aunt Malke in the leg. The terrified child ran to her mother; the killer dug a pit and buried them both alive. My aunt's husband and son were able to approach the spot after dark, but both were dead by then.

This hideous murder and the two precious martyrs who had been killed so gruesomely were mourned by all of Ludmir.

My uncle Motl Zavidovich was murdered a week later in Lwow[4] immediately after it had been invaded by the Germans. He was taken away "for labor" when the Germans first took the city, and never returned home.

The death of all the Jews of Ludmir was fast approaching. The Jews

Avner Tsuker and his wife Malke

[Page 139]

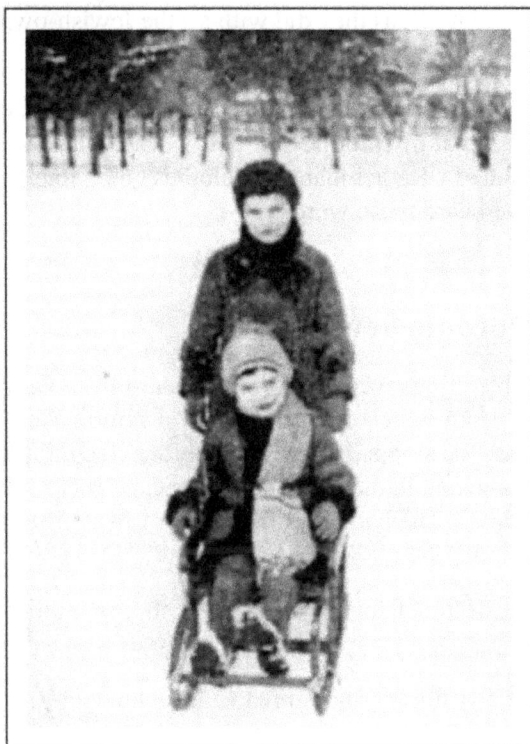

Sarale and Chanale, Mordechai Zavidovich's daughters

Mordechai Zavidovich and his wife Malke

lay low in hideaways. But the Germans ordered the Judenrat to supply people for forced labor. On the eve of Yom Kippur, 1941, the Germans removed as many as two hundred Jews from the labor camp, and tortured them horribly all night long. In the morning, they were taken to an open area near the prison, ordered to dig pits, murdered, and buried in these pits.

Among those slaughtered that day were my brother Moyshe Perlmuter, and Berl Grosburd, as well as the brothers Ben-Tziyon Zuberman and Yisro'el Zuberman, and their brother-in-law Re'uven Shtayn. All three were snatched up for forced labor burying war casualties, and never returned.

[Page 140]

The Situation in Horodlo After the Attack on Russia[5]

Conditions in our town worsened from day to day. New orders against Jews were announced daily, and death was the penalty for the slightest infraction. Normal, everyday actions counted as infractions, such as walking in the Christian neighborhoods, leaving the house after 7 p.m., possessing a bit of flour, etc.

The Jewish households gradually ran out of food, which was unobtainable at any price. We survived by bartering household objects and clothing for food. However, after two years of shortages and oppression, and exchanging possessions for food, homes were emptied of valuables.

I was busy with these exchanges, not wanting my mother to deal with such negotiations for fear she would be exposed to danger. I believed that if I would be arrested and killed for bartering, my mother would continue living for my younger brothers and sisters.

The cold winter and shortage of firewood forced us to dismantle the walls of the warehouse. After that was gone, we tore up the wooden floor of our shop, the wooden stairs, and other wooden objects in our home. The Christians dismantled the wooden fence and carried it off, as they did with all the Jewish-owned fences.

I recall the events of those days at our home. A Polish woman named Ladja, the daughter of Wlodka (who would light the ovens for Jews on Shabbat), demanded that my mother sell her my last winter coat, which I was wearing. "You'll be killed in any case," she reasoned. "Rather than your clothes going to others, you should sell them to me." A shudder ran through us as we heard these words.

[Page 141]

Expulsion of the Horodlo Jews

A pall settled over the town. There was a sense that terrible things were in store. We heard from various sources that the Jews would be sent to unknown locations, from which they would never return. We also heard that people were being sent to the concentration camps. We stopped undressing before sleep, for fear Jewish homes would be invaded during the night, as had happened in other towns. We packed rucksack in order to be ready for expulsion. We drifted around like shadows. The bad news from other towns froze the blood in our veins. This was the horrific situation, on Pesach of 1942.

Eight days after the holiday, our town suffered the fate destined for the entire Jewish community of Poland.

"The Jews are being driven out of Horodlo!" was the fearful cry that spread throughout the town. Naturally, the Gentiles came running to "take" the remnants of Jewish property, which the Jews were forced to sell for next to nothing.

In addition, the Ukrainian mayor went from house to house, to list household items to prevent their sale.

I went to a peasant named Matjewko Budniewski, offering our wardrobe for sale. I remembered that once, on a visit to our house, he had expressed his admiration for that handsome piece of furniture. Now he took the wardrobe and promised to pay one thousand zloty – a very good price. I was surprised at the amount, and expressed my astonishment in words. Budniewski responded, "The wardrobe is really worth that much. I want to pay full price, and not exploit the problems of others."

I feel it is necessary to mention this fact, because the wardrobe sale marked the start of my

[Page 142]

acquaintance with the Budniewski family – a relationship that later saved my life, as will be described below.

We still hoped that the expulsion order could be rescinded, by paying a ransom in Hrubieszow, where the murderers' central command was located, and where the evil decrees originated.

Some members of the Judenrat went to Hrubieszow to try to annul the decree. On their way back – after their efforts with the Germans were in vain – the enemy detained them near the village of Kobyle, separated Petachya Blat from the group, and killed him. Petachya Blat was the first martyr of Horodlo.

The news of the failed mission and the murder of Petachya Blat crushed the Jews of Horodlo. The town was seized by terror. Jews mourned, and fell into faints. We

The wedding of Yosef (Yuzhe) Rozenblum

[Page 143]

gathered at the home of Sore Mindl Rozenblum to say Psalms (people had prayed at her house constantly since the war broke out). We hoped that the murderers might withdraw the frightful decree.[6]

But the edict was enforced.

Eight days after Pesach (1942), all the Jews – men, women, and children – were ordered to assemble in the marketplace for deportation.[7]

The sisters Sheyndl and Fradl Rozenblum

People who worked in the fields as employees of landowners and of peasants, were exempt from the order. Jews ran to the peasants, begging to be hired as laborers without pay. In many cases the unlucky victims promised the peasants payment for their own labor.

It is impossible to imagine the horrifying scene when an entire community – men, women, and children – was taken out of its

[Page 144]

homes and town, where they had lived for generations, and taken, exhausted and demoralized, to an unknown destination. I remember my mother and her children – her little chicks – leaving our home. When they had gone some distance, my mother looked back in the direction of the house, sighed, and said, "Only God knows whether I will ever see my home again."

I was one of those who was able to get a job, and thus could stay in town. I hoped that I could supply my mother with food, once I knew their new location. When I parted from my dear ones, I thought my heart had shifted within me. I stood, staring at my mother and sisters, who were going further and further away…

I returned through the empty marketplace, sobbing. I wouldn't have cared if the Germans had heard my sobs and killed me. Eventually I came to our house, but entrance was now prohibited. A Christian named

Nazhli stood at the door and said, "What do you want here? The house is mine now, and you have no right to enter."

The few who remained requested a house to live in, and were given one. We were among them.

All the Jewish houses were now occupied by Christians. Many houses had been plundered and destroyed by the new residents. The streets of the town were shockingly different.. The town and its streets seemed to be mourning the destruction. I looked in the direction of our home and gazed at the trees that my brother had planted; they had budded, and were covered in spring blossoms… My heart contracted at the sight.

Fear and terror reigned everywhere. We were afraid to be in our own home town.

[Page 145]

Massacre of the Remaining Jews

Several days after the expulsion, the Germans arrested Rokhl Blat, Avrom Zaydl (Rivka Zaydl's son), and Moyshe Berger, took them to the Jewish cemetery, and murdered them.

A few days later, the Germans sent Khayim Vayntroyb, with a letter, to the village of Matsz, where he was murdered. Two days later, the murderers sent Avrom – Taybele's son – to the same village, with an identical letter. When we told him to try to run away and hide, he responded, "Where would I run, where would I hide? I wouldn't escape my fate in any case. Things will happen as they must." This was the period when Shmuel (Shmulke), the rabbi's son, was killed, and buried near the Polish school.

We were overcome by dismay and panic at the loss of personal safety, and afraid of our own shadows.

Displaced from Horodlo to Uchanie

After about a week, I found out that my mother and the children were in Uchanie, together with all the Jews of Horodlo. We also heard that there had been a dreadful mass murder of the Jews of Uchanie. We were told that the Germans had taken the local Jews to the Jewish cemetery and shot them. Among the dead were twenty-two Jews from Horodlo. The two who survived were ordered to bury the dead. These were Yankv Zeydl (Rivka Zeydl's son Yankele) and the son-in-law of Motl Soyfer (Rishle's husband). Their description of the barbaric carnage was blood curdling.

[Page 146]

The Last Jews of Horodlo are Sent to Uchanie

Eight days after Shavuot (1942), after the peasants had finished planting, we young people were also expelled from Horodlo and taken to Uchanie.[8] I was elated to meet my mother, brother, and sisters once again, in Uchanie.

The children of Note Perlmuter

I was so happy to see them run up to me with their pale faces, hug me, and cry; and so glad that I had brought them a heap of potatoes as well as firewood in the cart that followed us with our bundled belongings. I had gotten the provisions from the peasant, Budniewski, as part payment for the wardrobe that we had sold him. He promised that he would send the rest of the payment along once we sent him our new address.

[Page 147]

Life in Uchanie

The Jews of Horodlo had changed considerably in appearance since they had been banished to Uchanie. The few men had been forced to cut their beards, which transformed their appearance. The town rabbi, however, was an exception: he guarded his beard until the last day of his life.

Gitl Fayl and her children

Our paltry rations constantly declined. The food we had brought proved enough for four weeks. The bread became moldy – bread we had baked in Horodlo, and were eating in small portions, with great thrift and care. In spite of the shortage, my mother occasionally made sure to share her bread with those who had no food, remarking that thanks to this good deed, she hoped her children would be saved from death by starvation.

[Page 148]

The shortage of firewood was even worse. Even if we somehow obtained some potatoes, there was no way to cook them. My mother would walk into the forest – eight kilometers away – to bring a bit of firewood, risking her life. We often heard of people who had been shot for the very same "sin." Nevertheless, the instinct of life was stronger than any threat or danger. People sought ways to stay alive, hoping to overcome the edicts and hardships.

The Annihilation of the Horodlo Jews

We were not allowed to be together for long. A week after I arrived in the village – about two weeks after Shavuot, the 24th day of Sivan – the Jews of Horodlo were taken on their last journey, to the extermination camp of Sobibor, one of several such camps the Nazi murderers constructed.[9]

The death march of the Horodlo Jews is engraved on my heart, and I can never forget it. On that bitter day, they took the Jews of Horodlo to Miączyn, near Zamość, and gathered us at the train station. Men in their prime were ordered to one side, whereas the elderly, mothers, and children, were crammed into the freight cars, and egged on by blows and shots.

Oy vey! Where are the words to describe the horrifying scene that I witnessed that day in Miączyn? We see our dearest ones jostling and squeezing to climb into the freight cars as quickly as possible, so as to escape the murderers' bullets. We, standing to one side, cannot do anything to help them escape this calamity. The cars are very high, and the unfortunate deportees have trouble climbing up into them. People pull and push each other up, and the murderers fire at them constantly.

[Page 149]

Here and there, human corpses drop out of the train cars; these victims were shot while climbing in. I see my unlucky mother dragging her children and helping them into the freight car; in the crush, she runs back for the package of food and the bottle of water she took when we left Uchanie. A German murderer notices her in the crowd, and aims his pistol at her. I could not help myself and screamed, "Mama! Run! Save yourself!" Hearing my scream, the murderer turned his gun aside, pointed it at me, and fired. What happened next was strange. Frumet (the daughter of Eli, Yidl's son) was standing next to me, and tugged at me to stop me from screaming. The tug forced me to bend down. This happened simultaneously with the shot, and the bullet flew over my head. The German motioned with his hand, and my mother was able to climb into the freight car.

The cars are bolted shut, and the train moves slowly, taking away our suffering, unlucky nearest and dearest, on a road of no return. Our staring, terrified eyes follow them sorrowfully, painfully.

We spent the night sitting on our bundles, while the corpses of those murdered in this Nazi operation were strewn all around. We wept and mourned the bitter fate of our dearest ones, along with the rest of the Jews of Horodlo. All were exterminated in the most gruesome, horrific manner, by the German bloodsucking monsters.

Classifying the Remaining Jews into Groups: Extermination, or Labor

The day after this horrible event, a committee of murderers, reclassified the remnants as "capable of work"

[Page 150]

or "weak." Those capable of work, including me, were sent back to Uchanie; the "weak" were taken to the Staw concentration camp (near Chelm). That was a nightmarish camp. The miserable souls were naked as the day they were born. Reports of the horrors of the camp came from Yaakov Zaydl, who had also been among the unfortunates taken to Staw, but managed to escape and join us. Another escapee from the camp was Itshele, Moyshe Boymayl's grandson. The camp elder, a Ukrainian murderer, realized that they had fled. During the chase, he caught Itshele, returned him to the camp, and hanged him in view of the inmates.

When we came to Uchanie, I entered the room where my mother and the children had lived during their stay. I found souvenirs of my dear ones, and was deeply stirred: the small hat of my younger sister, my mother's reading glasses in a corner, and her prayer book with its pages discolored from her tears. Here was a small bundle of firewood for cooking, gathered in the forest by my mother at the risk of her life, and brought indoors. I could no longer look at these souvenirs, which evoked the pain my family underwent, and lost consciousness. I don't know how long I lay there, in a faint; but when I came to, I realized that I was still grasping the bundle of firewood.

We, the Horodlo survivors, were taken back to our town from Uchenie, and then began working on the Starzyn estate.[10] We found Jews from the village of Stryszów, as well as a few who had managed to escape from the Warsaw ghetto.

[Page 151]

The Atmosphere in Horodlo

It is interesting to describe the atmosphere in Horodlo as we walked through the town en route to our work at Starzyn. We had arrived in the town on Sunday, the Christian day of rest. When the Christians heard of our arrival, they began scurrying around in panic. Their astonishment was clear, as was their fear that we would stay in the town and they would have to return the goods that they had stolen. We sensed the danger in their glances. Only one Christian woman seemed truly happy at our return, especially when she saw me. This was Katja, the wife of the peasant Matjewko Budniewski. The moment she saw me, she gave me a hug and a kiss, ignoring the angry looks of the Christians who gathered around us.

On the Estate

We worked on the Starzyn estate all summer. We were given very little food, and were unable to change our clothes; we had only work clothes. Occasionally, we were able to pay a brief visit to Horodlo (disregarding the great danger of such a "ramble"), and asked the Gentiles for foodstuffs, as compensation for the goods they had stolen. One of our group – a daughter of Hershl Fraynd – was arrested on the way to Horodlo and shot dead.

During our time at the estate, we occasionally heard news of the Jewish ghetto of Ludmir, and information about the Jews in the city. Thus, we heard that Grandmother Zisl Zavidovich and my aunt Chana and her family were still alive. Once, I received a short letter from Grandmother, sent with a Gentile. That was the last letter and sign of life from our family in Ludmir.

[Page 152]

Very soon, the murderers carried out another Aktion, in which many Jews were arrested.[11] Among them were my remaining family members in their hideaway (they were hiding in Ftidjen, near Ludmir).[12] They were murdered and buried in a mass grave, together with the victims of the Ludmir community.

Fradil Zavidovich (Fishl Zavidovich's
daughter) and Fradil Tenenboym
(Moyshe Tenenboym's daughter)

Mordechai Zavidovich and his daughters
Sore and Chane

However, I very much wanted to hear details about my family and the life of the Horodlo Jews in Ludmir. After some time, I was informed that my sainted grandmother had survived the first large pogrom, but was discovered during the second pogrom, in a bunker where she had been hiding with other Jews. They were all shot and killed.

[Page 153]

I was also told about the death of my two cousins, Moyshe and Yekutiel Zavidovich, the sons of Levi-Yitzchok and Perl Zavidovich. These relatives had been hiding out throughout the war at a Christian's house. Shortly before the war's end, they were murdered by the same Gentile who had hidden them.

News of the fate of my two uncles (my mother's brothers) also reached me: Yekutiel and Fishl Zavidovich, and their families. They had lived in the Warsaw ghetto until the ghetto uprising.[13]

Flight

Autumn arrived, and with it the end of our field work. Once we had harvested the potatoes and other winter vegetables, the Germans ordered us to report in Hrubieszow, the district capital, the next day. I decided to flee. That night, I sneaked out of the farm and headed toward Horodlo. I went to the house of Matjewko Budniewski, and asked them to help me hide. Once I heard their positive answer – they agreed to conceal me – I felt more at ease. His wife added that she had had a premonition that I would arrive, and had prepared a hideout for me. They took me to the barn and showed me the hideaway they had prepared under the haystack, before the harvest. Katja – Budniewski's wife – said that my mother had appeared to her in a dream and asked her to hide me, so that there would be a survivor of her family, which consisted of her and her five children. The Budniewski couple had had no children during their ten-year marriage, and Katja had just reached the seven-month point in a new pregnancy. They believed that this blessing had occurred because they were concealing me. They therefore looked after me with devotion until the liberation.

[Page 154]

I lay in the refuge, which was quite dark. But, thanks to a crack in the wall, I could see daylight and watch life on the street. I could hear the peasants talking, and so learn about news and various events. In this way, I learned of the bitter fate that had overtaken my friends, the unfortunate survivors who worked at Starzyn, and did not flee as I did. When they reported to the authorities that next morning, they were taken to Hrubieszow, where they were murdered. The date was January 10, 1942. Some weeks later, I learned that several of my friends had in fact fled the estate that night, but had nowhere to hide. The poor souls wandered around like stray animals, and no refuge was offered. Not only that: they hid in haystacks, but the savage Gentiles found them and turned them over to the Germans. Among these unfortunates were some Jews from Stryszew, and some from Horodlo: Fishl Shek, his brother-in-law Mendl, and Yaakov Zaydl. Yaakov Zaydl had escaped from many dangerous situations and suffered unspeakable torture during the war, but had managed to dodge the danger until the last moment, when he was exposed by the Gentiles and murdered. Kopl's daughter Mirele was captured because of Stach Shmitzki, who pulled her out and handed her over to the Germans.

Two Years in Hiding

The space where I hid for two years was the size of a bed. I had to be seated the entire time, as standing was impossible. The entire time, I spoke to no one, and no one spoke to me. The days and nights moved at snail's pace, and seemed endless.

[Page 155]

It was so cold in winter that the water in a jar near my bed actually froze, and in summer the heat was stifling. The Germans often conducted searches, and I could not relax. The fear robbed me of my appetite, and I grew thin to the point of emaciation. I was depressed and wept constantly, thinking of the fates of my mother and young brothers and sisters, and the fate of all the Jews. The gruesome events live on in my memory, and often materialize before my eyes.

At this moment, I remember the horrible night in Miączyn. I see my mother trying vainly to retrieve her shabby bundles and bring them on board the freight car. The Germans are firing in every direction, and she is forced to leave the bundles behind. Suddenly, my little brother Yosele asks, "Mama! Where are my tefillin? When he hears that they had been left behind, he pushes through the crush, finds the bundles and the tefillin, and places them inside the clothes he is wearing. He adds a phrase of Kiddush Ha-Shem: "If I am alive tomorrow morning, I will need to lay tefillin."[14] It was clear that he grasped our situation. How important the tefillin were to him, and how deeply he loved them! After all, he had only become Bar-Mitzvah the previous Passover.

These mournful, depressing thoughts stayed with me during that desperate year I spent in hiding.

The new year, 1943, came, with fateful news. The German army was retreating from Russian soil. As a result, a large group of retreating German soldiers arrived in Horodlo, preparing to function as a town along the Bug borderline. My situation now changed, for the worse. The Germans

[Page 156]

confiscated all the peasant barns for their own use, including the one over my hideout. At night, I compressed my body, and tried not to fall asleep, so as not to be noticed by the Germans who were sleeping in the same barn. I could not risk even the slightest movement.

The danger that I would be found out increased as the German army horses ate their way through the hay over my refuge. Budniewski, the peasant owner, realized that the horses would consume all the hay before the next harvest, and ordered unripe hay to be cut in order to cover my hiding place. This aroused the curiosity of his neighbors.

The last weeks before liberation were especially difficult. I felt my strength ebbing, and my powers of resistance were almost gone. Thunder came from the front, and airplanes were attacking loudly. A bomb falls on a house, which disappears in smoke. Panic reigns outside as the peasants rush about aimlessly. Budniewski, the peasant, creates an emergency exit for my hideout, to serve in case of fire, and I felt that my legs could no longer carry me, let alone run. I could barely stand upright.

Now the Germans are retreating. They've crossed the Bug westward, setting fires as they go. The residents are ordered to leave Horodlo. The peasants pack their bundles, with commotion and panic. What can I do on my own, if the peasant family – my benefactors – are forced to leave? The explosions of gunfire and bombs grow stronger, and I hear the agitated Germans scurrying.

[Page 157]

I am constantly overrun by fearful thoughts, which cloud my consciousness… I want to fall asleep … it would be easier… anguished, I fell asleep. When I woke from a deep sleep, I saw that the Russians had arrived in town. Is this really the end of my suffering? Is this actually freedom? I emerged from my hideout, gulping the fresh air and daylight. I asked someone about the date, and was told that it was July 23, 1944.

Warily, I considered the situation around me. The first thing I wanted to know was whether there were still Jews alive! Had my comrades-in-suffering been able to save themselves? My dearest family, where are you?!

Soon, several of us had assembled: Fishl Gertl, Leybl Berger, Shmuel Berger, Abish Berger, Dovid Berger, and Yaakov (Yankl), the son-in-law of Mote the melamed. A handful of survivors from an entire community. But our vile enemies were remorseless, and attacked the few survivors; two were murdered: Yaakov Berger and Yankl, Mote's son-in-law.

We Leave Horodlo

We realized that we could not remain in our Judenrein town, and went west, to join the Jewish survivors who had come out from their hideouts, from the forests, and from the Russian steppes.[15] I was overjoyed to find my father, Note Perlmutter, among the wretched refugees. We were convinced that we couldn't stay here any longer, and began searching for safer shores.

[Page 158]

Below is the text of a postcard that Chana Zavidovich (daughter of Mordechai Zavidovich) wrote to this writer. She describes the murders and massacres perpetrated by the Germans, reports that her mother and her sister Sara had been sent to an extermination camp, and asks that Grandmother Zisl go to the grave of Grandfather Leybl to ask for his intercession.[16]

The card is dated August 1942, and was sent from Lwow to the Starzyn estate, where this writer was working. A translation from the Polish follows below.

Lwow

Dear Fradl!

I want to inform you that I am now an orphan, like you. Mother and Sara left on August 10, 1942, on the same road as your mother. I am staying with my mother's friend. I have enough food, but I am very miserable. Madame Shechita is queen.[17] There is no news from Warsaw which makes me very worried. If you write to Grandmother, ask her for me to go to Grandfather Leybl for me, and tell him everything. Write more often, as I am very lonely, and a letter from you will console me a bit.

Be well,
your Chana.
P.S. I have no news at all as regards my dear father.

[Page 159]

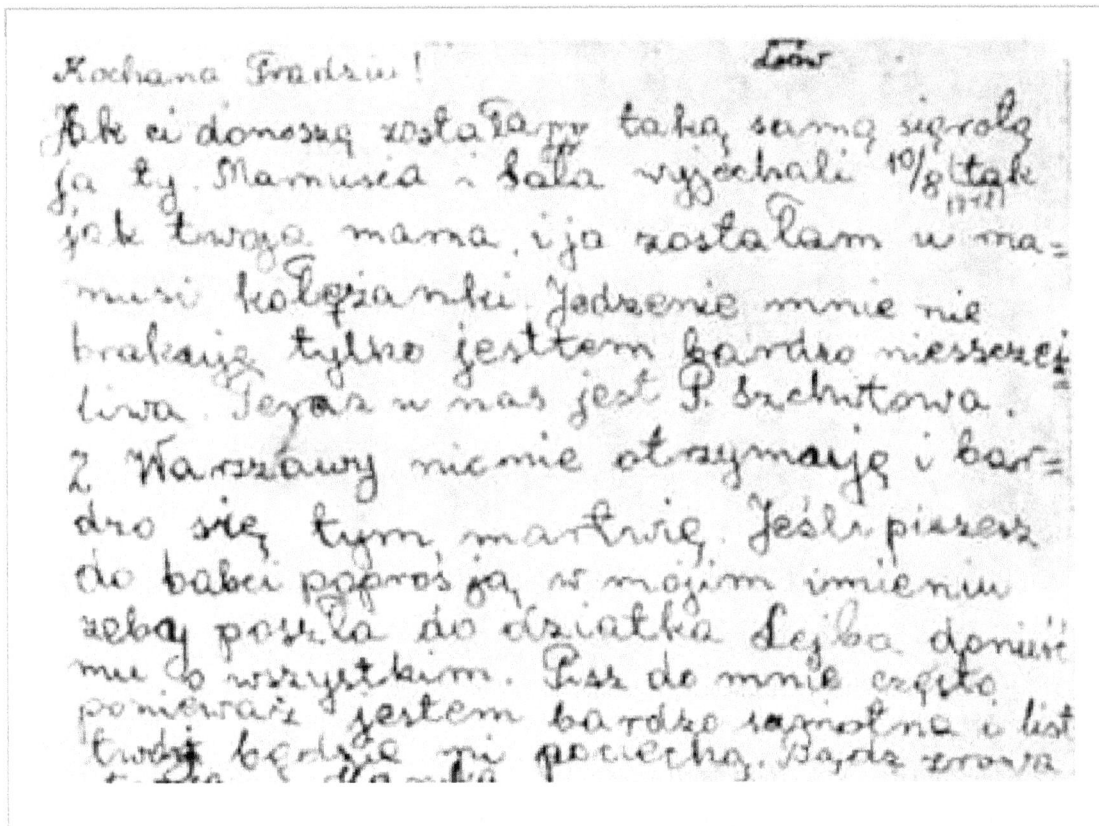

Image of the Polish text on the postcard

[Page 160]

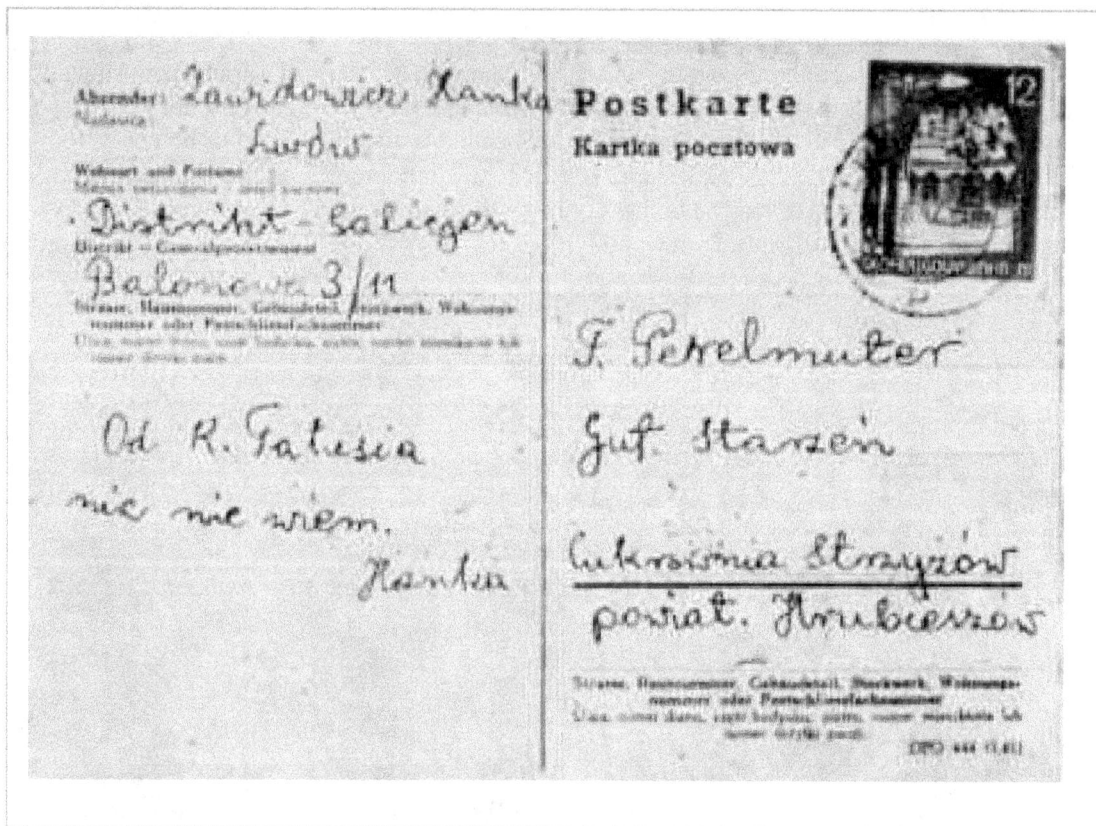

Image of the Polish text on the postcard

Translator's Footnotes:

1. Belzec was a German death camp, built as a center of extermination for the Jews of Poland.

2. Shiva is a traditional week-long period of mourning observed by first-degree relatives of the deceased.

3. The Judenrat (literally Jewish Council) was an administrative body comprised of local Jews appointed by the Germans to help them manage the Jewish population before they were ultimately murdered.

4. Sometimes spelled Lvov, today known as Lviv, Ukraine.

5. The German invasion of Russia took place on June 22, 1941

6. Jews have traditionally recited Psalms for solace, guidance, catharsis, renewal, etc.

7. Pesach that year was on April 4, 1942.

8. This was on May 30, 1942.

9. June 9, 1942.

10. I was not able to identify this estate and have done an approximate transliteration.

11. Aktion was the German Nazi term for a military or police operation of mass assembly, deportation, and killing.

12. I was not able to identify Ftidjen.

13. The uprising was during April-May 1943.

14. Kiddush Ha-Shem ("sanctification of the holy name") is any action by a Jew that brings honor, respect, and glory to God. The tefillin (phylacteries) are put on by adult male Jews during morning prayers.

15. Judenrein is the German term used by the Nazis during the Holocaust to designate areas that had been "cleansed" of Jews.

16. This widespread custom consists of praying to God and asking for compassion on account of the merit of the dead.

17. The Hebrew shechita, which normally denotes ritual slaughter, is often used for a massacre of Jews. The Hebrew word is transliterated in Polish on the postcard, possibly for fear of censorship.

[Page 161]

The Jews of Horodlo During the War, and their Dreadful Death

by Aryeh (Leon) Berger, Be'er-Sheva, Israel

Translated by Pamela Russ

When the first news came concerning the German attack on Poland and the bombing of Polish cities by German aircraft, fear and depression settled over the Jews in Horodlo and throughout Poland.

The anxiety over the possibility of occupation by the Germans, whose hatred of Jews knew no bounds, was immense, although the complete annihilation of Poland's Jews was beyond anyone's imagination. Quite understandably, the Jews of Poland, and those of Horodlo among them, received the news about the rapid advance of the Germans, and the rout of the Polish army, with trepidation.

Horodlo was occupied by the Germans about three weeks after the war began. Upon their arrival, they broke open the locked Jewish shops (helped by Polish youth) and flung the merchandise out to the Poles, who gathered for the loot.

I was at Pinches Berger's house, when the Germans burst in to ransack the house. The German captain who accompanied the soldiers told us, "We came to Poland for the Jews. We'll exterminate you like mice." However, they did not attack the Jews physically yet, and were satisfied with grabbing Jewish property.

The next day, the Germans retreated from Hrubieszow, and were replaced by the Russian army. But only six weeks later,

[Page 162]

the Russians returned to the eastern bank of the Bug River, and the Germans came to Horodlo once again.

A small part of the Horodlo Jews took this chance and left the town along with the Russians.

As soon as they arrived, the Germans ordered a list to be made of all the Jews in Horodlo. Jews were also forced to wear a white armband bearing a Star of David. The Germans began to hand out Jewish houses and expensive items of clothing. Jews were ordered to report daily for forced labor, which was accompanied by torture and humiliation.

Appointing the Judenrat[1]

In May 1940, the Germans appointed a Judenrat and put it in charge of supplying Jewish forced labor according to their demands. On May 20, they required "Jews who were suitable for physical labor to be sent to Bełżec."[2] The town was panic-stricken. Jews sought hiding places for fear they would be sent to Bełżec, and the Germans prowled among the Jewish homes, hunting for concealed Jews. When I saw German soldiers at our door, I slipped out of the window into the courtyard, jumped over the garden fence to the bank of the Bug River, and hid in the grass. I lay there until the end of that particular Aktion.

Arrest and Torture

However, it was not always possible to evade the conquerors. One night, they knocked at our house door.

[Page 163]

When we opened the door, about fifteen German soldiers burst in, holding Petachya Blat captive. They woke the entire family and drove us out into the adjoining garden (including my mother and her small children). The east end of the garden was bounded by a curved wall that extended down to the Bug River. They stood us in a line and said that they knew we had thirty thousand marks, and demanded that we hand it over to them. When we said that we had no money, they told Petachya to convince us to admit that we had the money, and to give it to them. Suddenly, they pushed Petachya and me down the steep hill. We rolled down to the river, and were so badly bruised by the clods of earth, thorns, and shards of glass that we could not get up. We were ordered to climb back up the hill. My mother and the young children were told to go back home, while my father and I were taken to headquarters. Once there, we were tied up, and the torture began: endless blows on my shoulders. I lost consciousness several times, and was revived each time by the shock of cold water cascading over my body. My shirt was shredded by the beatings. The captain told me that I would not leave the room alive if I did not hand over the money – 'think of your own life'. I told him that he was torturing me in vain, as I had no money. Then he took my father into a small cell designed for torture. We stood in the cell all night, as there was nowhere to sit. Water constantly dripped on our heads. The next day, at 10 a.m., the captain opened the door and asked us, mockingly, "Are you refreshed after the shower?" We were ordered to leave the cell, driven into the courtyard, and forced to jump through the sports equipment on the grounds, to the accompaniment of blows. We were then released.

[Page 164]

At the Outbreak of Germany's War with Russia

After war broke out between Germany and Russia (in June, 1941), a new edict was published: each Jew had to show that he was working for a Christian peasant. Anyone who could not prove this would be expelled from town. Jews began rushing to the peasants asking to be hired, and willing to pay in return for a work certificate. My family and I were hired by Swietlinski (the town elder), as was Petachya Blat's family. This temporarily saved both families from expulsion.

Various decrees were published daily, and transgressors were placed on the death-list. This was in addition to the evening home curfew law. Any Jew found outdoors after curfew was risking his life. The Jews realized that their lives were free for the taking by any bully.

As we stand in Swietlinski's courtyard, two German youths go by on bicycles. One calls to the other, "Look, Jews!" They come into the courtyard, draw their revolvers, and order my father Avrom Zaydl – who just happened to be there – and Rokhl, Petachya Blat's wife, to follow them. They took them to the cemetery, and murdered them.

The Expulsion of the Horodlo Jews

One summer day in 1942, the Germans published an order expelling all the Jews from the town to Uchanie. This was the worst of decrees, which we had feared for a long time. Yet not everyone realized that general expulsion meant the extermination of Jews in the death camps. Obeying this order, all the Jews – men, women, and children – reported to the marketplace. The entire community was then deported to Uchanie.

[Page 165]

The terrible scene of their departure from the town where they and their ancestors had lived for many generations, not knowing where they were going and what the murderers would do to them, defies description. It was shocking to see the unfortunates leave the town, shuffling along on their way to an unknown destination. Exhausted physically as well as emotionally, the oppressed exiles reached Uchanie, where thousands of exiled and tortured Jews like them, expelled from nearby towns and villages, were assembled. They were crammed into small, tight rooms, where other families, including mine, were already quartered. We awaited the newcomers in fear. Yet it was hard to imagine that the next stop would be the death camp.

Our lives were free for the taking in Uchanie as well. One day, a few cars carrying SS agents drove through Uchanie and noticed Jews assembled in the marketplace. They stopped, exited the cars, and selected fifty Jews. These Jews were ordered to lie on the ground, and were murdered with machine guns. They then ordered us to clear the area of bodies, while they themselves sat by the well and ate sandwiches.

Deportation to the Death Camp

The order came after eight days: we were to gather in the Uchanie marketplace. About two thousand people assembled. We were loaded onto peasant wagons that had been brought for this purpose, and taken to Miączyn, without being told where we were going or for what purpose. As we were riding along, the Gentile coachman asked me, "Do you know where you're going? You're going to the crematoriums." I repeated these words to the rabbi, who did not want to believe me. When we arrived at Miączyn (an intersection fifteen kilometers from Zamość),

[Page 166]

we were taken to the railroad station, where a train of fifteen freight cars was waiting. A band of SS murderers came and ordered the women and children to climb quickly into the cars. The murderers started to fire in all directions, including the mass of wretched Jews. A stampede began, there was nowhere to flee, and many were killed on the spot. I was near Rabbi Yehuda Leyb HaLevi Berman (may his righteous memory be for a blessing), the Rabbi of Horodlo, who was shot by the Germans and who dropped over me. The unfortunate women and children rushed around in the crowd, trying as best they could to climb into the cars in order to

"Dogs surround me, a pack of villains encircles me" (Psalms 22)
The German murderers and their victims

[Page 167]

Sheva Hirsh
(daughter of Hinde, Simtshe's daughter)

Tova Goldberg

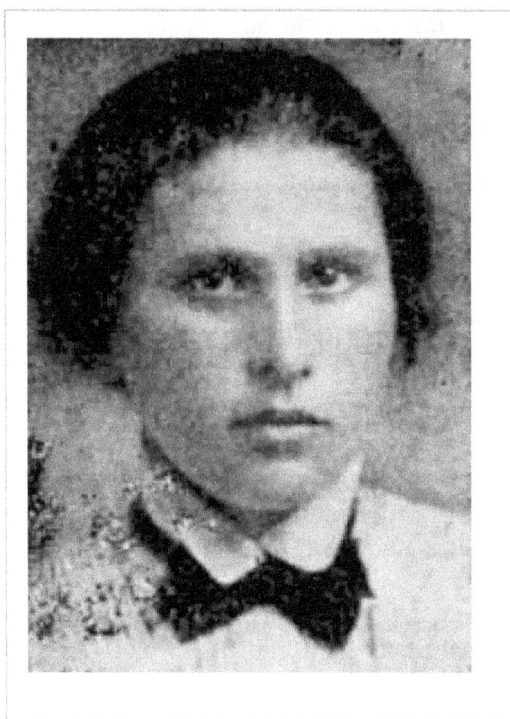

Malka Valakh
(daughter of Moyshe Mandil)

escape the German bullets. The cars became filled with human victims, and started to roll, while we remained on the platform, bewildered, staring at the train that was carrying our dearest to us into the crematoriums of Bełżec. Among them were my beloved mother and her three children, Miriam, Gitl, and Binyomin.

The Fate of The Survivors

We stayed there all night, not knowing what they wanted to do with us. The next morning, a group of Germans came, classified the survivors, and divided them into two groups. One group

[Page 168]

consisted of youth, women, and men. The other group included the feeble elderly, as well as boys and girls below working age. This second group was wrenched away from us violently, and also taken to the death camp. My 13-year-old brother Yehuda was in this second group, and parted from us with heartrending screams.

We were told that we survivors would be sent to do farm work in the vicinity. The same day, estate owners showed up, selected people for work, and took them away. The Jews from Horodlo and Stryszów were not chosen for labor, and the Germans ordered us to start working on an estate near Horodlo. We returned to Horodlo and went to Straszyn, where we worked for approximately five months. The owner designated me as his personal coachman. In the course of this position, I witnessed an unspeakably distressing murder incident that still chills me to the bone. This indescribable event underscores the depth of cruelty to which the Germans sank.

The gruesome, indelible event unfolded as follows:

One day, the landowner ordered me to drive him to Hrubieszow. When we arrived, he went off to run his errands, while I stayed back to watch the coach, which was standing near the Jewish ghetto. I used this chance to talk with a Jew who was standing nearby. Suddenly, Germans came up and ordered us to go with them. We were brought to the cemetery, and taken to a group of Jews who were digging a pit – for a purpose unknown to us at the time. Shortly afterwards,

[Page 169]

61 young Jewish children were brought in. Their tiny arms were bound together, and their cries reached the heavens. They were followed by a German murderer with a band of killers. After some preparations, he began to smash their tiny heads with a rock and to throw their bodies into the pit. This horrible, barbaric murder shocked all the remaining Jews, and crushed them completely.

When we had been in Straszyn five months, the estate manager, Pisecki, came over to me and said that a German had arrived on a bicycle and wanted to speak with me. Naturally, I fled in panic into the field, not knowing what to do. After waiting some time, I went back to the estate manager and asked him to find out what the German wanted. He came back after a while and told me that the German had brought me a letter. I went over to the German, who told me that he had come from Ludmir, knew my brother Tevl, and was giving me a letter from him. In the letter, my brother Tevl and sister Rivke wrote that I should come to them in Ludmir, and that it was safe to talk with the German.

The German suggested that I ride to Ludmir on his bicycle. Of course, I managed without his offer of service. I left the estate and began walking over a rough road until I reached the Bug River. I knocked on the door of a peasant named Bilecki, close to the river, and proposed that he help me across, in return for payment. As he had no boat, we swam across the Bug. I made two bundles of my clothes and possessions.

Bilecki carried the larger bundle with the clothing. As soon as we had crossed, Bilecki returned to the other bank with the bundle; I was left in nothing but underwear.

[Page 170]

My Visit to Ustyluh and My Arrival in Ludmir

I started out for Czerniawka and stayed overnight with a peasant named Tarbil. Waking up early, I left for Ustyluh. There, I met Eliezer Halperin's son, who told me about the catastrophe that had overtaken the Jews of Ustyluh as well.

Shloyme Blat and his family

I continued from Ustyluh to Ludmir, and went to the Ludmir Jewish ghetto immediately upon my arrival. The first person I met was Mordechai Zuberman; later I found many Jews from Horodlo. These included Yaakov Zuberman's family, Perl Zavidovich and her sons Yekutiel and Moyshe Zavidovich, Moyshe Zisberg, and other families. I stayed in the ghetto for four weeks.

I worked at odd jobs in the Ludmir ghetto, but life was not safe

[Page 171]

nor were there any opportunities. There were roundups nearly every day, and Jews were taken to be murdered at the nearby village of Piatydni. It was clear that the Germans had pledged to annihilate the distinguished Jewish community of Ludmir. This community had grown larger thanks to the Jews who had fled there during the Russian occupation.

Escape from the Ludmir Ghetto

Mordechai (Motl) Zuberman, Itshele Zuberman and I had agreed to escape from Ludmir and find a safe site in the Horodlo area. Motl disguised himself as a peasant carrying a box on his shoulder when we left Ludmir, dressed in our own clothes. We had decided to leave separately. The first problem was going through the Russian police station, near the military post at the entrance to town. We tried to go through carefully, but, unfortunately, were noticed by a Ukrainian policeman. He fired first at Itshele, who dropped; then he began chasing me. I squeezed through the fence of the police station, and tried to shelter behind the buildings. Each time, the Ukrainian found me. Having no choice, I jumped over the last fence, swam across the Huczwa (a small local stream), ran dripping wet into the small wood, and stretched out on the ground, believing that I had shaken my pursuer. Yet, glancing back across the stream, I saw the Ukrainian undressing and getting into the water, leaving his rifle on the other side. I decided not to flee any more but rather to fight him. I found a sturdy tree branch, and greeted him with a fight challenge. He immediately turned back to the stream, dressed himself, and left the area, while I followed his every move.

Once I had rested and calmed down a bit, I

[Page 172]

continued on my way to Horodlo. Imagine my astonishment at encountering Motl Zuberman once again! He told me that he was never stopped en route, as all the passers-by took him for a peasant.

As we were passing Piatydny, we heard machine-gun fire and loud screams. These were the screams of Jews from Ludmir, who were being taken to their deaths. We continued on our way, pained and fearful. Motl took the road to Chelm, while I went to the Starzyn estate.

At Starzyn Once Again

Back at Starzyn, I met Jews from Horodlo again. Among them were my cousins Shmuel Abish and Shmuel Berger, Fishele Gertl, Bashe Berger, Fradl Perlmuter, and others. I asked the estate owner and the manager not to let the Germans know that I had returned, and began working there.

The Order to Leave Starzyn

About three weeks after my return, the Germans announced that we had to report to the command center at Hrubieszow. This was approximately in December 1942. The day after this order, we rode in carts supplied by the estate's owner. Arriving in Hrubieszow, I went to visit my 74-year-old uncle. He was surprised to see me, and asked me why I had come to Hrubieszow and not found a hideout. Incidentally, Fradl Perlmuter and my cousins Abish and Leybish Berger, as well as Genia, did not join us on this trip and decided to hide.

At dusk, Fishl Gertl, Fishl Shek,

[Page 173]

and Yaakov Zaydl came to my uncle's house and told us that they knew the Germans were preparing to carry out mass murder the next day, and they thought that it was better to leave Hrubieszow. We planned to meet up at midnight. We sneaked out of Hrubieszow that night, en route to Mruczin. We had to cross the ice-cold stream of Laczewy, and arrived in Horodlo at dawn.[3] We stopped near the hay and grain barns, and looked for a hiding place. We went into Wobriszewicz's barn, climbed up to the hayloft, and lay down. Searching for food, we found a piece of bread in a peasant jacket that was hanging there, and divided it between ourselves. We were motionless the entire day. At night, we decided to go into Wobriszewicz's house and ask for food. He was very surprised when we appeared in the house. I told him that we had escaped from Hrubieszow, were looking for food, and asked permission to hide in his barn. He gave us food, but wanted us to leave the barn, as he feared the Germans. We had no choice, and left our hiding place for the fields. A blizzard was raging, and the snow pelted our faces. Despairing, we asked ourselves where we could go. I suggested returning to Starzyn and hiding in the lofts of the long stable buildings. I assumed that those lofts were rarely visited, and we would be able to stay there for some time.

We arrived in Starzyn exhausted, and hid in the loft of a stable. Down below, the horses were munching on white beets. One of us climbed down and took a few bunches of beets from the feeding trough; that was our food.

The next morning, we heard steps approaching, and realized that the newcomers were speaking Yiddish. Raising our heads, we saw Itshele from Stryszów with his son, followed by

[Page 174]

three more Jews from that village, whose names I do not remember. They were frightened of us and began to run away. In low voices, we called them by their names, and they turned back and came up.

Going for Bread

We developed a plan to assure us of food and bread. Someone from Stryszów told us that he had fabric for a woman's dress, and that we should plan to barter it with a peasant for food. Who would do it? We cast lots, and it fell to Fishl Shek and me. Fishl Gertl announced that he had taken a solemn oath never to leave my side, and insisted on coming along. We said that a band of three would arouse curiosity, so Fishl Shek stayed in the stable while Fishl Gertl and I left.

We went to Horodlo, and knocked on the door of a peasant named Yashke Meruniya. Once inside, we spread out the fabric and proposed the exchange. The peasant's wife told us that she had no bread at the moment, and instructed us to spend the day in her barn loft. This would giver her time to knead the dough and bake bread, time-consuming though it was. We did as she said. Late the next night, she gave us a few loaves of bread tied up with string, and we left Horodlo for Starzyn. I remember that we asked her for a bag and promised we would return it to her, but she refused for fear that we would be murdered, and she would lose the bag.

As soon as we started on our way back, a powerful wind came up, and the snow that began falling was so thick that it wiped out the way to Starzyn. As we came to Murciak's brick kiln, we could not see the way. We tried to discover the way as best we

[Page 175]

could, but in fact we kept going around the kiln. We realized this only at dawn.

At that point I told Fishl that we would not be able to go on by daylight, and we needed to find a hiding place. We went to Wlodka Dobrovolski's barn, which was far from his home, and found it to be securely locked. Fishl climbed up on my shoulders, removed the bunches of hay from the thatched roof, and let himself in; he then opened the window at the barn's end. We climbed into the loft, and had a good rest.

We spent the day peering through the cracks, and heard Kwiszniewski, Dobrovolski's neighbor, tell him about the horrific scene he had witnessed as he drove his cart through Starzyn: the bodies of nine murdered Jews. He recognized Fishl Shek, Yankele Zaydl, and Itshele Arnshteyn. He also said that he had heard that their hideout in Starzyn had been discovered by the estate watchman, who had reported it to the Germans. They were then killed.

Thus, we found out that our unfortunate friends had been caught, after all the suffering and dangers that they had been able to evade. We knew that returning to Starzyn was out of the question.

We lay in that temporary hideout for about a week, living on the bread that we had gotten in exchange for the fabric. Yet, we were discovered one night by the barn's owner, who feared the Germans and ordered us to disappear.

Once again, we faced the terrible problem of finding a hideout that would be suitable in the freezing conditions. We remembered the many barns and stables near Swietlinski's, and started out in that direction. We climbed into

[Page 176]

Swietlinski's hayloft and lay there. We would emerge at night and knock on the doors of certain peasants with whom we more or less acquainted, and ask for bread. Among those we visited was Tomki Bilecki, whom we asked for food.

Once, he told us that he could give us no more bread, unless we stole a sack of flour from one of the peasants and brought it to him. He would then bake us bread. We began thinking of the best way to get a sack of flour. Our problem was solved the next night, when we went to ask for bread at the house of a peasant named Slavtinski and noticed a sack of flour in the entryway. Naturally, we did not go inside the peasant's house but heaved the sack onto our shoulders and brought it to Bilecki.

In the meantime, we had noticed that there was a locked underground cellar in the barn where we were staying. Fishl was able to open the top of the cellar with a special key, and we discovered a winter store of apples, which we used to refresh ourselves.

We lay in this refuge for sixteen weeks. Our boldness and readiness to take risks increased during those weeks. Bilecki, the peasant, demanded that we join him and his brother in an attack that they wanted to carry out on the administrative director in Rivne.[4] He also trained us in the use of rifles. Sure enough, he called us over one night to join them in the operation, and gave us two rifles. The Bilecki brothers ordered us to knock at the door of the administrative director's house, and go inside; they would cover us and stand guard outside. We knocked at the door. "Who's there?" came the question. "Open!" we said in German. They apparently took us for Germans. The door was opened by the director, who found himself

[Page 177]

confronting our rifles. We ordered him, his wife, and another man who was there, to face the wall and stand motionless. Then Bilecki came in and began taking various household items and foodstuffs. We heaped the loot onto our cart, and quickly left. At Bilecki's house, we asked for some of the goods; he cut off a small piece of meat and gave it to us. He even took the jacket that Fishl had taken from the director's house.

We would go out almost every night, looking for opportunities. One night, we heard the footsteps of a man singing in German. A German soldier was staggering as if drunk, singing soldiers' songs. When he drew near, we emerged from our refuge and ordered him to put up his hands. We took his fur jacket as well as his revolver, objects that we needed in our situation. We laid him on the ground and tried to tug his boots off, but without success.

On one of our nocturnal rambles, we were almost captured by the Germans. The peasant Lucilo Farkavich, from whom we often begged for food, apparently informed on us to the Germans. One evening, as we approached his house for a bit of hot soup, we noticed that the building was dark. That seemed somewhat suspicious. We became more careful and pricked up our ears to catch any sign of disturbance on the street. Suddenly, we heard the rustle of people moving. We bent low immediately, as a spotlight came on and illuminated the surroundings. This was followed by a hail of bullets directed at us. We responded by firing our guns, whose barrels enhanced the sound, so that one could think that we were firing heavy artillery. The Germans did not

[Page 178]

dare to approach us, and we retreated very warily.

We set ourselves up in the loft of Swietlinski's barn, but here, too, we were discovered by the owners. This is what happened: one day, Swietlinski's wife was milking the cow in the barn, with her husband standing nearby. We hear her say, "Edziu, what smells so bad?" "You're imagining things!" he responds. When she leaves the barn, leaving her husband there, he says to himself, "Yes, the barn stinks of human excrement." We see him searching for the source of the smell, and discovering the place where we performed our bodily functions. He came up into the loft and found us. We begged him to keep his discovery to himself, and not share it with anyone. We also asked him to allow us to continue hiding there.

The next day, he came up to the loft and told us that he had had strange, sad dreams about us, and asked us to leave.

Once again, we faced with the problem of a hiding place. This time, we did not know which way to go and where to seek refuge.

We went into the Christian cemetery, and found a locked crypt. Breaking the door open, we saw that it belonged to a princely family. We moved the two coffins aside and lay down. However, we couldn't stay there for more than two days, as the air was so bad and polluted that we couldn't touch the food we had brought. Leaving the crypt, we went to the priest's housekeeper to seek shelter. She proposed that we hide in the church cellar, but we couldn't stay there either, as creatures with glittering eyes scampered around at night, frightening us even more.

[Page 179]

Leaving the church cellar, we remembered that Koblocha, the peasant, owned a neglected ruin that no one visited. By this time it was summer, the days were hot, and we thought that the ruin would be suitable as a summer hideout.

We hid in the ruin, believing that no one would discover us there. But, once again, we were discovered through an odd coincidence: Golombuski, who lived near the ruin, was missing a hen. He asked Koblocha's granddaughter to climb up to the ruin's attic and see if the hen was there. She climbed up, found us, became terrified, and let out a loud shriek before running back home. Koblocha climbed up to see what had frightened her so badly. I sprang up and calmed him down, telling him that we were only hiding here, and asked him to be quiet. He went back down and told the neighbors – who had gathered after hearing the girl's cries – that nothing unusual had happened. After the neighbors had scattered, he climbed up again, plucked a few hairs from our heads, charred them in a flame, and told his granddaughter to inhale the smell (a superstition which was meant to calm fears).

That evening, he came up to the attic and told us that we could hide in his barn, in return for supplying him with stolen goods. We began roaming around at night, looking for stolen goods to bring to our benefactor. In fact, we found various surprises: flour, grain, clothes, and once, even a calf. In return, he would make food and bring it to us in the hideout.

His wife knew nothing about us, and Koblocha

[Page 180]

for his part, was careful to say nothing to her about our hiding place. However, she was surprised at the number of objects that her husband was suddenly bringing home, as well as their unexpected affluence. Apparently, she decided to find the reason. One day, she came into the barn – something she had not done for a long time – and discovered us. Her husband, who also arrived, and found her in the barn, slapped her face. We became frightened at the family dispute that had erupted over us and could become a problem. We kept the wife inside, until we had convinced her husband to ask her forgiveness, and they reconciled over a glass of brandy.

During one of our nightly "strolls" we were almost captured again by the Germans. This was when we risked a burglary in their command post.

We knew that the warehouses of the command post contained many necessities, such as food and clothes, and decided to steal from these warehouses. We tried to break the gate open, but the massive locks proved too difficult to tackle. Then, Fishl climbed onto my shoulders, crept into the warehouse through the small window, and began flinging out food and clothes. However, he ran into trouble when it was time to climb back out through the window. Holding my breath, I waited for the results of his efforts. After a struggle, he was finally able to climb up to the window and jump out. However, we did not know that the gate was secured by an alarm system. We had apparently activated the alarm wiring; less than a hundred meters away, we were fired on from several directions. We lay on the ground silently. When the shots stopped, we quickly slipped away towards the barn, holding the sack of food and bread. When we

[Page 181]

sliced the bread in order to eat, we found bullets inside. These were the bullets that the Germans had aimed at us, and that had lodged in the bread. We had been saved by a miracle.

The next morning, Koblocha brought us a German newspaper, with a report of our attack on the command post warehouse. It was presented as a robbery attempt done by partisans.

It seemed that we would stay in this hideout until the end of the war. It was April 1944. We were hearing about the German army's defeat on the battlefield, and we knew that Germany's downfall was near.

Ya'akov Gruber

However, the following unusual circumstance forced us to leave Koblocha's barn. Two Germans and their horses were resting near our stable refuge. One of them pulled out the clump of hay that concealed

[Page 182]

our entry and exit hole. Some hay slid out, along with our revolver and the belt to which it was attached. The Germans immediately rushed to the command post to report the incident. We promptly fled into the fields, towards Murciak's brick kiln. Wandering through the fields, we did not know what to do next. In the distance, we saw a peasant spreading fertilizer over his fields who was driving a cart harnessed to two horses. We approached and recognized Dumek Amndrich. He greeted us and said, "Fellows, stay strong, because the defeat of the Germans is very near." He gave us news of the war, and the collapse of the German army, news which cheered us up a bit.

We stayed in the field until evening. After dark, we left to try and hide with a Gentile named Michalka . We told him that the Germans would soon be defeated and the war would be over, and we would then reward him for his consent to hide us in the attic of his house. We were able to convince him, and he agreed.

That was our last hideout, after a long period of living through suffering and hardships, and being hunted like animals. Looking out of our refuge several weeks later, we noticed some unusual military maneuvers. Soldiers wearing unfamiliar uniforms began coming from the other bank of the Bug. Our host appeared in our refuge and announced that the Russian army had captured Horodlo, and the Germans had retreated. We emerged from the hideout. After a very long period of suffering, we stepped out onto the street in broad daylight for the first time. We were lonely and miserable. Everything looked strange and crushed. – 'Where are you,

[Page 183]

Jews of Horodlo?!' we asked. Had other Jews been able to save themselves from the massive annihilation??!

We went out to search for Jews. During that day, several survivors who had lived through the deluge, like us, gathered.

We knew that we could no longer live in Horodlo. Some time later, we left the town and went west, to the displaced persons' camps, seeking a safe shore.

Translator's Footnotes:

1. A Judenrat (Jewish council) was an administrative body established in German-occupied Europe during World War II which purported to represent a Jewish community in dealings with the Nazi authorities.

2. Bełżec was the first Nazi German forced-labor extermination camp in occupied Poland.

3. I could not identify Mruczin and Laczewy.

4. The town of Rivne (Rovno, the capital of Volhynia), became, under the Nazi occupation, the administrative center of Ukraine.

[Page 184]

The German Occupation and Liquidation of the Horodlo Community

By Abish Berger, Be'er Sheva, Israel

When World War II broke out, I was a boy of sixteen. I did not properly understand what the terrible war meant, and did not foresee the bitter fate that awaited the Jewish community of Horodlo and Poland as a whole.

1. The Jews of Horodlo During the German Occupation, Prior to Expulsion

The Germans took Horodlo on September 26, 1939, and instituted a regime of terror immediately upon their arrival, imposing forced labor. They appointed a Judenrat, which included Petachya Blat (may his memory be for a blessing), Mendl Lerner (may his memory be for a blessing), Shmuel Berger (may his memory be for a blessing), and Shmuel Goldberg (may his memory be for a blessing), and made them responsible for supplying Jews for forced labor. The Judenrat members managed to evade this task. But when no one reported for work, the Germans beat and tortured the members of the Judenrat.

The Germans generally set the Jews to do tasks that were difficult and shameful, and humiliated them in various ways. They harnessed Jews, instead of horses, to wagons loaded with earth, and forced them to pull the wagons to the German command post, in the Polish school; they were also forced to sing derisive songs.

The workday most commonly ended with the following terrible scene. The Jews were usually brought back from their labor in

[Page 185]

a procession that stopped at the marketplace, where they were then shot at indiscriminately from all directions. It is hard to describe the ensuing shock and panic, and the stampede of the Jews, who fled for as long as they were able.

Sometimes, S.S. soldiers from the county would come and demand that a number of Jews go with them "for work." Those who went never came back. One night, Germans came to our house and demanded that my father send his sons with them for work. We were hiding in the attic, and could hear our father saying that he did not know where we were. We were afraid that the Germans would search the house, and quickly slipped out of the attic into the night.

2. The Expulsion

It was a bitter, unexpected day when the decree to drive out the Jews of Horodlo came from the German county authorities in Hrubieszow. I remember that a Ukrainian Gentile appeared in our house, and proposed that my father sell him our house; in any case, it would belong to others after the Jews were banished. I can still hear my father's reply, "I believe that Hitler (may his name be blotted out) will not be able to exterminate all the Jews, and those who remain alive will exact revenge for the Jewish blood that was shed."

The day of the expulsion, all the Jews were collected in the marketplace. We were taken to the town of Uchanie. Once there, we were placed in a sheep barn, and kept there for two weeks. Naturally, the Germans gave us no food or other necessities. We subsisted on the little food we had been able to bring with us from home. We did nothing in Uchanie, and awaited the future with great dread.

One day, the Germans informed us that we had to move on,

[Page 186]

and we were taken to Miączyn. Exhausted and dejected, the crowd of expelled Jews trudged, accompanied by the German murderers on horseback. When we arrived in Miączyn, we saw that we were being led into a sheep barn that was surrounded by barbed wire fencing. On our way into the barn, we were harassed and tormented. German soldiers stood at either side of the entrance and beat the incomers severely.

3. To the Extermination Camp

The same day, at dusk, the Germans forcibly took away the women and children, beating them savagely, loaded them onto railroad freight cars, and took them to Belzec – the ghastly death camp, from which they never returned. It is difficult to describe the savagery of the murderers as they separated the families. It was a black, bitter day, as the entire crowd was shattered and devastated.

Night fell. We lay unmoving, anxious and fearful, unable to sleep.

The next morning, a German Commissioner of Police arrived with a group of murderers. After a short consultation with the Germans who had taken us to Miączyn, they sat down at a table near the entrance to the second sheep barn, which we had not noticed earlier. They began classifying the survivors, who consisted solely of men; the women and children were no longer there. Each of us left the barn and passed through a double row of soldiers until we reached the "classification commission." Young people were sent to the right, the old and the weak to the left, where they were placed inside a fenced area. The Judenrat members were also taken to this area.

After the classification was completed, several hundred young people were left. The Germans informed us that we would return to

[Page 187]

Uchanie, and would have to obey the orders of the Judenrat. They also warned us against anyone trying to escape. If one person was missing, they would kill the Judenrat members. After these threats, they ordered us to stand and return to Uchanie. Our

Peshi Ayzen

Ts. Barenholts

Rokhl Royter

[Page 188]

parents and dearest ones were left behind in the other barn. We asked the Germans to allow us to kiss our loved ones and part from them, and were turned down. Accompanied by German guards, the group of young people slowly walked to Uchanie. We stayed there for eight days.

4. At Work

Owners of the large estates came and selected people for work. The managers of the Keszinowski and Starzyn estates also arrived, and chose Jews from Horodlo for work on their properties. My three brothers and sister-in-law Genia (the wife of my brother Shmuel, both now living in Haifa) and I, along with Eliyahu Rozenfeld and his sons Mukl and Aharon, Eliezer, and Chantshe, were chosen for work at the Starzyn estate. We were joined by Sara (Mindl's daughter), Shifra Shek, Leybl Berger, Fishl Gertl, Zalmen Rozenfeld, Gutta Rozenfeld and other young folks from Horodlo.

We worked on this estate the entire summer.

Shimshon Fayl   Eliyohu Berger

[Page 189]

5. The Escape

One day, at the end of the work season, the estate manager came up on his horse, called me aside, and told me that the Germans had ordered him to deliver the Jews who worked for him to the German command post. I asked his permission to leave the job in the middle of the work day, and he agreed. I went to the site on the estate where the Jewish workers would gather to eat, and gave them the news. I said that I believed we should flee that very night. My uncle Eliyohu and his sons said that they had no strength for more wandering, regardless of the consequences. I agreed with my brothers and with Genia to make a break for it that night. We prepare bread and other food items, and ran away from the estate in the dark.

We made for the fields, heading for the village of Janki, about three kilometers from Horodlo.[1] At Janki, we went to the area of the barns. Under cover of the darkness and silence, we went into a barn full of hay, which belonged to a peasant woman whom we knew. We immediately burrowed into the hay and lay still. We emerged at night, but spent the days in our hideout, being very careful to stay hidden.

On our nighttime excursions for food and water, we erased our tracks as we returned to the barn. We hoped that we would be able to stay there for a long time without being discovered.

Once, the peasant's daughter noticed tracks leading to the barn loft. She followed the tracks and discovered us. She was very frightened at first, as she had stepped on one of

[Page 190]

of our faces, and let out a shriek. We calmed her down and asked her to keep silent, so that the Germans wouldn't find us. We also asked her to let us stay there as long as possible. Two days later, she told us that people in the village knew about our hideout, and insisted that we leave the place.

We left that night and went to the village of Czołki (seven kilometers from Horodlo). We tried our luck with a Gentile we knew: we knocked at his door and asked him to hide us. However, he closed the door in our face, saying that he was afraid of being punished by the Germans if he hid us. We begged him to let us stay a day or two, to replenish our energy, but he refused. He did give us bread, and told us to prepare a "bunker" in the fields. He knew, after serving in the Russian army, that an underground cave would stay warm in winter as well.

6. The Bunker

We retraced our steps, and arrived at the outskirts of Horodlo. Searching around Murczak's brick kiln, we found nowhere suitable. We thought about the best course of action, and decided to dig a covered underground "bunker." A mound off to the side, which people did not visit, seemed right. The bunker we dug was large enough for four. We concealed it with the clothes and rags we collected at night, and began living under the surface of the earth, emerging only at night. Under cover of darkness, we went into peasant farms, and took chickens to roast inside the bunker, over a fire in a bucket. We

[Page 191]

sometimes dared to knock on a peasant's door at night, and ask for bread and other food. We ended up spending the entire winter like this, lying in the bunker.

On one of those nights, we returned to Janki. We remembered that a peasant women owed my parents money, and decided to approach her and demand repayment in food. The Gentile woman seemed willing to help us, and said that she was going to bring us bread. However, she did not come back for a long time. We wondered about this and deliberated what we should do. One thought we had was that she might have gone to bake fresh bread for us. Suddenly, we were shocked by the appearance of a number of her relatives; they demanded that we surrender to the Germans. Instinctively, I charged at the door, broke it open and jumped out. I was followed by my brother Shmuel, and the two of us started running. Shmuel was nearly caught by the end of a scarf that he was wearing. Luckily, he was able to wriggle out of the scarf, which remained in the hands of his pursuer. We fled into the darkness, and they gave up the chase.

7. Summer in the Fields

Spring was here. The air grew milder, and the snow began to melt. However, this pleasant season created a problem that we had not foreseen. Our "bunker," which was on a down-slope, became filled with water from the melting snow. We were forced to spend all day sitting in cold water, as we were afraid to come out; we suffered from the damp and the cold. It became clear that we would not be able to continue using this hideout.

[Page 192]

At nightfall, we set out for the village of Rybne (three kilometers from Horodlo).[2] We knocked on the door of a poor peasant. After appealing to him and promising that we would do him favors and bring him many valuable objects, he allowed us to hide in the attic of his barn.

We would leave our hideout at night, steal chickens and potatoes from the peasants in the vicinity, and even kernels of grain, and bring it to our peasant. With time, he appreciated us more, and even prepared cooked food for us. He was extraordinarily cautious – not even the members of his household knew about us.

We stayed with this peasant until May, and then went into the fields to search for a refuge, heading for Starzyn and the property where we had first worked. We met the field watchman, and told him that he had to pretend not to notice us. If he did not cooperate, we would liquidate him. We told him that we were part of a partisan group numbering 500. The watchman actually behaved accordingly, and we stole foodstuffs from the property. We even milked the cows in the cow barn, and roamed the wide fields.

This continued for two months.

At that time we met a Gentile who told us that a Jew was hiding nearby just as we were doing, and that this Jew wanted to see us. That very evening, we were joined by Velvl Stryszever and his rifle. Our confidence increased a bit. Our raids on the peasant farms became more daring, and the food we gathered was quite valuable.

[Page 193]

8. The New Winter Hideout

As winter approached, we were able to promise the peasant payment for hiding us in his horse barn. Our hideout was now quite comfortable; and we were experienced at hideouts. We lay there during the day, and roamed around at night, bringing the Gentile many tidbits. We spent the entire winter in that hideout.

9. On the Eve of Liberation

It was summer once again. We left our hideout and returned to our summer refuge in the fields. The roads were full of retreating Germans, and we understood that the front was drawing near. Anxiously, we awaited liberation by the advancing Russians. We were well hidden in the grain fields, and were careful not to be discovered by the many Germans in the area.

At night, we would come out of the grain field to see what was happening in the vicinity. We went as far as the village of Łuszków, which was now very near the front.[3] En route to Łuszków, we saw a German vehicle parked at the side of the road. We approached gingerly and saw that the driver was asleep over the wheel, his gun beside him. My brother David slashed the canvas and drew out the gun.[4] We ran off quickly and returned to our hideout.

We were able to see that massive bridge over the Bug at Ustyluh was in flames, and understood that the Germans had retreated from that town.[5]

My brother Shmuel and sister-in-law Genia then went to seek food on the Rogl property. After the war, they told us

[Page 194]

that they had approached a peasant, who told them that they could stay on his property at night, because the front was close by. The next morning, he showed them how to go over to the advancing Russians.

At this point, we parted, and did not see them until the end of the war.

Once again we – Velvl, my brother David, and I – hid in the grain fields.

During that period, we were almost caught by the Germans. As we lay in the field, we heard the grain stalks rustling in an unusual way. Velvl raised his head to see what was happening, and told us that two German officers were riding towards us in the field. We quickly rose and began running. The Germans fired at us with their revolvers, as Velvl took a hand grenade from his pocket and hurled it in the direction of the Germans. The grenade exploded with a deafening crack and covered the Germans in a cloud of dust. We fled as soon as possible, running non-stop across the fields, until we came to our first hideout – the "bunker" near the brickworks. We stayed there until dark.

After nightfall, we checked the vicinity. When we realized that all was calm, we stood up and went to the Rogl farm. No one was there – it had been abandoned. We climbed up to the attic of one of the barns and spent the night there.

10. Liberation

The next morning, we saw that the front was raging around us and the farm was caught in the crossfire. Peering through the cracks of the barn, we saw Germans scampering around like lunatics, holding their rifles, while the Russians were bombing and firing incessantly. Our

[Page 195]

barn caught on fire. We leaped from the attic to an adjoining building, noticed a cellar underneath it, and quickly went in. The cellar was already occupied by dozens of peasants and their families who had found refuge there. They called us to come near, and gave us bread and milk.

Suddenly, someone announced that the building's roof was on fire. Everyone fled from the cellar in a panic and ran to the fields. We lay in the grain all day, hearing the shots and explosions resounding.

Tova Tsukerman
(known as Tova, Mekhl's daughter)[161]

That night, we decided to cut through the front line and join the Russians. We figured that the Germans were in Janki village, and the Russians were in Luszkow village. Anxiously and cautiously, with great difficulty, we began making our way towards the Russian trenches. We were able to penetrate the barbed wire that blocked the Russian trenches.

"Halt!" someone shouted in Russian, pointing his rifle barrel at us. We raised our hands. Russian soldiers approached and asked, "Who are you?" We answered that we were Jews who had been hiding from

[Page 196]

the Germans. They let us go, instructing us to move away from the front and go to Ustyluh. From there, we continued on our way to Ludmir. The destruction and desolation was evident in both these places, which had been the home of large Jewish populations. We met some downcast Jews in Ludmir. Clearly, that city was no place for us. We decided to return to our home town, Horodlo.

Yitzchok Ling

Shmuel (Velvenyu's son)[7]

In Horodlo, we once again met up with my brother Shmuel and my sister-in-law Genia, as well as Leybl Berger, Fishl Gertl, Fradl Perlmuter, and Tzipora Tzigler. Fradl and Tzipora had survived the entire war by hiding with Christian families. When they heard that we had arrived, they joined us. All of us lived together in the home of Berl (Dov) Grosburd.

[Page 197]

We stayed in Horodlo for about a year. During that year we tried to do business with the peasants across the Bug River. We would go to Ludmir, buy horses from the Ukrainians, and sell them to the peasants around Horodlo. Sometimes, we would take them to sell in Hrubieszow. However, this business culminated in great tragedy. My brother David (may his memory be for a blessing), who was the most active and the boldest in this enterprise, was captured and killed by Polish anti-Semitic gangsters on one of his trips to Ludmir. We mourned him bitterly. After having survived so much suffering before being liberated, he was murdered.

We realized that Jews no longer had a place in their home towns. We moved to Hrubieszow, where we would await the end of the war, and then join the Jewish survivors who planned to go to the Jewish homeland.

Translator's Footnotes:

1. Janki is located south-southeast of Horodlo on the road to Łuszków.

2. Modern day Hrebenne, located southwest of Horodlo and west of Janki.

3. Located southeast of Horodlo.

4. The car's window was apparently covered with canvas.

5. Destroying the bridge behind them to slow advancing Soviet troops.

6. The possessive that follows her name could indicate either her husband or her father.

7. There seems to be a typo in the name; as Velvl is mentioned several times in the text, I've made this correction. Velvenyu is an affectionate diminutive of Velvl.

[Page 198]

Events in Horodlo, 1939-1942
(Memories of an Eyewitness)

by Aharon Fuks, New York, United States

The first German soldiers to arrive in Horodlo following its conquest were border guards. Their main task was to watch the new border between Russia and Germany – according to the treaty between the two countries, it ran along the Bug River.

These soldiers occupied whichever Jewish houses they fancied; the Jewish occupants had been turned out into the cold wintry streets of 1939. A considerable number of these former occupants died of hunger and cold during the first winter of the German occupation.

I remember that January 1940 witnessed the first horrific acts and systematic torture directed at Jews. Simultaneously, the Germans published announcements threatening retaliation and penalties towards those who helped Jews in any way.

Before 1941, when the Germans attacked Russia, the murderous actions of the Germans were limited, and stopped short of mass murder. In June 1940, the border guards were replaced by other soldiers, with the mission of establishing a Nazi regime in the town.

As the German army advanced further into Russia, the Germans began to ensure that the existing roads were in good shape

[Page 199]

and that new roads would be paved. That was when Jews were forced to remove the gravestones from the Jewish cemetery to use as paving stones for the road between Horodlo and Stryszów. When the gravestones were gone, the peasants in the vicinity brought their livestock to graze in the destroyed cemetery.

I also remember that the Germans turned the synagogue into a horse barn. Once, when a horse had died, the Germans forced the rabbi to arrange a funeral for it, wrap it in a tallis, and bury it in the Jewish cemetery.

Conditions for the Jewish residents worsened from day to day. A leader of the Jewish community was designated as accountable to the Germans, and responsible for supplying workers according to their demands. The German demands, however, were vast and horrific, and the Jewish community leader was unable, as well as unwilling, to fulfill them. Therefore, Germans themselves raided the Jewish homes and snatched Jews up for labor; as a by-product, they murdered Jews who were weak, elderly, or anyone they did not like.

During one of these raids (April 1942), which took place in the morning, my father, Ben-Tziyon Fuks (may his memory be for a blessing) was snatched and murdered by the Nazis, along with four other Jews. Before being murdered, these unfortunates were forced to dig their own graves.

This state of affairs -- of oppression, decrees, and murders of Jews -- continued until June 1942.

In June 1942, the Germans began the total liquidation of the Jews of Horodlo.

One day, all the Jews of Horodlo and its environs were taken out of their homes, assembled in one place, and taken to Miączyn. When we poor souls arrived in Miączyn, we were concentrated near the railroad station. We were told that we would be sent to different work places.

[Page 200]

The following is what happened to the Jews of Horodlo and its environs, in Miączyn:

We arrived in Miączyn in the late afternoon, and found the bodies of many Jews who had been murdered sprawled there. They had been killed by the Germans for not climbing into the rail cars fast enough during that day's liquidation operation.

One day before we came to Miączyn, Jews from the nearby towns of Uchanie, Grabowiec, and other sites had been brought in. When we arrived, fifty thousand Jews were still crammed together in a small area near the railroad station. Twelve freight cars stood in another part of the station.

The Nazis issued a new order to the mass of despondent souls: they had to separate into two groups, one of Jews less than 18 and over 50 years old, and the other of Jews between the ages of 18 and 50.

This was the most tragic moment for the Jews of Horodlo and the surroundings, on their last journey to the death camp.

The families were ruthlessly separated and divided according to age. Men and children under 18, and men and women aged 50 and over, were forced violently into the freight cars of the train bound for Sobibor.[1] Men in the other group, between the ages of 18 and 50, were mostly loaded aboard other freight cars, after having been separated from women in the same age group. I was then under 18, but I thrust myself into the older age group. Our train left Miączyn that night, heading for Chelm, where we arrived the next morning.

[Page 201]

On arrival in Chelm, we were taken off the freight cars and marched to Staw. When we came to Staw, we numbered about 200. Our homicidal guards took us to an abandoned flour mill. I was immediately taken to work in the kitchen. Conditions in the camp were horrible, and the death rate among the prisoners was high. I knew I wouldn't be able to survive, and decided to escape. After extraordinary efforts, I finally got away, arrived in Chelm, and went into the Jewish ghetto. There, I met Petachya Blat's two daughters, who had been living there for some time. The Blat sisters helped me economically. Eventually, I escaped from the ghetto.

After leaving the Chelm ghetto, I lived under an assumed name until the war's end.

* * *

After the war ended, I decided to leave Poland, with its blood-soaked soil. I left for America and came to New York. I'm now living here with my oldest brother Shmuel and my oldest sister Sara. My parents were murdered in the Holocaust, together with my younger sister Toybe. My uncle's family of seven was completely wiped out.

Translator's Footnote:

1. Sobibor was an extermination camp built and operated by Nazi Germany as part of Operation Reinhard. It was located in the forest near the village of Żłobek Duży in the General Government region of German-occupied Poland. As an extermination camp rather than a concentration camp, Sobibor existed for the sole purpose of murdering Jews.

[Page 202]

"The Last Journey"

By Fradl (Perlmuter) Shiffer

The sun appeared on the ashen-blue horizon, which seemed to have awoken from sleep on a spring night. Once again, it spread its rays and light over the world, as it did every year, as though nothing had happened and no unusual event could take place.

We, a large group of Jews, stand in the marketplace of the Uchanie ghetto. We've been waiting since the late night hours, overcome with the fear that fills in our eyes. One question hangs in the air: What awaits us? What will happen?

However, these unfortunate souls actually knew what awaited them. Even the small children felt it. Here they stand, the young saplings, sleepy, shivering with cold and hunger, wearing identification tags so as not to get lost in the crowd of evacuees. They are silent. It is very still, except for an occasional groan accompanied by the question of an ill, weak person: "What will happen to me, if I cannot walk when the order to move comes?" Here and there mothers weep, swallow their tears, and hug their small children who ask for bread.

Obtaining bread was an important project for the Jews of the ghetto. Anyone who possessed bread was considered blessed and happy, even if the bread was crude and baked with bran and flour that had been ground in the old-fashioned way, using stones. The problem of finding

[Page 203]

bread occupied the thoughts of the ghetto population, and continued to worry us even as we stood in the marketplace for the last time, awaiting the order to set out on our last journey.

A sudden murmur broke the general silence. "Here they come!" people told each other, and a large number of German savages appeared riding their horses, holding whips. A cold sweat drenched us as we saw the murderous faces.

My mother gathered the children in her arms, as if wanting to protect them from the oncoming evil. We children pressed ourselves against Mother, hiding behind each other like sheep around their faithful shepherd as ravenous wolves appear.

"Into the wagons!" the order slices through the silence of the group. All obey in terrible silence and docility, and climb into the wagons. The peasant drivers whip the horses and they start moving.

Where to? Everyone knows where we're going, but no one dares to say the truth, and articulate the horrible thought.

We weren't allowed to stay in the wagons for long; the drivers ordered us to get off so as not to exhaust the horses. The mass of oppressed, hungry, and thirsty people dragged itself towards extermination.

I glance at the crowd of evacuees, looking like a group of corpses just arisen from the graves to which they will soon need to return. But even in these last despairing moments, the life impulse wakes and arouses hidden hopes. "Something might happen after all, and we'll escape," the hopeful thought creeps in. At the same time, we look up at the sky and a murmured Sh'ma Yisro'el[1] is heard, hoping for a miracle.

[Page 204]

Thus does the world look on silently, as innocent masses are taken to the slaughter.

The sun shone warmer, as if mocking, and warms the group of parched people, who peel off articles of clothing one by one, attempting to ease their pain and exhaustion.

We meet up with small bands of tired, crushed Jews, returning from the same journey as us. They are a small part of a Jewish group that was on its way to extermination, but were selected for labor, and temporarily saved. They shout out, "Run! Run! Don't go in the direction they are driving you!" But where and how can we run, if all the roads are blocked, Gentiles are watching every Jewish movement, and turning in Jewish escapees. And the journey continues…

It is midday. The sky is covered in clouds and a powerful wind suddenly comes up to shake the world and attack it. The forces of nature seem to have come to help the dehydrated, suffering people, and to ease their thirst. The wind strengthens and becomes a full-fledged storm, stirring up clouds of dust and sand that obscure the sky. We cannot see each other, and we hear only cries and screams. The horses try to break loose of their harnesses and disobey their masters. Mother and I stretch our arms over the children, so that the wind doesn't push us apart.

A hopeful thought occurs: Could the storm separate us from the German murderers? However, when the storm was over we realized that we were still in the hands of our torturers.

Night fell. We come to the railroad station of Miączyn, somewhere near Zamość, in pitch dark. Our feet trudge through deep mud. Our clothes are

[Page 205]

damp and cling to the skin. My little sister wants to take off her clothes; she is cold and wet… Mother is considering how to do this, how to get a change of clothing.

However, we weren't allowed much time for thinking and considering. The murderers set us up in rows, administer beatings,, and then fire at the rows of sufferers.

Confused, I ask Mother how the children are doing. I hear no screams or groans. The people in the rows are so tightly pressed against each other that there is no space for the dead to fall down.

The final order comes. Mothers and children are to climb into the dim train cars, and the young people are to remain.

My last question to Mother is, "What shall I do, Mama?!" She replies, "Save yourself, my child! Perhaps a trace of my family will survive."

Her words were fulfilled. We, a handful of boys and girls, were kept back for labor and hardship. However, through all the anguished years that followed, Mama's words rang in my ears.

We stood there, the remnants, and watched, in pain and sorrow, as our dearest ones exert their last bits of strength to shove each other up into the dim freight cars. They move as fast as their waning strength allows, in order to avoid the German bullets that strike the sides of the cars.

The freight cars are closed up.

That was the last time that I saw my dear mother, my brothers and sisters.

The train began to move. We, the remnant, sent aching glances at the fast-disappearing cars, which carried so many beloved, sacred souls to the crematoriums of Sobibor that were built by the gruesome murderers, the human scum.

It was the 24th day of Sivan, 5702.[2]

[Page 206]

Let the Jews of Horodlo remember, wherever they may be, and may the Jewish people remember, the sacred, beloved souls, blameless and pure, who were annihilated by these despicable creatures.

A memorial assembly commemorating the martyrs of Horodlo, Tel Aviv, June 17, 1957

A memorial assembly commemorating the martyrs of Horodlo, Tel Aviv, June 17, 1957

Translator's Footnotes:

1. The Sh'ma (Shema) is a central prayer in Judaism, said three times each day by observant Jews.

2. June 9, 1942.

[Page 207]

Customs and Personalities

[Page 208]

[Blank]

[Page 209]

Customs and Personalities

This section is an attempt to portray life in Horodlo through descriptions of some residents, their appearance and personalities, and some events of bygone days. These details can provide an idea of Jewish customs and social life in the town.

The people portrayed were not unusual. On the contrary, in their personalities and qualities they embody the Jews of Horodlo and their different classes and positions. Each person described below is typical of people in the same social position.

There was no one in Horodlo who could create an artistic depiction of the town and its residents. Similarly, those who contributed to this section are not professional writers, but wanted to follow the instructions in the Sayings of the Fathers: "In the place where there are no men, strive to be a man."[1] True to this maxim, these writers made efforts to recount and describe according to their storytelling abilities, and portray the figures of men and women who were characteristic of our beloved residents of Horodlo.

Thus, the descriptions in this section were written not only to represent particular persons, but to provide an idea of the entire community as well.

[Page 210]

Our Nearest and Dearest

by Yosef Chaim Zavidovich, Israel

1. Aryeh (Leybl) Zavidovich (may his memory be for a blessing) and his wife Zissele (may her memory be for a blessing), may God avenge their blood.

Leybl Zavidovich and his wife Zissele were considered to be some of the most interesting and central figures in Horodlo. Leybl was a rabbi's son-in-law, and his wife Zissele was the daughter of the local rabbi, Rabbi Yekutiel Gelernter, himself a descendant of great rabbis and a link in the golden chain of rabbis over 24 generations. These facts alone guaranteed their honored standing in the life of the town.

In addition to his family lineage, Leybl Zavidovich was remarkable for his personal aristocratic appearance. His face, that of a Torah scholar, was adorned with a long beard. He was distinguished for several noble qualities: handsomeness, wisdom, knowledge, kindness, and discernment. His righteous wife, Zissele, was renowned for her honesty and modesty, and was also exceptionally intelligent. She was considered a woman of refinement. It is therefore not surprising that their home was a gathering place for the local notables. People who sought good advice and instruction consulted the couple.

My grandfather and grandmother (may their memory be for a blessing) had a large, ramified family. They were deeply and extensively rooted in the past, and active in many different areas.

They themselves had eight children, five sons and three daughters, all of whom were gifted and who possessed fine character and qualities. The oldest was Levi-Yitzchak (may his memory be for a blessing), my father, who married Perl

[Page 211]

Biderman, my mother (may her memory be for a blessing). Second was Yosef, who moved to Ludmir after his marriage to Rokhl Fishl, a member of an important Ludmir family, whose father, Yeshayahu Fishl was a distinguished person. The third son, Yekutiel, moved to Warsaw after marriage. The fourth son, Fishl, also moved to Warsaw after marriage. The fifth son, Mordkhe (known as Motl Zavidovich), moved first to Lutsk following his marriage, and then to Lemberg.[2] The daughters were Khaye, who married Note Perlmuter; Malke, who married Avner Tzuker and moved to Ludmir; and Khane, who married Moyshe Tenenboym.

My grandfather (may his memory be for a blessing) was an expert assessor of forests and classifier of wood – a very respectable profession in those days – and was permanently employed by the Heller brothers in Warsaw, who were forest owners and timber merchants. The Heller brothers valued my grandfather's knowledge and professionalism, and agreed to pay him his high salary in foreign currency (dollars).

Arye (Leybl) Zavidovich and his wife Zissele

[Page 212]

Because of his work, Grandfather spent long periods of time in Warsaw and other large cities, and would usually return home for longer vacations around the High Holidays. The time he spent in large cities, and his many other trips, to various cities, taught him urban mannerisms and gave him much experience in world affairs.

Naturally, whenever he appeared in Horodlo after many months in the world outside of the town, he made a great impression on the town, and caused much excitement in our household.

I remember the major preparations in Grandfather's house, in our house, and my uncles' houses, before his arrival. The day he arrived, we grandchildren were dressed in festive clothing, and ran towards him to greet him. With bated breath, we awaited Hershele Fraynd's cart, which had taken a special trip to the railroad station to bring Grandfather back home. He never returned empty-handed. We watched with curiosity as the large, heavy valises were heaved off the cart, and tried to guess which presents he had brought us.

The Hasids of his synagogue received him with deep respect. After greetings, they invited him to sit in a seat reserved for dignitaries, crowding around to hear the latest world news, as well as news from the Radzin Hasidic court. During the High Holidays, Grandfather was honored by chanting the prayers for dew and rain, as an expression of their respect and esteem.[3]

The family customs in Grandfather's home were those of a refined, observant family of great lineage. I will never forget the mutual understanding, respect, and love between Grandfather and Grandmother. Their family life, calm and genteel, provided a paradigm and an example for the entire family.

[Page 213]

Grandfather and Grandmother were the undisputed authorities in the family, and their opinion was accepted without argument. As noted above, Grandfather's work caused him to spend months away from town. In his absence, we considered Grandmother, who was exceptionally intelligent and practical, to be the family's guide. They all had full confidence in her words and advice, which was always level-headed and prudent. Her home continued to serve as the gathering place for the entire family.

Even after the death of Grandfather (may his memory be for a blessing), the home continued to be revered in the same way; there was no change of attitude. We considered Grandmother the keeper of the beautiful family tradition, as well as someone gifted with high morals and refined qualities.

The children and grandchildren who moved to other towns, as well as those who moved far away, also stayed in touch with Grandmother by letters, and thought it appropriate to write about their lives and hear her opinion about various matters. And indeed, Grandmother was able to write everyone, give detailed answers, and express her opinions and provide guidance in matters as required.

* * *

Grandmother was quite elderly when World War II broke out. She was forced to leave her home and the town in which she had spent her entire life, and where she had founded a large, fine family. She moved to Ludmir, to be close to her son and daughter and their families.

Woe is us! She could not avoid the destruction of Ludmir. She, as well as many family members, was murdered by the Nazi killers and their accomplices.

[Page 214]

2. My beloved parents: My father, Levi-Yitzchok Zavidovich, and my mother, Perl Zavidovich (may their memory be for a blessing).

When I was very young, not yet Bar Mitzvah age, my father (may his memory be for a blessing), died, and left my mother with small children; all of us lost our teacher and guide.

I was a small child at his death, but his beloved image is before my eyes. I remember his height, his powerful figure, his broad face and the blond beard that surrounded it, his high, imposing forehead, and his kind, gentle expression.

My father (may his memory be for a blessing) was boundlessly devoted to his family–his wife (my mother) and children. His love for us was fatherly and steadfast, and simultaneously that of an educator and guide. We, his children, were attached to him like eagle nestlings to their eagle mother, and treated him with obedience and love. He was a hero figure to us, and we felt safe in his care.

Father (may his memory be for a blessing) was beloved and respected by the Jews of Horodlo. He was a member of the Radzin Hasids, who prayed in the small synagogue, and was the regular Torah reader. He raised his children to follow the rules of the Torah and be pious. Even when times were hard, we were poor, and he had to work hard to feed his wife and five children, he wouldn't allow my oldest brother Moyshe (may God avenge his blood) help to make a living. "The children must study and become religious scholars," he would say. He therefore included among his duties regular tuition payments to the melamed.[4] Even in the most difficult periods, when he himself did not make enough for a living, he made sure that the melamed would get his wages on time.

Father had profound faith in God, and did not

[Page 215]

turn to other people for help. He believed in hard work and initiative, and wanted to raise his children in the same spirit. He wanted to see us become Torah scholars, as well as people who were familiar with worldly things, and believed that the sages' proverb "Excellent is the study of the Torah when combined with a worldly occupation, for toil in them both keeps sin out of one's mind" was the best course in life.[5] However, he also thought that general subjects should also be learned in a context and under conditions that would not adversely affect an observant education. He therefore ruled out any chance that we would go to a Polish school.

All week long, Father was busy with his livelihood, while we children spent all day in cheder under the watchful eye of the melamed. However, when Shabbat came around, he devoted much attention to us, and would quiz us on our studies of the past week.[6] We stood before him respectfully and listened to his questions. Often, these were not easy, and the responses required much effort.

When Father died, we felt that the entire order of the world had changed. Mother was confronted with the bitter problem of making a living. "How will I be able to sustain my children?" she asked herself. We children, young as we were, very much wanted to help her. Our living was derived from a haberdashery shop, and we wanted to help her there. However, Mother was firmly opposed to anything that would disrupt our cheder schooling, and she took on the entire burden. She worked in the shop from early morning until late at night, and travelled to nearby towns to buy merchandise. She continued to bring us up, as Father would have wished. She was happiest when the melamed reported that we were making progress. Her greatest desire was that we should grow up to be Torah scholars.

On Saturday mornings, Mother would rise at the crack of dawn

[Page 216]

to pray in the House of Study. However, it was still early. We, the boys who studied in the House of Study, were used to rising very early and studying for several hours before the morning prayers. Mother (may her memory be for a blessing) would listen in from the women's section, and was happy to hear her sons chanting the Talmud. This was her greatest reward for all her labor.

Perl Zavidovich with her sons Yekutiel and Yehoshua,
Chaya Zisberg, and Moyshe Tenenboym's son

As we grew older and gained understanding, we persuaded Mother that it was time for us to join her in the job of making a living. However, she clung to her principles and insisted that we continue our studies. She did agree to bring our oldest brother Moyshe (may his memory be for a blessing) into the business; he was old enough and had completed his cheder schooling. Once he joined, Mother's burden was much easier. He replaced her in

[Page 217]

the exhausting journeys, and showed an aptitude for business. Our livelihood grew a bit less precarious.

When I was older, I replaced my brother Moyshe in the shop. He wanted to become independent, and I wanted to support Mother's work and efforts. I was young and energetic, and stepped into the business world enthusiastically.

Moyshe Zavidovich and his daughter

But my mother demanded that I devote several hours a day to religious study. She would come into the shop at specific hours each day to remind me that it was time to go to the House of Study.

Mother had a gentle nature. For us as well as for others, she was a model of modesty and honesty. She was a righteous woman, who would save her own money to give to charity and aid to the poor. She made do with little, and raised her children to be honest and unpretentious.

* * *

[Page 218]

1934 – 1935. Conditions for Polish Jews grow worse, politically and economically. Anti-Semitism surges, and daily life is more restricted each day.

I decided to leave the world of business and start training for emigration and settlement in the Land of Israel, at one of the training centers run by HeChalutz HaMizrachi.[7] I consulted with my mother, and asked for her opinion. Without saying a word, she clearly approved of my decision. On the one hand, she, too, grasped the hopeless situation in Poland, and understood that I, like all the young people, needed to think of a safer shore; on the other hand, my departure greatly distressed her.

* * *

In 1939, Hitler (may his name be blotted out) invades Poland.[8] His armies stream through the country and reach Horodlo in about three weeks. Survivors told me that my brothers helped Mother load the shop's merchandise onto a cart that she had rented, and she fled to Ludmir. In that city, which was still in Russian hands, she joined our relatives. Like many other Jewish refugees, she and my brothers thought that the enemy would not advance further and they would be able to evade the war by staying in Ludmir.

Alas! The monstrous foe was allowed to continue his murderous advance of conquest and occupation. He attacked the Russians in June 1941, and within a few hours reached Ludmir, with its large Jewish population. The city was now full of displaced Jews. The German butchers and their allies killed and murdered the Jews of Ludmir gruesomely. Among them were my mother, brothers, elderly grandmother, and members of my large and ramified family. These innocents were slaughtered for no reason at all.

[Page 219]

3. My uncle (Mother's brother) Shmuel Biderman (may his memory be for a blessing).

Shmuel Biderman was one of the most respected Jews of Horodlo. He was held in high regard by the entire town, and was one of the local notables.

He had achieved this position thanks to certain qualities. First, his Hasidic appearance: he had a pious, scholarly face, surrounded by a long beard. He had a secure livelihood (an important factor in a town where making a living was difficult), his daughters were admired and important, and his sons-in-law were considered great scholars. He brought up his only son, Moyshe Biderman (now living in the United States) to be just as pious and scholarly as himself. In spite of his preoccupations, he devoted many hours a day to studying Torah at home, in the small synagogue, and in the House of Study.

I still remember the delightful melody of his Talmud study in the early mornings as it penetrated the wall of our house, which adjoined his. We would hear his chanting in the morning and at night. The melody gave us pleasure and a sense of security as we slept. We always asked, "How is he able to do with so little sleep, with all his concerns and businesses?"

My uncle Shmuel had a tavern. During the day, he did business with drunken Gentiles who expressed themselves crudely. He felt that his studies lifted him up from his everyday life: his Torah and Talmud studies during every spare moment in the evenings enhanced his spiritual life.

Shmuel was considered one of the important Radzin Hasids, and was esteemed by the local Jews. Following is an example of their high regard for him. When I was still a cheder student, we learned about permitted actions that an important person had to be strict about: "Even more so for an important person"

[Page 220]

(Mishna Berachot, 19b; Bava Metzia 73). When the rabbi was teaching, and wanted an example of an important person, he would say, "Take Shmuel Biderman, for example." This example would be understandable and persuasive.

Shmuel was strict, and held his family (including us young people) to high standards of education and upbringing. This was because he himself was careful about every detail, small or large. The death of our father while we were still young children, which placed the entire burden of livelihood on our mother, caused him great concern. He was deeply affected by our family's difficult situation and by Mother's hard work, and sought ways to ease her load and living conditions in our home.

We obeyed him and loved him, despite his strictness. We obeyed him because of his righteous and observant way of life, which served as a shining example.

5. Yosef (Yosele) Bergman (may his memory be for a blessing).[9]

Broad-shouldered, short, his face round and cheerful, rimmed by a long blond beard, with clever, laughing eyes and a penetrating look mixed with kindness – that was Yosef Bergman as he appeared in Horodlo. Yosele, as he was known, was pious, a Radzin Hasid, quick and cunning, active, and rich in original thoughts about improving the Horodlo economy. His vision called for developing the town into a large city, which would afford economic possibilities.

Yosef Bergman had many economic plans, which he presented to the town institutions. Although some of these plans were clearly impractical, he never stopped believing that they could be realized. He would propose holding "fairs" and convince the town

[Page 221]

council to assume responsibility for organizing these events. He believed that these occasions would be great opportunities for providing the residents with more means of making a living.

By nature an activist, he would devote time to community affairs, while at the same time he himself had no means of making a living, and struggled to provide for his large family.

In spite of his own concerns regarding a livelihood, Yossele was quick to help others, as he had influence with the town institutions and with the Polish authorities. He also knew the county officials, and was able to do much to achieve results. Many residents turned to him at times of trouble, and he helped them as best he could. Everyone in town loved him. People consulted with him, and he was unparalleled at finding solutions to complicated situations. He was an unofficial "institution" in Horodlo, recognized and liked by all.

6. Aaron-Khayim Feder (may his memory be for a blessing).

Aaron-Khayim Feder was a respectable Hasid, very learned, intelligent and sensible, clever and discerning.

He was one of the important members of his Hasidic small synagogue, and was highly esteemed in the community. His shrewdness and vast Talmudic knowledge gained him the admiration and respect of the young students in the synagogue. Few could match his keen mind and good sense.

After the death of Levi-Yitzchok Zavidovich, who had been the Torah reader for many years, Aaron-Khayim assumed that significant position. He liked to study with others of his caliber. His best friend was Mendl Lerner, who was just as shrewd and knowledgeable,

[Page 222]

with a quick intelligence – qualities much prized by Aaron-Khayim.

Aaron-Khayim was the official leader of the community for a long time, and the title suited him perfectly. He possessed several rare qualities: cleverness, good sense, moderation, authority when needed, and a practical way of thinking. He fulfilled his community role with great honesty and devotion. He was highly respected by the town residents, who valued his opinions and his pronouncements.

7. Mendl Lerner (may his memory be for a blessing).

Mendl Lerner was a great scholar, astute, and well versed in the Talmud and later commentaries. He enjoyed high status in his small synagogue, fought for his opinions and was knowledgeable in many general areas.

It was hard to challenge him and win a discussion, because he was unusually quick-witted and logical.

At that time, new ideas were penetrating the Jewish community, with the notion of a modern "return to Zion" chief among them.[10] This ideology of Jewish revival, which captivated most Jewish young people, was opposed by Mendl and the Radzin Hasidic community; they considered Zionism a deviation from accepted Judaism. His weapons, however, were words, and his arguments were firmly grounded. It was therefore very difficult to have discussions with him.

His teaching method was lofty and profound. When we young synagogue students came to him with a question about a complicated Talmudic question, he was never satisfied with a simple answer, but helped us to find the solution by explaining and clarifying the issue at hand.

[Page 223]

We soon found the answer, thanks to debating with him. He would present parallels, references, and justifications from other sources. A clear, understandable answer would emerge.

As mentioned above, Mendl was opposed to Zionist ideology, and believed in the continued existence of Jews in the diaspora, especially in Poland. It seemed that he would never change his mind.

Before I left for Palestine, Mendl sought a chance to have a talk with me. I was extremely surprised at the nature of his talk, and his conversation, which was rich in new ideas.

Anti-Jewish politics was widespread at the time. Members of the Polish government began to implement policies of discrimination and publish edicts against Jews. People were saying that the Jews were alien elements in the Polish economy. Mendl began to acknowledge the situation of the Jews, and their unclear future. He wanted to talk with me about his son Dovid's chances of settling in Palestine.

Mendl was not well off. I therefore suggested that he investigate possibilities in the religious Zionist movement. Though this route would be long and hard, it was less costly. I knew no other ways to achieve this goal, and could offer him no other suggestions.

Woe is us! The tragic catastrophe came, and put an end to the Jews of Horodlo, with Mendl's family among them.

8. Ayzik Arnshteyn (Ayzik the Tailor).

Ayzik was a simple Jew, observant and God-fearing. Yet despite his simplicity, he was smart, and possessed natural and practical wisdom.

Ayzik made his living at tailoring.

[Page 224]

Like all tailors of the time, his home also served as his workshop. He was renowned in the vicinity as a good tailor. Anyone who wanted a well-made kapote, coat, or suit turned to Ayzik.[11] As he was busy with many orders, it was difficult to set a date for the finished product. We therefore spent many days at his house, to encourage quick completion of the piece. In the process, we marveled at his professionalism and speed. He lived a modest life, despite his intensive work – a life without special conveniences or luxuries. "I always have much work and a poor livelihood," was his motto.

Ayzik raised a generation of tailors. His sons helped him, once they were old enough. Over time, they themselves became professional tailors. After they married and started their own business, they wanted to learn from their father's experience, and Ayzik hurried from one son to the other with fatherly advice.

He worked two shifts a day, and considered that normal. He would rise very early, rush to the House of Study for early prayers, after which he would return home and sit down at his sewing machine. He worked with no breaks, except for the meals (breakfast and lunch) that his wife Royze prepared. After lunch, he continued working until it was time for afternoon prayers. He would then stop work and rush to the House of Study, pray, and stay for evening prayers.

He loved sitting in on the sessions of groups studying Talmud, Mishna or *Ein Ya'akov*, and especially enjoyed the wonderful legends in the texts.[12] When a text praising a profession or handicraft came up, or references to people who earned their own living, his face would radiate joy.

After he returned from the House of Study, Ayzik would begin his

[Page 225]

night shift with fresh energy. After supper, he would fill the lamp's bowl with kerosene, carefully clean the glass chimney, light the wick, and continue working until late into the night.

Ayzik enjoyed complete Shabbat rest starting on Friday afternoons. "Nothing compares to Shabbat," he would say. "The only person who fully appreciates Shabbat is one who works with his hands." He would spend long hours in the House of Study, and listen to the studies in a calm, elevated mood. His face, with its clever black eyes and black, well cared for beard, shone with bliss on that day.

9. Yosef Hecht, the Carpenter (may his memory be for a blessing).

He was tall and broad-boned, with the strong hands of a carpenter a kind, gentle face, and innocent, laughing eyes, framed by a wispy blond beard. Yosef was typical of his carpenter comrades. We children considered every carpenter a hero with strong hands and iron muscles. Yosef, with his athletic form, symbolized wonderful craftsmanship.

In those days, Horodlo was still unfamiliar with carpentry machines, and all the heavy work was carried out by hand, requiring much laborious effort. We loved to watch Yosef working, his powerful hands maneuvering a manual plane that was over a meter long. Yosef ran the plane back and forth and raised it energetically. Wide curly shavings sprang out through the opening, and the heavy piece of wood gradually metamorphosed into something new. Yosef Hecht's swift, agile motions left us stunned. How powerful and capable he was!

On weekdays, he was characteristic of his social group – that of a hardworking Jewish artisan who lived by his talents. On Fridays, though, he shook off his toil and

[Page 226]

readied himself for Shabbat. The next day, he left all his cares behind and took on a princely appearance. He would sit at a table in the House of Study and quietly listen to the voices of people studying or telling a lovely legend, enjoying himself. It was fascinating to watch the transformation of this man, a hard worker all week long, as he relaxed completely on the sacred Shabbat.

Yosef Hecht was different from the other carpenters. He had an additional specialty, which he took up at a certain time of year,

Yosef Hecht

when his home became a focal point of the town thanks to this specialty. Yosef Hecht was one of the two bakers who prepared matza for the town's Jews. At that time of year, he put away his carpentry tools, packed up his workshop, and readied his house for Pesach. His home turned into a matza bakery.

[Page 227]

The long tables were surrounded by women and girls of the town wanting to augment their family's income, as well as the members of Yosef's family. Production went on in two daily shifts, while Yosef himself was responsible for the most important task. Like a ship's captain, he stood at the blazing oven holding long-handled paddles. With amazing speed, he filled one side of the oven with matza dough, and lifted baked matzos out of the other side, placing them in the large basket that stood ready alongside.

Before Pesach, at matza-baking time, we would go to Yosef Hecht's home and watch the agility of the men and women

Leybl Hecht

baking the matza.[13] All the stages of work linked with the mitzvah of matza-baking were carried out with amazing speed, swift hand movements, and perfect assignment of tasks.

Preparing matza for the Horodlo Jews was the responsibility of two men: Yitzchok (Melech's son) and Yosef Hecht. Both carried out their sacred task faithfully, and never disappointed those who relied on them.

[Page 228]

Yosef Hecht, and the other artisans, were closely connected to Jewish life in Horodlo, and were distinguished by their Jewish simplicity and modesty.

10. Cart Drivers.

Almost all areas of commerce in Horodlo were run by Jews. The shopkeepers bought their merchandise in three neighboring towns: Hrubieszow (14 kilometers to the west), Ustyluh (across the Bug River), and Ludmir (18 kilometers away, on the eastern bank of the Bug). They made small, urgent purchases in Ustyluh, whereas larger and more important purchases were made in Hrubieszow and Ludmir.

Four cart-drivers supervised the traffic between Horodlo and its nearby supply sources: Hershele Fraynd, Notele Shruver, Moyshe-Mikhoel (commonly known as Moyshe-Mekhl), and Moyshe Hak. At that time the small towns had no buses or other means of transportation; the roads were dominated by four-wheeled carts harnessed to horses, driven by experienced cart-drivers. Thanks to them, people could go where they pleased.

Communications were handled by the same four cart-drivers. However, whereas Hershele Fraynd and Notele had good horses and sturdy carts with broad, long ladders along their sides that enabled the proper loading of packages for transport over long distances, Moyshe-Mechl and Moyshe Haks' carts were rickety and creaked, with squeaky, wobbling wheels, pulled by a single weak, undernourished horse. Obviously, the latter two men knew that they could only

[Page 229]

undertake short trips to nearby destinations, such as Ustyluh. This route thus became their monopoly. They often walked alongside the cart. The Hrubieszow-Ludmir connection, on the other hand, remained in the capable, experienced hands of Hershele Fraynd and Notele.

Almost every day, two carts set off in the directions of Hrubieszow and Ludmir, driven by these expert drivers, each cart carrying four or six shopkeepers; they returned laden with merchandise. The trip was slow and patient.

As soon as the morning star became visible, but while it was still dark, the carts would appear in the middle of the marketplace, ready for the journey. The coachmen yelled loudly to inform the shopkeepers of their "imminent" departure. It was rare for a cart to start moving before ten a.m. or even later, and to return as late as ten p.m. or midnight. Obviously, these trips were quite traumatic, despite the short distances.

There were still no paved roads at the time, only muddy tracks, and the cart dawdled along: it took three hours to arrive in Hrubieszow, and even longer than that – to Ludmir. If you traveled the day after it had rained, or on a snowy day in winter, the trip seemed interminable and you thought you would never arrive at your destination. On such arduous journeys, everything depended on the driver, whose behavior and confidence calmed the passengers.

The drivers differed in character; these differences dictated their driving style and habits. When you traveled with Notele, he immediately began telling his jokes, as well as his experiences on the road. Your mood would lift instantly, and you would forget the mud and the exhausting trip. Incidentally,

[Page 230]

Note would teach his passengers the craft of the road. At each stage of the difficult trip, especially on inclines, he would take pity on his horses, jump off the cart, put his shoulder to the cart, and push it and its passengers. Who could stay seated and feel his face growing red?! The passengers would immediately disembark and add their shoulders to his, helping the cart to go along.

Hershele was quite different in nature and character. He did not say much, but was often immersed in thought. Once his passengers were in the cart, and the horses began moving, Hershele became immersed in thought. His eyes gazed at the horizon, and his lips murmured entire psalms from memory. Hershele was renowned for his honesty and his modest nature. A shopkeeper who had asked him to bring merchandise could be certain that his property would be taken care of. Hershele went to great lengths to pack merchandise properly in his cart and make sure it would not be affected by rain or be otherwise damaged.

When the cart and its riders arrived at their destination – the big city – the driver went to his regular inn, and the shopkeepers left for various large shops to buy their merchandise. The driver immediately started preparing his cart and horses for the return journey. He unhitched the horses and set them in front of a trough full of barley. While they ate, he performed maintenance on the cart, removing its wheels for re-greasing, and tightening various parts where necessary. After taking care of the cart, he went into the inn for a hot meal.

The shopkeepers began returning in the late afternoon, carrying large packages of merchandise and accompanied by a porter who carried the largest packages. They would hand the packages to the driver, who placed them in the cart so as to protect them from any kind of damage. During this time, the shopkeepers would say their evening prayers and eat supper. In the meantime,

[Page 231]

the driver would hitch up his horses, make a last survey of the cart, and urge the shopkeepers to take their seats, as it was time to start the return trip. He mounted, picked up the reins, and the horses started moving.

The loaded cart made slow progress. It started out at twilight, and kept rolling, as the evening grew darker, going through several villages, where impudent dogs greeted them with loud, terrifying barks. The dogs continued running alongside the cart with its passengers even after they had left the village. Somewhere, a drunken Gentile would let loose a hoarse song. The travelers sat sunken in their own thoughts, not talking to each other, while the driver constantly urged the horses on, with calls they knew. The passengers wanted only to be back at home as soon as possible.

After three or four hours on the road, the first houses of Horodlo came into view. The passengers woke from their doze, and their mood lifted. The lights were on in several houses – these belonged to the passengers, whose families were eagerly awaiting their return. A cheerful "giddyup" resounded through the stillness in the spacious marketplace, announcing a safe return. The merchandise was quickly unloaded, and the cart-driver hurried home for a few hours of sleep. After all, he had to be at the marketplace early, to take other shopkeepers to town. He couldn't disappoint them!

A cart driver could enjoy some rest on Friday, when traveling long distances was out of the question, for fear of desecrating Shabbat. On Friday, he would busy himself with cart repairs and taking orders from shopkeepers for the following week; he would also help with Shabbat preparations at home. He enjoyed total rest on Shabbat. On that holy day, he would rest from his hard labor of the past week

[Page 232]

on the roads. He was pleased with his conscientious service, and thanked God for protecting him and his passengers from all dangers and harm on their trips back and forth.

11. Borech Shmid (may his memory be for a blessing).

He was powerfully built, of medium height, with a broad, olive-skinned face, a long beard, and a high, wide forehead that radiated seriousness and scholarship, but his black smiling eyes were those of a friendly person who loved long conversations.

He was a frequent visitor at the House of Study, where he spent every free moment studying Torah and Talmud, Mishna, *Ein Ya'akov*, Midrash, etc. "Studying Torah is the best," he would say, and he practiced what he preached.

His home was far from the town center, on the road to Dubienka, almost at the edge of town. Yet he was not too lazy to walk the long route, through the Gentile neighborhood, to the House of Study. On most days he went home alone. He was respected in the town, by the Gentiles as well. Even the most unruly Gentile children did not dare to bother him as he walked their streets, even on his way home at night.

Jews who had to walk along the lengthy streets where Gentiles lived, because of work, would see two non-adjoining Jewish houses, which belonged to Moyshe Babes and Borech Shmid. Jewish passers-by treated these homes as rest stops, where one could catch one's breath. They would stop for water, or a glass of tea, and refresh themselves so as to continue their journey.

Borech Shmid, too, had once been a melamed, but his methodology was different. Teaching, in his opinion, was not only a means to make a living, but a mission. He taught Torah for its own sake. No one knew how,

[Page 233]

but he made a success of it. Learning did not come easy to the boys who studied with him, yet he taught them very patiently. His relationship with the students was very proper and direct; he did not respect the disobedient students, though some of them came from rich families. It is worth noting that most of the Jews of Horodlo did not think much of rich people; on the contrary, they had high opinions of scholars and Torah experts.

Borech was completely unable to understand why the young people were eager and impatient to leave Poland. He would not even admit that the decrees and discrimination were factors. "The Gentiles will never attain our lofty status, because the Jewish people are the people of God. Our power lies in the spirit," he explained. "A Jew must take up his spiritual armor, so as not to feel the harassment by the Gentiles." He himself would provide a practical example of his view, which was shared by most of the Jews of Horodlo.

12. Dovid Yosef Zuberman (may his memory be for a blessing).

The Zuberman family was extended, and its members were scattered. Most of them lived in Horodlo, though some moved away after marriage. They were interesting people, and played a significant role in Horodlo social life. Their leaders were important among the scholars of Horodlo, and headed the community of the House of Study and the small synagogue.

Members of the second generation of Zubermans followed in their fathers' footsteps. In the House of Study, they were distinguished by their scholarship. Later, when they were no longer students and began to be occupied with worldly affairs, they were at the forefront of social and community activity in Horodlo, and were responsible for Zionist activities.

[Page 234]

The family was headed by five brothers: Dovid Yosef, Yaakov, Tzvi, Moyshe, and Aharon. Each had his own particular position in Horodlo. However, all five shared their scholarship, decency, and general knowledge. They had acquired their spiritual values thanks to their impetus toward learning and knowledge.

First and foremost was Dovid Yosef, with his imposing presence and personality. He was a great scholar, who was interested in many things and an expert in many fields. No one knew how and when he had gained all his knowledge. He was unassuming; his modesty and simplicity concealed his knowledge.

He was always in the House of Study, and had his own spot, where he would study for long hours. He was the regular Torah reader there, and chanted like an experienced reader. He never wasted time: even in his shop, when there were no customers (a common occurrence in the economic circumstances of Horodlo), he would open one of the scholarly books he always kept close by – Torah, Talmud, Mishna, etc. -- and immerse himself in that spiritual world.

Dovid Yosef loved the Hebrew language and its riches, and liked to delve into scientific matters and books. When *Ha-Tsfira* resumed publication, under the editorship of Yosef Heftman (may his memory be for a blessing), Dovid Yosef read its important, erudite articles with great interest and pleasure.[14]

Along with his love of books, he loved physical labor. He preferred work that required effort, and undertook such projects in his yard and home.

[Page 235]

He lived his life with simplicity and honesty, and approached the world with the same qualities, which he recommended to others as well. It is therefore not surprising that he was beloved by everyone and had no enemies. He respected everyone and was himself respected in turn.

Translator's Footnotes:

1. *"Sayings of the Fathers,"* 2:5.

2. Lemberg is now known as Lviv.

3. These special prayers, which follow the seasons in the Land of Israel, are said at the appropriate times of the year. Chanting them is an honor.

4. Melamed is the term for the teacher of boys under 18.

5. *Sayings of the Fathers*, 2:2.

6. This was a common practice in observant families.

7. One of the religious Zionist youth movements oriented towards settlement in Palestine.

8. Germany attacked Poland on September 1, 1939.

9. The system of numbering used for the description of personalities omits number four in the original text.

10. This term appears in the biblical books of Ezra and Nehemiah, which depict the return of the Jews of the Kingdom of Judah, subjugated by the Neo-Babylonian Empire in 589 BCE and freed from Babylonian captivity following the Persian conquest of Babylon (539 BCE).

11. The kapote is a long coat that was worn chiefly by Jewish men in Eastern Europe, and is now used by ultra-orthodox men of that origin.

12. *Ein Ya'akov* is a compilation of Aggadic texts in the Talmud

13. Tradition requires the matza to be made and baked within eighteen minutes, as grain begins to ferment after that length of time.

14. *Ha-Tsfira* was the first Hebrew-language newspaper to appear in Poland under Russian rule (1862), and emphasized the sciences. It closed down that year, and re-opened in 1874, becoming a daily in 1886; it ceased to appear in 1931.

[Page 236]

Unforgettable Figures

by Aharon Pelech (Wallach), Haifa, Israel

1. Matisyahu the Melamed (Mates Melamed) (may his memory be for a blessing).[1]

Mates was my first melamed and the one who began to teach me the Torah. I spent most of my childhood in his cheder. That period is engraved deep into my memory, with its indelible experiences of the melamed, the young pupils, and the courtyard. The Torah classes I took with Mates have become an enduring part of my knowledge.

To this day, I can hear the melody that Mates used when he taught us the passage in Genesis, "As for me, when I came from Paddan, Rachel died to my grief in the land of Canaan on the way, still some distance to Ephrath," with a wonderful explanation of the entire Torah portion.[2] I recall that I knew the section and delivered the melamed's explanation better than my classmates, and was rewarded by a pinch of the cheek, which flooded me with emotion. I boasted of the experience to my sister and friends, and the excitement at this expression of the melamed's feelings towards me persisted for a long time.

2. Yitzchok, son-in-law of Henech Shtayn (may his memory be for a blessing).

After having been a pupil of different melameds in various cheders, and making very good progress. I began studying on my own in the House of Study. My father thought that I still needed to be supervised by an older scholar, and he

[Page 237]

arranged supervision by Yitzchok, a fine scholar and a follower of Kotsk Hasidism.

Yitzchok and I studied together that winter, and made fine progress. I studied *Yoreh De'ah*[3] and *Choshen Mishpat*.[4] When my father (may his memory be for a blessing) returned home before Pesach (Passover), and tested my knowledge of Talmud, I noticed his amazement at the progress I had made. However, his pleasure did not last for long. It vanished after his conversation with Yitzchok, when the latter informed him that I had gone astray, and he could no longer be my melamed.[5]

The great sin I was found guilty of was quoting from the poems of H. N. Bialik and M. Z. Fayerberg, two poets of whom I was very fond, and whose names I had written on the first pages of various sacred books in the House of Study.[6]

3. Mendel Lerner, the son-in-law of Hershl Novizhents (may his memory be for a blessing).

I moved on to studies in the small synagogue of the Radzin Hasids, where I grew close to the other students.[7] It was not easy to break into that circle, as some of them considered me non-observant and showed no desire to become my friends.

The only person who respected me was Mendel Lerner, and it was thanks to him that I stayed in the synagogue community. He influenced me to add a blue string to the fringes of my ritual undershirt, in the manner of the Radzin Hasids.[8] I did not take into account the offense it would cause my father, who belonged to the Ger Hasids, and thus considered my addition of the blue string a sure sign that I had forsaken the Ger court and joined the Radzin court.[9] However, I did not fully acclimate to the Radzin synagogue either. By then, I was already striving to acquire a general

[Page 238]

education, which I could not obtain in Horodlo. I went to study in Lida, near Vilna.

4. Zissele (may her memory be for a blessing, known as the Rebbetsin).[10]

Zissele was of my mother's generation and her best friend. She was one of the most interesting persons in Horodlo: a righteous woman who did many good deeds, had an aristocratic appearance and was very clever. She was kind and had a noble spirit. She extended her counsel and help to all who were in need.

Although women did not play a great role in community life at that time, I felt great respect for those virtuous and honorable women whom Zissele represented. When times were hard in our house, Zissele would appear at the right moment with good advice and good deeds. She was renowned for her wisdom, and everyone held her suggestions in high esteem.

May her memory be blessed!

5. Shmuel Biderman (may his memory be for a blessing).

Shmuel Biderman was well-known as an important, respected person. As a highly observant Jew, whose piousness bordered on fanaticism, he was clearly not too fond of me. Yet fate would have it that he actually gained my sympathy.

It happened in this way:

During the Austrian occupation following World War I, Shmuel Biderman – a Radzin Hasid -- used to say his weekday prayers in the House of Study.[11] He would come in early, and after prayers would study until late afternoon. I was almost the only young person who studied there until

[Page 239]

late afternoon. Shmuel and I were usually the only students during that time, sitting and studying and hardly conversing.

One day, the Austrian police were snatching up people on the street for forced labor, and were approaching the House of Study. Shmuel quickly took me into the women's section and hid me. When they appeared on the threshold of the building, he informed them that he was the only person in the place. He did so at the risk of his life if the policemen had searched the building and found me. I was very moved by this evidence of Shmuel's devotion and care.

6. The Town Rabbi, Rabbi Moyshe Leyb Ha-Levi Herman (may his righteous memory be for a blessing, and may his merit protect us).

The Horodlo rabbi was distinguished by his wonderful qualities and honorable ethics, which were above and beyond the conventional. He was a great scholar, God-fearing, and renowned for his knowledge of the Talmud and its commentaries. He had written a number of important religious works, and his bearing was imposing. His remarks and sermons in the synagogue before shofar-blowing, and on other occasions, were very impressive and aroused my great respect.

The rabbi and my father (may their memories be for a blessing) exchanged letters on matters of Jewish law and Talmud. I still appreciate my great privilege in being the go-between in their exchanges. These were the letters of two scholars who, though they argued over halacha (interpretations of Jewish law), were simultaneously

[Page 240]

profoundly moved by deepest respect, friendship, and comradely feelings for each other.

Horodlo was a small town, and was very proud of its rabbi. The rabbi (may his righteous memory be for a blessing) had great spiritual influence over his community, and his deep knowledge of Jewish learning was renowned. He was respected by all, and a source of wisdom.

7. My father, Moyshe Mendl Valach (may his memory be for a blessing).

He was known in the town simply as Moyshe Mendl. Though he was famous as a great scholar, he befriended ordinary, decent people, and led an unpretentious, modest daily life. He was a wonderful family man and loved to be at home. His relationship with my mother was attentive and respectful. As was common among observant Jews of the time, he never referred to my mother by her name, but they had a complete and mutual understanding. I can't remember him ever raising his voice or showing anger at home. His attitude towards his daughters, my sisters, was fatherly and generous.

With me, on the other hand, he was very strict; he had high expectations of me as far as education and religious knowledge were concerned. However, I was also rewarded. It was a moment of generosity and good will, on the eve of Yom Kippur, just before we left for the synagogue, for Kol Nidre.[12]

At this emotional, anxious moment, he focused my attention by winking and beckoning me into his room, where he laid his hands on my head and blessed me quietly. His tears, falling on my head,

[Page 241]

refreshed my soul, dew-like. Memories of that moment still move me to tears.

The last time I saw him was in November, 1939, in Chelm, when I was preparing to cross the border towards Russia.

Moyshe-Mendl Valach and his daughter Esther

We were already hearing that Jews were being killed by Hitler (may his name be blotted out), and the Jewish population was in a panic about the future. But my father (may his memory be for a blessing) continued his methodical routine, studied Torah and was busy with community affairs. He had faith in God, to whom he entrusted his future.

[Page 242]

Horodlo, My Home Town

After years of absence, I returned to Horodlo. The situation was tragic, completely different from the case years earlier, when I had left. The years of peace and stability were over, and the town – along with all of Poland – was suffering from a harsh wartime regime and conditions that were terrible for the Jewish community.

I arrived on a Friday afternoon in November 1939, hoping to cross the Bug River (the then-border between Poland and Russia). The cart-driver who had driven me to Horodlo stopped at the Polish school, on the town's outskirts. He was afraid to take me into the town proper. I left him and tried to enter the town through side roads, taking precautions not to encounter any Germans.

Exhausted and terrified, I went to Gitl-Roize's house. A few friends and relatives came to see me when they found out that I was coming, and advised me to leave the town immediately and return the same way I had come, although it was almost night. These dear Jews recounted the cruel laws that ruled the town, and maintained that if the Germans discovered me I would bring disaster upon myself and upon the town's Jews. They were fearful and terrified by the pervasive climate of persecution. Afraid to go to the synagogue for the pre-Shabbat services, they locked themselves in their homes to pray by the light of the humble Shabbat candles.

When I saw those candles shining through the windows of a few Jewish houses, I was overcome by a longing for the distant peaceful days. Fearful and agonizing, I quietly slunk out of my home town, my birthplace. I felt lonely and abandoned, unable to bid farewell to family and friends, and continued to seek respite for my weary soul.

Translator's Footnotes:

1. Melamed is the title for a Teacher of Hebrew and Jewish religious subjects. Most often it refers to a teacher in a school for young children, known as a cheder.

2. Genesis 48:7.

3. Kotzk is a Hasidic dynasty originating from the city of Kock, Poland, where it was founded by Menachem Mendel Morgenstern (1787–1859). Kotzk is a branch of Peshischa Hasidism, as Menachem Mendel Morgenstern was the leading disciple of Simcha Bunim of Peshischa (1765–1827).

4. These works are sections of *Arba'ah Turim*, Rabbi Jacob ben Asher's compilation of halakha (Jewish law) (1300).

5. This phrase implies deviation from traditionally observant Jewish culture.

6. The poet Chayim Nachman Bialik (1873-1934) wrote primarily in Hebrew and Yiddish, and is considered a pioneer of modern Hebrew poetry, part of the vanguard of Jewish thinkers who gave voice to a new spirit of the time. Mordechai Ze'ev Fayerberg (1874–1899), was a Hebrew writer, a pioneer of psychological realism, neo-romanticism, and symbolism.

7. A dynasty of Hasidic rebbes. The first rebbe of this dynasty was Rabbi Mordechai Yosef Leiner, author of Mei Hashiloach, in the city of Izhbitza. (Izhbitza is the Yiddish name of Izbica, located in present-day Poland.) Mordechai Yosef founded his own Hasidic movement in the year 5600 (1839), leaving the court of Rabbi Menachem Mendel of Kotzk. His son and successor, Rabbi Yaakov Leiner of Izhbitza, moved to Radzin. The dynasty today is therefore known more as the "Radziner Dynasty".

8. The corners of an observant Jew's undershirt are typically garnished with fringes that hang down. Different groups of Hasids use different types of fringes, some with blue strings as referenced in the Torah.

9. Ger is a Polish Hasidic dynasty originating from the town of GÃ³ra Kalwaria, Poland, where it was founded by Yitzchak Meir Alter (1798–1866), known as the "Chiddushei HaRim". Ger is a branch of Peshischa Hasidism, as Yitzchak Meir Alter was a leading disciple of Simcha Bunim of Peshischa (1765–1827).

10. Rebbetsin is the traditional term for the Rabbi's wife.

11. During a short period in World War I, the southeastern part of Congress Poland, encompassing the areas east of the Vistula and the towns of Radom, Kielce, and Lublin, was administered by Austria-Hungary.

12. Kol Nidre marks the start of the Yom Kippur evening service.

[Page 243]

Matisyahu (Mates) the Cheder Teacher
- *dedicated to his sacred memory*

by Yisroel Barg, Tel-Aviv, Israel

The melamed (teacher) of the youngest boys in our town was different from other melameds. Those who could not make a living otherwise became melameds, to whom parents entrusted their small children so that the boys would learn traditional Judaism. These melameds employed different methods to fulfill their mission – some with the whip, others with a plain stick.[1] Thus, the children absorbed learning and blows simultaneously. Our melamed, like the others, did not spare the stick. But his pedagogical methods were completely new. He had acquired his profession thanks to his experience at work and teaching, and he was truly proficient at it.

He had begun his career as a melamed's assistant in the towns of Galitzia, and was trained as a melamed in the modern fashion. He had diplomas, recommendations, and testimonials for his pedagogical work. We loved learning and having the Hebrew texts explained in Yiddish. He knew how to make every class period pleasant; he understood us and familiarized us with the texts. This was how he formed scholars who admired him and that went on to tell their own children, "Go, my boy, go to rebbe Mates! I, your father, studied with him." The love he inspired in his students gave rise to his reputation.

He was generally a cheerful person, understanding and wise, good-natured and satisfied with his life. He gained the love of all the social classes in town: scholars as well as the

[Page 244]

unlearned, and suited his conversation to each person's understanding and knowledge.

I remember one occasion. We were learning Leviticus 21, which states that a priest may not be in any proximity to, or in the same space as a dead body, because this confers ritual defilement.[2] However, the Talmud commands a Kohen to do all in his power to bury an unknown, unclaimed dead person, even though he may become defiled.[3] Our small class suddenly grew very quiet, and the melamed's voice rang out: "Dear children, please think about this question: What is the rule in a case when a priest is on the road and sees a dead person running away? Is he allowed to care for him or not?" The class went completely silent. We did not know what to say. This happened in the presence of a guest, when the melamed wanted to boast about how knowledgeable we, his best students, were. There was silence. Each of us sat speechless and looked at a friend, who looked at another in turn, etc. We finally looked at the melamed, begging him to solve this very serious problem and not shame us in the presence of a guest.

We knew what we were doing. The melamed quickly came to our aid, saying, "It is in your nature. When a guest enters the classroom, you don't listen to the subject matter. If you had listened, you would have immediately asked, 'Rabbi, how can a dead man run?'" This was how we were saved from an insoluble situation.

Once the guest left, we all began trembling with fear, waiting for the melamed's physical response, which we deserved. However, we were wrong this time. He did not strike us, but rather gave us a lecture on ethics: "Shame on you, Gentiles! Every penny of hard-earned money your parents are paying for you is wasted. The efforts and pedagogical experience I invest in you are also wasted! Close your Torah books and go feed the animals." We sat there as if turned to stone, acknowledging our guilt and justifying the lecture. We wanted

[Page 245]

to fall at his feet and beg forgiveness, embrace and kiss him out of respect, but were afraid to move. We just sat with downcast eyes, ashamed. He came to the rescue once again. "That's enough! Go and eat, and have a rest. I'll try one more time. If you don't change your ways, I'll leave you and go wherever my feet carry me." We were not disappointed. We devoted ourselves to our studies, listened and learned. The melamed noticed this and said, "You see? I wasn't wrong about you. I had the right idea: if you studied, you would succeed, and all would be well." He was very pleased with our progress, as well as with his own pedagogical expertise.

The weekly schedule of our studies was as follows: we all studied together for the first three days of the week, and studied individually on the other three days.

I remember what he told me once, when I was no longer under his supervision. One winter night, he was standing at the cantor's position in the synagogue, leading the afternoon and evening prayers. Two of his students were standing in conversation., talking. One said. "This evening we should be studying separately. We're not up to the melamed's expectations, and he'll probably beat us. If I had a knife, I would stab him in the back." The other said, "If he were standing on the riverbank, I would push him into the cold river for a dunking." When the two returned to the cheder, they were beaten as they expected, for not knowing the Torah portion, for the stabbing, and for the dunking." When the melamed finished his story, he presented the moral. "In spite of the beating, their children are also my students. I resemble the Patriarch Abraham, who converted the Gentiles.[4] I turn the small ignorant children into 'little Jews' and their later teachers enjoy ripe fruit."

His private life was sad. His wife Beyle

[Page 246]

had given birth to sixteen children, of which only three girls had survived. I remember that when one of his daughters died, his wife nearly went out of her mind with grief. When his youngest son died, his father's favorite, and the one who was supposed to say the mourner's Kaddish, the melamed was despondent.[5] The ritual slaughterer Ya'akov (may his memory be for a blessing) paid a consolation visit, during which he told him the following story:

Rabbi Meir's two sons died on the same day. His wife, who did not want to give him the news all at once, greeted him at the door as he was returning from the House of Study, and posed the following dilemma: "A few years ago a person came and asked me to keep a valuable pledge safe for him. I was overjoyed to have the pledge in my possession, and considered it my own treasure. Today, the person came and asked me to return his pledge. What do you think I should do?" Rabbi Meir immediately said, " Of course, you need to return it." She then took him into the children's room, where he saw the lifeless bodies of the two beloved children. He raised his arms to heaven and said, "God gave, and God has taken away." The slaughterer's visit and the story had a positive effect on the melamed. He was comforted, and began to return to his everyday life.

Just like the Patriarch Jacob's request of God, "Bread to eat and clothing to wear", the melamed achieved these through hard work at different jobs.[6] He did not make his living solely through being a melamed. His house was inherited, and he rented out several of its rooms. He also repaired overshoes, especially those of the Gentiles in the area. He had a rich brother in Ludmir, a sister in America, and a brother in England; these three did not neglect their brother, the melamed.[7]

He would often recount a dream that he had had, in which his father came and gave him a cupboard full of sacred books and a sack of money for his brother in Ludmir. That was why he remained poor

[Page 247]

whereas his brother was extremely wealthy. He often complained about his hard life, despite the help he received from the above-mentioned sources. He would compare his situation to that of other Jews in the same situation, yet were able to make a respectable living. "I, too," he said, "would like to spend time studying Torah for its own sake in the House of Study, and not have to use my religious knowledge as a means to subsistence.[8] Following up on this thought, he once tried his luck in business.

When Poland was under Austrian occupation, the authorities enabled the cultivation of tobacco without special permission. The melamed began to grow tobacco for his own use as well as for sale to individuals. At that time, people began to deal in tobacco and sell it in Lemberg.[9] The Jews were very successful and made good profits. The town businessmen thought of the melamed and persuaded him to try his luck in the tobacco business. He finally agreed to try, found a partner in Moyshe the carpenter, and after the holiday of Sukkot (a period of vacation) borrowed money from all those who paid his wages and wanted him to succeed in business as well as to try his hand in a different economic field.[10] He added the little money that he had, as did his partner. The two of them made efforts to purchase tobacco, hired a cart with two horses, and set out for Krakow and Lemberg, accompanied by the good wishes of their acquaintances.

Halfway through their trip, a downpour began, drenching the ground and everything above it. The cart overturned, and all its contents were soaked and ruined. Obviously, the melamed could not continue – who would be interested in such spoiled merchandise? Shamefaced, they

[Page 248]

turned back to the town. They arrived at night, so as not to draw the attention of the townspeople. As they walked back into the house, the melamed said, "Oy, Moyshe, Moyshe, you've lost your money and wasted your time, and all because of me. Before we left, I forgot to tell you of my dream about a cupboard full of books that I received. I realize that I must continue being a melamed, and prepare the community's sons for life as good Jews. I will never be a merchant; teaching is my mission for the rest of my days. Moyshe, please forgive me for the damage I have caused you."

Thus did the melamed return to teaching small boys, and he continued to do so until the end of his life in our small town in Poland.

May his memory be blessed!

His student, Yisroel Barg, in the Land of Israel.

Matisyahu (Mates) the melamed and his daughter Mindl

Translator's Footnotes:

1. A small whip was commonly used for discipline in cheders.

2. Leviticus 21:11.

3. Kohen is the Hebrew term for male descendants of the priestly families.

4. A midrash on Genesis 12:5.

5. Traditionally, only boys may say Kaddish.

6. A quote from Genesis 28:20.

7. Melameds were stereotypically poor.

8. Mishna Avot, 4:5: "Do not make your scholarly knowledge a spade with which to dig."

9. Present-day Lviv.

10. One period of vacation time in traditional Jewish schools begins immediately following Yom Kippur (10 Tishrei), and runs at least until the end of Sukkot; some schools extend the vacation until the end of Tishrei.

[Page 249]

Horodlo, My Home Town

by Avrom Kulish, Israel

It's a bit difficult, after thirty years away, to write down my memories of Horodlo and the Jews who called it home. In fact, I would not have written a memoir at all if Jewish Horodlo had still existed. But the terrible destruction that overtook Europe's six million members of Jewish communities, including the Jews of Poland (among them our parents, brothers, and sisters), who were all murdered by Hitler - the arch-enemy of the Jews -- and his helpers, obligates us to write down memories of our town and its beloved Jews.

May the descriptions below serve as memorials to the Horodlo community and its precious Jews, who existed and are no more.

The Jews of Horodlo during the Month of Elul[1]

As the month of Av drew to a close and Elul began, the air became suffused with a palpable sense of sanctity. The Jews of Horodlo shifted from their everyday existence to the sanctifying worship of God. They rose early in the morning to pray and study in the synagogue and the House of Study. At twilight, they hurried to leave their shops and businesses to take their places in the synagogue, where they would spend the evening in prayer and study until late into the night. As the time of selichot approached, the air of sanctity became more acute and pervaded the town.[2]

I remember Leybl the chimney sweep, who played an important role during the days of selichot, a role that was quite different from his ordinary manual labor

[Page 250]

all year round. It was he who woke people before dawn for these special prayers in the synagogue. Which native of Horodlo does not remember Leybl striding through the dark streets, holding a large lantern in one hand and a wooden hammer in the other? He would strike three powerful blows, which would mingle with his dry, high-pitched voice as he called out, "Jews! Wake up! Come to services!" His penetrating voice would echo through the dark distance.

Flashes of light appear in the windows: the kerosene lamps are being lit in the homes of waking Jews. Adult family members rise and dress quickly so as not to miss the beginning of the service. The synagogues soon fill with devout Jews, who are simultaneously apprehensive and full of confidence and hope for the new year.

Dovid Yosef Zuberman was the regular Torah reader in the House of Study. This ordinary man was kind and honest, and would be seen all year round holding a Pentateuch, as though he were reading the weekly Torah portion and preparing to chant it in the House of Study. He was the proper, trusted person to lead prayers during the Days of Repentance. He would ready himself, covering his head and body with the tallit, and his voice would ring out in the dark: "Righteousness and justice are the basis of your throne; steadfast kindness and truth go before you."[3]

During the High Holy Days, especially Yom Kippur, the sense of impending sanctity expanded and strengthened. The Jews of Horodlo searched their souls and devoted most of their time to religious obligations. They cleansed and purified themselves for their heavenly father, and were confident that he who heeds prayer would accept the prayers of his people, the People of Israel.

The Cantor, Kalmen Nayman (may his memory be for a blessing)

Kalmen Nayman (or, as he was known in town, Kalmen Moyshe, the son of Baba), played a very important role during the Days of Repentance.

[Page 251]

He was the regular cantor in the Great Synagogue. The souls of the members of the congregation would tremble at the sound of his passionate prayers and powerful lyrical voice. Like a conductor, he would stand at the lectern, surrounded by a choir of young boys. When his mighty voice would thunder, "Happy the people who know the horn's blast," the congregation shuddered, knowing that their cantor was a true messenger.[4]

He would be standing at the lectern, in ecstasy; his strong, pleasing voice filled the synagogue, pleading for the people who had delegated him: "Here I am, impoverished in deeds and merit. But nevertheless I have come before You, God, to plead on behalf of Your people Israel.accept my prayer as the prayer of one who is wise and experienced."[5] The congregation was carried away by Kalmen's devotion and excitement. After he had finished the Mussaf prayers, the congregation was clearly impressed by the dedication of their local cantor, whom they greatly appreciated.[6]

Kalmen Nayman and his family

[Page 252]

Guests in Town

The face of Hershl, the cart driver, beams even more than usual. He devotes extra attention to his horses and cart, taking care of every detail. He harnesses the horses and drives happily to the train station: important guests are coming today.

"Giddy-ap!" his voice resounds, galvanizing the horses. His voice echoes in the distance. The horses obey him, and he's sure he'll arrive at the station on time. And, indeed, he soon returns with the important guests, who had been away from town all summer. They had been in Warsaw and Lódz on business, and were returning home for the High Holidays. As the cart appears in the marketplace, the Jews of Horodlo come to the doors of their shops and houses, and inspect the guests.

Here is the imposing, aristocratic figure of Leybl Zavidovich, with the heavy valises that contain holiday gifts for his household and his extended family. His wife Zissele comes out to greet him, with great joy and respect. Here is Moyshe-Mendl Valach, the great scholar with his patrician face; here are the handsome Eliezer Tsung and the knowledgeable and Enlightened Leybl Kulish, as well as many others.[7]

The appearance of these important visitors and their return home after an absence creates the impression of good news, elevates the town above its ordinariness, and adds charm and glamour.

On the eve of Rosh Hashanah, preparations for the holiday intensify and are felt throughout the town. Women are busy baking challahs and sweets, and cooking the holiday dishes. The wonderful fragrance pervades the entire market. The men clean their holiday attire, shine their shoes, and offer to help their busy wives, all before they go to the mikvah (bath-house) for purification in the ritual bath.[8]

[Page 253]

Moyshe the Mikvah (Bath-House) Attendant

Moyshe, the bath-house attendant, is especially busy. Early in the morning of the day before the holiday, he begins to fill the ritual bath with clean spring water, after draining it of the water that previously filled it. Moyshe stands with the wooden bucket in the dim early light and pours the fresh water contents into the wooden trough that connects with the pure ritual bath. Drawing water takes many hours: again and again, he pulls the heavy bucket up and empties it into the trough, until the ritual bath is full. Then, he prepares the steam room by heating up the stones on the large oven. The first Jews start to come in late morning, to bathe and purify themselves for the holiday.

Zelig the Synagogue Manager

One of the busiest men in town before a holiday is Zelig, the synagogue manager. With his long, black, aristocratic beard, he evokes respect. Zelig was an integral part of the Horodlo scene, who was respected by everyone.

For years, he had taken upon himself an important community role: seeing to the good order and cleanliness of the Great Synagogue. He carried out this responsibility faithfully, and would personally polish the large, heavy lamps, as well as clean and refill the barrel of water for ritual hand-washing. He did not rest until the entire synagogue was spotless and gleaming with light and tidiness. He also remembered to prepare drinks and treats for the synagogue Kiddush on Saturdays.[9] "Have a drink, enjoy yourselves!" he would say graciously, "Le Chaim, folks. To life!" and his face would shine with joy.

* * *

Woe is us! All these dear, innocent ones were murdered by the Nazi killers (may their names be blotted out). May the holy memory of the community and its martyrs live forever!

Translator's Footnotes:

1. The Jewish month of Elul immediately precedes the High Holy Days, and is a time of introspection and repentance.

2. Selichot (Hebrew for pardon or forgiveness) are penitential prayers recited before and during the Ten Days of Repentance from Rosh Hashanah to Yom Kippur.

3. The talit is a prayer shawl. The verse is from Psalms 89:15.

4. Psalms 89:16.

5. This prayer is traditionally recited, in the first person, by the cantor prior to the Musaf (or additional) service on Rosh Hashanah and Yom Kippur. The cantor engages in a personal dialogue with God, asking for his prayers to be received favorably, despite any personal shortcomings.

6. Mussaf is the series of prayers that follows the morning service.

7. The Jewish Enlightenment movement was an intellectual movement, mainly among the Jews of Central and Eastern Europe (1770s-1881). It advocated against Jewish reclusiveness, encouraged the adoption of prevalent attire over traditional dress, while also working to diminish the authority of traditional community institutions such as rabbinic courts and boards of elders. It pursued a set of projects of cultural and moral renewal and the adoption of modern values, while working towards an optimal integration in surrounding societies. Other goals were economic production and the taking up of new occupations. The movement promoted rationalism, liberalism, relativism, and enquiry, and is largely perceived as the Jewish variant of the general Age of Enlightenment.

8. The Mikvah is a ritual bath used by religious Jews to fulfill for ritual purification.

9. A synagogue Kiddush is a blessing over wine said following Saturday morning services at synagogue, which often becomes a communal gathering with food and drink.

[Page 254]

The Heroism of Yitzchok Saller

by Melech Shechter, Israel

(This account is in memory of my murdered brothers, David and Mendl Shechter, and their families)

Let me tell you about the life of Yitzchok Saller (may his memory be for a blessing). You will most likely wonder why I chose to describe the life of this Yitzchok, rather than that of any other resident of our town. I can say that I'm doing this because he was my closest neighbor, whom I knew better than anyone else in the town. I saw him often, and was familiar with his difficulties in making a living. I'm qualified to do it, as I lived next door to him for over twenty-five years.

He was middle-aged, tall and thin, with a sparse blond beard. A Jew like all others, honest and decent, with a pure, virtuous soul. All day long, he would roam through the villages around Horodlo, trying to sustain his family. He would buy some wheat or barley from a peasant, some pigs' bristles, or the skin of a calf, and sell it. He was also a tobacco dealer, and kept a goat at home for milk. In short, he was a poor Jew, like most of the Jews in town.

He would be on the street from early morning until late at night, with his coat unbuttoned, his naked torso exposed. He liked to sing a Hasidic melody, clearing his throat loudly afterwards and saying, "Oy, God, my God! What will we do? After all,

[Page 255]

we need to prepare for Shabbat, and we need to stay alive until Shabbat too. There's not a penny in the house. On top of everything else, the High Holy Days are nearing, and afterwards – the long, cold winter. The children run around in tattered clothes and worn-out shoes. Oy! What can I do? Who can understand God's will? 'He punishes those he loves.'"[1] This was his refrain as he walked the streets.

He would rarely speak to anyone. Only two people were familiar with his moods, and to them he would pour out his bitter heart. They were Mendl Lerner and Note, Zissele's son. He would have scholarly conversations with them, and argue over a difficult point of law. They would also share their opinions about their business ventures: the price of wheat is rising, barley is cheaper, tobacco is in short supply, and so forth.

I knew him well. A glance at his face would tell me whether he had earned enough that day to sustain his family. If God had helped him to earn something, he would walk up to me with a smile, asking, "Well, Melechl, have you taken a dip in the river today?[2] How are things going?" And I would answer with a smile, "Well, Yitzchok, why are you smiling? What's the happy occasion?"

He would answer, "Oh, you're too young. When a Jew earns something to keep going, with God's help, he needs to rejoice." This would be followed by a Hasidic tune hummed under his breath. But his greatest joy was on Shabbat when he was well supplied. On such occasions, he would dress in his Shabbat coat and black velvet cap, comb his reddish beard, and go to pray in the Radzin small synagogue.

He had a wife, named Chashe, and three children: Moyshele (who was deaf, may God preserve us!), Shmulik,

[Page 256]

who also had a physical problem – he had a constant eye infection. As Melech could not afford medical care, he couldn't help his child. His small daughter, Rochele, was healthy.

Now I would like to tell you about several misfortunes that befell to Yitzchok Saller. One sad event happened on a hot summer day. His only goat died, and he began sobbing, "Oy, what will we do now? We have lost half of our household's livelihood! At least our children had a bit of milk, and I could sell some milk as well." I could see gloom spreading over his face, and his hair starting to go gray.

Another tragic event that made a great impression on me was after the High Holidays. Signs of the oncoming winter were beginning to appear. It was starting to rain, and the sky was covered with heavy clouds. One day at dawn, when the town was asleep, we heard terrible screams from the direction of the river. I got up and ran towards the river breathlessly. When I came to the river, I saw a dreadful scene: Yitzchok Saller and a Gentile were standing neck-deep in the water, holding a heavy sack, each pulling one side in order to take it from the other. When Yitzchok saw me, he started yelling with all his might, "Melechl, save me!"

When I began shouting 'Gevald' and calling for police help, he begged me, "Don't yell, just help me take the sack from the Gentile. You know that the contents of the sack are secret. They are my entire livelihood, my flesh and blood."

To tell the truth, although I knew that the sack was full of

[Page 257]

tobacco, Yitzchok's sole source of income, I truly did not want to go into the water. Instead, I picked up a large stone and began to threaten the Gentile, shouting,

"Either you drop the sack or I'll kill you on the spot!" Hearing the commotion, several Jews came up. The Gentile dropped the sack and fled across the river in his fishing boat. We grabbed the sack, which was full of tobacco and heavy with the weight of the water it had absorbed, and started off towards Yitzchok's house. On the way, he asked me to take the sack into our shop rather than to his house. He was sure that the police would eventually search his house, and would confiscate the tobacco if they found it, cutting off his source of livelihood. In addition, he would be sentenced to several years in jail. We hauled the sack into our shop, concealing it in rags and wood chips. I asked him, "How did you get into this situation?"

He answered, "A peasant from the neighboring village came to me and said that he wanted to buy thirty kilos of tobacco. We decided on the price, and he said he would pay me after I helped him take the sack to his boat, which was on the river. He knew I would not call for help, because I was prohibited from dealing in tobacco. Obviously, he wanted to rob me.

"Yitzchok continued: 'I'll tell you the truth. If it had been my money alone, I wouldn't have risked my life for the sack. But I'm using other people's money, people who gave me loans.' A single thought flashed through my mind: 'God,

[Page 258]

where will I get the money to pay off the loans? I don't even have a spare penny in the house!'"

* * *

This is how Yitzchok Saller, the fine young man, who had never done anything wrong, a delicate person who would not bother even a fly on the wall, who was silent about his hunger so that the town would not discover the extent of his hardships, who never wanted to take charity, whom the whole town called "Yitzchok Rooster," who did not mix with others and was not interested in politics and current events – this person exhibited incredible bravery and courage in his final hour.

When war broke out in 1939, and the Nazi boot trampled Poland, killing our town of Horodlo among other communities, our Yitzchok's situation was miserable. He had no hopes, and was resigned to his fate. The edict struck him like a thunderclap on a clear day. He had not a penny in his pockets. Doing business was impossible, as it was prohibited by the Nazis. He walked around in a depression, saying, "What will happen to us? How will we find a way out of these troubles? The Nazis certainly won't let us do business. Earning money is impossible. Where will I find food for my children?"

At this point, he couldn't imagine that the Nazis would not only demand money from the Jews, but their dearest possession, their lives.

As he saw people fleeing the town, he would ask his wife, "Well, Chashe? What do we do now? Where do we run? True, we still have about 200 kilos of barley and a bit of tobacco. But how long can we live on that? And what will we do when that is finished?"

[Page 259]

"Of course, we'll die of hunger. Wouldn't we be better off if we moved to a different town, where there are more Jews?"

His wife would reply, "Well what can I say. You're a man, after all. How would I know what we should do? I think we shouldn't leave our house. What will we do on the roads? It's hard to be wanderers, dragging our children with us. We worked so hard to get this house – should we now just abandon it? You know about the lives of the Gentiles around here. They know us; they know that we have no money. We don't need to run. The idea makes no sense, and won't help us."

He would then pucker his forehead and say, "How would I know? You might be right. Where would we run? Winter is coming. God might help us, and peace will come to the world. Maybe! But if things get worse, we'll leave in summer."

But the future showed that neither fleeing nor remaining could help save the Jews. Their bitter end had already been sealed, as we, the survivors of Horodlo, now know.

When the Nazis burst into Horodlo, the Gentiles were their best and truest friends. We suffered the same fate as everywhere in Poland.

The worst and most hostile Gentiles included the three Marczianik brothers (may their names be blotted out), the three Sarabakwicz brothers (may their names be blotted out), Bjanek Danczek, and especially the vile, heartless Zygmunt Szimnicki. These, and others, found great pleasure in robbing the unfortunate Jews of the town. They would go to Jewish homes and say, "Listen, I can make sure that you won't have to

[Page 260]

work for the Germans. Well, for a price, of course." Another time, they would say, "The Jews will be transported out of here today. Give me such and such an amount, and I won't show them your hideout." Or they would say, threatening, "Give me this much, or I will tell them where you hide your merchandise."

This was how, leech-like, they systematically sucked out the money and blood of the Jews.

That was when Zygmunt Marczianik came to Yitzchok Saller, saying:

"Yitzchok! Give me tobacco!"

Yitzchok would reply, smiling at first, "You want tobacco – where would I get you tobacco? You know that I haven't had any tobacco since the Germans arrived."

But the Gentile insisted, as his eyes sparkled with the robber's gleam, "Listen, Yitzchok, I know where you hide your money and your gold, and your tobacco, as well. You're rich."

"Dear Zygmunt, what are you saying! How would I have money and gold? You know that I'm a poor Jew and have always worked hard to make a living, especially these days."

Zygmunt answered, gnashing his teeth angrily, "If that's the case, I'll bring the Nazi police right now. They'll discover all of it and you'll never see the light of day again. You'll go where many of your brothers have gone – straight to Paradise."

Yitzchok considered this threat for a bit, and said,

"All right, Zygmunt. I have some from before, about a hundred grams. You know that I need it, too. Take some, and leave some for me. There's no food. Let me smoke, at least."

His wife sat in a corner while the children

[Page 261]

buried their heads in her apron, crying. Hearing the conversation, she spoke to her husband, weeping: "Yitzchok, don't give him any, or there'll be no end to it."

Let me note that these were daily occurrences. Each Gentile found "his" Jew, whom he would exploit like a blood-sucking parasite.

And the end came. One day in Nissan, Zygmunt walked into Yitzchok Saller's house with a Nazi policeman, with the following announcement:

"Yitzchok! We've been ordered to search your house, as we've been told that you possess gold and money. Give it to us willingly; if not, your end is near."

Naturally, this caused a panic. Heartrending cries came from the children, who clung to their mother. Yitzchok tried to show that he had no money or gold, and that he made a living only thanks to the generosity of his Gentile neighbors. Zygmunt (may his name be blotted out) began the search violently, tearing up the bedding, breaking the furniture and even the oven.[3] Finally, when he seemed to have given up on searching the rooms, he turned to the policeman, saying, "Stay in the room and make sure the wife and children don't remove anything."

He then addressed Yitzchok imperiously, smiling devilishly, though his face was crimson with anger: "You, take me into the warehouse!"

When they entered the warehouse, Zygmunt began angrily and wildly kicking and breaking everything within reach. Once again, he found nothing. Then he began to demolish the floor.

[Page 262]

At that moment, the embarrassed Yitzchok turned as pale as a sheet. Apparently, the Gentile was breaking open the floorboard that concealed the tobacco and barley that Yitzchok was keeping as a last resort. When he saw the Gentile bent over the floor, breaking up the boards, he realized that this was his last hour, and there was no escape. He and his family were facing death.

Without a thought, Yitzchok caught up the heavy stones on the weighing pans of his scales, and, mustering all his strength, began to strike the head of the bending man vigorously until it split, and the blood gushed out. The Gentile apparently died instantaneously. The wounded lion, Yitzchok – whose first reaction to the sight of blood was shock–leaped up agilely, leopard-like, and burst into the house as swiftly as an eagle. Before the Nazi policeman could react, he wrenched the rifle out of his hands and struck him with the butt.[4] The German swayed for a moment and fell face down, with blood pouring from his mouth. Quick as lightning, Yitzchok sprang upon him and stabbed him with the rifle's bayonet.[5] With the same agility, and fueled by a sense of revenge, he yelled to his family, "Come!"

He ran to the river, apparently intending to cross it and so save his family and himself, never looking back. His family ran with him. When they came to the river, he impulsively grabbed his wife and children, and hurled them into the water, knowing that none of them could swim. Yet it must have seemed the only way to rescue them. He then threw himself into the river.

That was how Yitzchok Saller and his family were murdered.

May their memory be blessed!

Translator's Footnotes:

1. Proverbs 3:12.

2. Attaching "l" at the end of a name signifies a diminutive, and can be a sign of affection.

3. The oven may have been the old-fashioned type, made of bricks.

4. The description of Yitzchok's movements is traditional, and taken from the exhortation in *Mishna Avot* 5:20, "Be strong as a leopard, and swift as an eagle, and fleet as a gazelle, and brave as a lion, to do the will of your Father who is in heaven."

5. The rifle was most likely a Karabiner 98, which has a knife bayonet attached.

[Page 263]

Figures of Horodlo

by Mordechai Herbst, Argentina

One rainy Sunday afternoon, a group of Horodlo natives sat with me in the home of Ya'akov and Rivke Mededrut, and reminisced about the small Polish town of Horodlo, in the province of Lublin; specifically, about a number of characteristic persons, and events that occurred there.

The rain outside was pouring, but here, indoors, the portrait of the bygone town spread light and warmth all around, through the memories of the surviving sons and daughters, who carried these memories deep in their hearts, longingly and sorrowfully.

Each person recalled a different character and a different episode. These brief depictions and short characterizations combined to create a beautiful image of bygone Horodlo: a town rich in sacred scholarship and good deeds. I was overcome with pride at having been born in such a place.

After long consideration, I concluded that the emergence of great geniuses and sources of light for the Jewish world in such small towns was not a coincidence. This is why we are still inspired by those small towns in Poland, Lithuania, Hungary, Russia, etc., which dipped into and imbibed the finest qualities of our nation.

* * *

The conversation evoked a rich gallery of Horodlo Jews, each of whom could be the central character of a book about the Jews of Poland.

[Page 264]

Here, we will present only a few short strokes on each character, enabling the reader to create a portrait of the local Jewish personalities.

Chaim Hirsh Vayntroyb, the Magistrate

Chaim Hirsh fulfilled an official function. He was the unofficial magistrate of the town and its Jewish community. When the town's authorities (the council and the police) or the community's leaders wanted to announce a topic, regulation, or ordinance, they would do so through Chaim Hirsh. He could also revoke and cancel harsh decrees.

He was charitable and kind, one of the first to enter the House of Study in the morning, where he spent hours praying and chanting Psalms. When a visitor or an emissary from a yeshiva came to town, he would eat at Chaim Hirsh's home. Chaim Hirsh was remarkably healthy, and took long strides with the powerful, focused gait of a strong person. Before each meal, he would drink, and enjoy, a strong, lip-burning brandy. He also treated each guest at a meal to the same brandy drink. The guest would have a coughing fit, to the host's astonishment.

He was busy almost daily doing acts of charity and kindness, visiting Jewish homes with a sack on his shoulders, collecting bread and money for yeshivas, who considered him a faithful representative. The receipts and acknowledgments from the yeshivas were collected in a special bag, which, according to his will, would be placed at his head after his death.[1]

When an emissary or a roving preacher arrived and gave a sermon

[Page 265]

in the House of Study, Chaim Hirsh would chant the Kaddish prayer in his resounding voice. The boys' choir would then respond "Blessed is He, blessed is His name" and conclude with "Amen" after the cantor's blessings.

His good health and stamina continued into his old age. He was always vigilant over Horodlo, its House of Study, and matters of charity and kindness.

Isser Peretz Mederdrut

Ya'akov Boymeyl

Ya'akov Boymeyl was honest, pious, and renowned for his many good deeds. He was a simple, decent man, and made his living by working at rope-making. This righteous, modest man set up a hostel in his own home for travelers and local indigents, which offered a bed for the night, and shelter during winter nights and rainy days. His piety and sincerity led him to observe the mitzvoth related to hospitality throughout his life.

[Page 266]

Gitl Mederdrut (Isser's wife)

She was pious and charitable, always seeking to help others. This was her way of fulfilling the mitzvah of charity: she would go to all the Jewish homes and collect candles for lighting in synagogues, and money for secret charity. The Jewish homes always welcomed her. Everyone appreciated her good deeds; even the poorest would give her a donation.

Rivke Mederdrut recounted the kindness of the Horodlo Jews: when she visited Jewish homes seeking bread and challah for the town's indigents, she naturally avoided the homes of the poorest. However, they would come to her home carrying a challah, and complaining, "Rivke, why did you skip my home? I too want to give charity." They would hand over their contribution.

Yitzchok Hirsh Fayl, with wife Elka and granddaughter Miriam

[Page 267]

Isn't such sincerity and modesty moving and inspiring? Such decency and kindness touch one's heart and soul and arouse the most profound feelings and sensations!

Yosef Shmuel, the Melamed

Learned and scholarly, an expert on the Talmud and later commentaries – such was Yosef Shmuel the melamed. He usually taught older boys who knew the Talmud well enough to take on in-depth study. Those who started studying with Yosef Shmuel were considered able of studying an entire page of Talmud without assistance, and came to him for more sophisticated, shrewd, and subtle study.

He was certified to have the final word on matters of rabbinical law. If the town rabbi was absent, people would turn to him for permission or prohibition. He himself had created many manuscripts containing new interpretations of rabbinical texts, written with a goose feather pen.

In his old age, a group of his students undertook his support and sustenance.

He devoted his entire life to study and pious worship, and produced many students and scholars.

Rabbi Ya'akov Tshetner, the Shochet (ritual slaughterer)

Rabbi Tshetner was a great scholar and very pious, in behavior as well as in personality, and was careful to heed every mitzvah, whether great or small. He was very meticulous, and even forbade himself things that were permitted. He was just as observant of mitzvot concerning his fellow men as those concerning God. Most of his time was spent studying Torah, working, and giving charity.[2] Most of the time, day or night, he could be found studying in the Hasidic small synagogue. Passers-by in the late hours of a winter night

[Page 268]

could see him there, hunched over a volume of the Talmud. More than once, he would study through the night, and put on his tallis and tefillin for the morning prayers. He was truly a holy man.

His honesty, decency, and modesty were exemplary, and he was justifiably considered a Hasid and a man of great devotion to worship, outstanding in both learning and piety. His qualities earned him a place among the Hasidism. All Jews treated him with respect and awe.

Yoel Yitzchok Zuberman (Yoel Itshe)

Yoel-Itshe was God-fearing, a cantor with a pleasant voice, as well as an expert mohel. He carried out this sacred duty mostly free of charge. Jews from the surrounding villages invited him to circumcise their sons, a mitzvah that he always performed joyfully and in a timely manner.

He prayed with warmth and ecstasy. When he led the prayers during the High Holy Days, the hearts of the congregation would quiver with emotion.

Shmuel Herbst

Shmuel Herbst was known as a prayer leader who roused and impressed the congregation; he was also a well-known Radzin Hasid. Listening to him pray during the High Holidays was especially wonderful. I particular remember him chanting the *Akdamut* on Shavuot, to a beautiful melody.[3]

When the town rabbi, the great scholar Rabbi Moyshe-Leyb HaLevi Berman (may his righteous memory be for a blessing) would render the sugar factory (in Stryszów village) kosher for Pesach (Passover), he would appoint Shmuel Herbst, Yosef Bergman, and Yehuda Biterman as supervisors. Under their supervision, the rabbi was certain that the right people made sure the factory was kosher.

[Page 269]

Bashe (Yankel's wife) and Chaye-Toybe

Two righteous women of Horodlo worth mentioning considered themselves knowledgeable in medicine. Many townspeople respected their knowledge and applied their medical advice. They were especially well-versed in childhood diseases and respiratory ailments, which they treated with traditional medicine. People trusted their medical advice.

The Young People of Horodlo

The Jewish youth of Horodlo were remarkably serious, knowledgeable, and educated. They achieved this by their efforts and diligent self-education, and were famous in the nearby towns as well. These young people were activists, who were renowned for their devotion. At the same time, they were unusually serious and scrupulous in all areas: business, society, public activities, and personal relationships. Most of their public work was concentrated on personal relationships. Most Horodlo youth were

From right: Chana Shturm, Tzvi Zuberman, Yekutiel Zavidovich, Feyge Gruber, Tzvi Zaltzman, Fishl Gertl, Tova Goldberg, Moyshe Gruber, Rokhl Blum

[Page 270]

From right: Rokhl Datelgeld, Yosef Zavidovich, Tcharna Halperin,
Eliezer Lerner, Fradl Zavidovich, Yosef Rozenblum, Chife Fayl,
Feyge Gruber

[Page 271]

From right: Charna Halperin, Rokhl Datelgeld, Chife Fayl, Chaya
Zissberg

[Page 272]

idealists, who were prone to moral thinking and ethical ideals. Personal and social honor were higher-ranking than materialistic considerations. Feelings of mutual brotherhood and mutual aid were hallmarks of the young people of Horodlo.

Their thirst for religious and general knowledge was outstanding. The breadth of their education, despite a shortage of financial resources, is praiseworthy. The town could truly be proud of its young people.

* * *

When I began to set down these short notes delineating some characters of Horodlo, I thought that I was stringing together the most beautiful pearls of our past; but it seems to me now that the town of Horodlo itself was a shining gem, a worthy section of the golden crown that is the history of the Jewish community of Poland.

Translator's Footnotes:

1. This is linked with the belief that a person's good deeds during their lifetime ensure a good afterlife.

2. These three forms of religious observance are quoted from the *Sayings of the Fathers*, 1:2: "The world stands on three things: On Torah, on works, and on kindness to others."

3. The *Akdamut* prayer is a liturgical poem, written in Aramaic. It consists of praise for God, his Torah, and his people, and is usually recited by Ashkenazi Jews on the first day of Shavuot.

[Page 273]

The Liturgy of Shabbes[1]

by Mordechai Herbst, Argentina

Those who are curious about the nature of Shabbes, its importance, and its essence, should page through the Siddur (Prayer Book) and read the prayers it includes; they contain the soul of the people and the soul of Shabbes. The sublime poetry that shines forth from the black glow of its lettering contains the spirit of the people, the beating of one's own heart, and the reader will feel the depth of his own soul.

They will discover that Shabbes provides rest for the body, whereas the spirit, the soul, and the heart "work" on Shabbes, arousing aspirations, longings, love, memories, and blessings, in the sublime state of joy, rest, and sanctity…

* * *

A Jew welcomes Shabbes with love and poetry, poetry that wells up out of love, and a love that flows from poetry.[2]

The Friday afternoon prayers therefore begin with the biblical "Song of Songs," a song of love between the Jewish people and the Holy One (blessed be he). The love in each Jewish heart strengthens until the prayer continues with *Yedid Nefesh*. Now it flares up to "My Soul Pines for Your Love," and the speaker longs to witness the power of God's strength

Following this "hallway" that introduces God's love, the Jew enters the "parlor" of worship: "Come, let us sing joyously to the Lord". The emotional outpouring of the sweet singer of Israel in a few chapters of Psalms are conveyed in a prayer that expresses the joy

[Page 274]

of a bridegroom welcoming his bride. He calls out ecstatically, "Come, bride!" The Shabbes bride is as beautiful as a queen ("Queen Shabbes").

At this sublime moment, he begins to call out, "A song of praise for Shabbes. It is good to thank God." Yes, he overflows with gratitude for these moments of elation. Now he recalls the fourth of the Ten Commandments: "Remember the Sabbath day by keeping it holy" and senses the sanctity of the day ("You sanctified the seventh day"), which was blessed from the very beginnings of the world ("God blessed the seventh day and sanctified it, because He rested from all the labor of Creation"). The head of the family therefore rejoices, as stated in the Shabbes prayer "He who keeps the Sabbath and call it a delight will rejoice in Your kingdom." He prays with profound sincerity, "Our father and the God of our fathers, be pleased with our rest ," then continues with a description of God's greatness ("Protector of our fathers by His word… the God like no other, who grants His people rest on His holy day"). Therefore, "we will serve Him with great fear and trepidation, and thank His holy name."

* * *

The head of the family goes home joyfully, after his passionate prayer in the synagogue. Here, he meets important and honored guests – God's messengers – whom he greets with a heartfelt Sholem Aleichem. He knows that God loves him as much as he loves God, and has therefore sent him messengers to bless him ("Bless me with peace, you messengers of peace") and protect him ("He will order His angels to protect you wherever you go"). After parting from his guests, he prepares for the festive Shabbes meal.

The house is illuminated and neat, and the wonderful fragrance of food fills the air. He remembers

[Page 275]

his wife's hard work, and utters the song of praise beginning, "A woman of valor, who can find?"

He blesses the wine, and senses God's generosity: "You have chosen us and blessed us of all nations, and given us Your sanctified Shabbes day with love and goodwill." Therefore, he blesses God, "Blessed are You, God, who blesses the Shabbes."

He fulfils the Shabbes commandment to have a festive meal, and joyfully sings "He who keeps Shabbes properly is richly rewarded." Happy and satisfied, he ends the Shabbes evening ceremony with the blessing after food, and expresses the wish that the afterlife will be an eternal Shabbes.

* * *

During his prayers, he cannot forget Zion, and implores, "When, sweet God, will You reign in Zion?" He hopes that this will surely happen "soon, in our time, Your presence will rest forever (in Zion)."

As he remembers Zion, his national consciousness is roused, and he is proud that "You did not grant the Shabbes to the other nations of the world, but to the nation of Israel, your people." At that moment, the supplicant's soul is bound up with the nation as a whole. He mentions the "Jewish communities that gave their lives for the sanctity of the Holy Name" and begs God to bless the Jewish communities and "all those who work faithfully for the community." He longingly recalls the radiant past of the nation: "You planned the Shabbes and accepted its sacrifices," and has a single desire: "Bring us to our land joyfully and establish us within its boundaries,"

[Page 276]

so that "we can serve you faithfully."

He ends the Musaf prayer with the "Song of Honor," which details the greatness of God and His actions. Addressing God, he prays for the following prayer to be granted: "Let my discourse be pleasant to You, for all my being longs for You."

He makes the blessing during the midday Shabbes meal, praising God with the piyyut "Blessed is almighty God who granted rest." In the afternoon, after a day of spiritual joy and before the end of Shabbes, he recites a summary of his impressions of Shabbes: "Rest of love and generosity, true and faithful love, rest of peace and quiet, the complete rest You desire."

* * *

The sun is setting, darkness falls, and Shabbes fades away…

Weekday cares resurface. The burden of Exile lies heavy once more. His soul prays at the close of Shabbes for the coming of Elijah: "Elijah the prophet…may he come to us soon, with Messiah, son of David…"

Translator's Footnotes:

1. I have chosen to transliterate the Yiddish Shabbes (rather than the Hebrew 'Shabbat') in this section.

2. In the next few pages, the writer provides a detailed moment-by-moment description of the Shabbat liturgy and domestic customs, from Friday evening to Shabbat evening. The text is replete with quotes from the Bible, prayers and religious poems (piyyutim), and with references, which would have been familiar to the readers at the time of publication.
    [I have added some background information below, which follows the order in which the terms appear in the text. The *Song of Songs* is an erotic poem, construed in Jewish tradition as an allegory of the relationship between God and Israel. *Yedid Nefesh* is a 16th-century collection of psalms usually sung to welcome Shabbat, which includes the phrase "My soul pines for Your love." "Come, let us sing joyously to God" is the beginning of Psalm 95. The "sweet singer of Israel" is a traditional term for the biblical King David, whom tradition presents as the composer of the Book of Psalms. Shabbes is often depicted as a queen. The "Song of Praise for the Sabbath" is Psalms 92. The phrases "You sanctified the seventh day" to "thank His holy name"… are from the Friday evening blessings. "God's messengers" refers to the popular poem – "Shalom Aleykhem, mal'akhey ha-shalom" -- sung in many homes to welcome the Sabbath through greeting the heavenly messengers accompanying it. "He will order His angels" is from Psalm 91:11. The "woman of valor" poem is in Proverbs 31. "He who keeps the Shabbes" is a well-known liturgical poem of the piyyut genre. The following phrases are taken from the liturgy. Zion is the traditional Jewish homeland. The Yiddish phrase I have translated as "sweet God" is gotenyu, a diminutive form of Got, God, which connotes endearment, and is often used as a form of address to God in personal prayer. "When will You reign in Zion" is from a liturgical poem. You did not grant it to the nations of the world" is from the Musaf prayer. "The Jewish communities that gave their lives" is from the Shabbes morning service. The memorial prayer "Father of Mercy," a piyyut from the 11th or 12th century, said every Shabbes. The phrases "You planned the Shabbes" and "Bring us to our land joyfully" are from the Shabbes Musaf (additional morning service). The "Song of Honor," and the piyyut "Thanks to God who granted rest" date from the 12th century. "You did not grant it to the nations of the world" is from the Musaf prayer. The text of the popular song "Elijah the prophet" is taken from the prayer book.]

[Page 277]

The First Theatrical Production in Our Town[1]

by Yisroel Barg, Tel Aviv, Israel

When the young people of Horodlo decided to arrange a theatrical production for the town's residents, they faced a task that was not easy. Their only resource was the wish of those individuals who wanted to supply the cultural nourishment that the town clearly lacked.

As our sages said, "Nothing can block the will."[2] They resolved to work towards preparing such a performance. They invited a director from out of town; the artists were the young people themselves. Everything, of course, was done in great secrecy, so that their parents wouldn't discover the project.

Rehearsals began in the abandoned house of the Russian priest. Those who knew what was taking place in that house respected the attempt. When they passed by the house, they knew that a room in that house was the home of culture, a secret component of life that they had not yet experienced.

The evening of the performance drew near. The secret was discovered on Friday evening, one day before the actual performance. All the performers were ostracized. Those in charge of the performance told the participants to prepare for battle, and housed them in the building where the event was slated to take place. The uproar was great: the young people's parents knocked on the house doors, yelling, "Give us back our children! Stop the apostasy!" There was a feeling that

[Page 278]

war was imminent between the progressives and the conservatives, who wanted to keep their heritage and traditions intact. Those who saw themselves as champions of culture knew that this day and this performance would be a litmus test for both sides. Cancellation of the performance would mean the complete defeat of all our hopes of escaping from the boundaries our parents had set. These young people, who were completely inexperienced in cultural battles, decided to stand their ground and fight for freedom of ideas, and above all – for culture. The rabbi (may his memory be for a blessing) called, like the biblical Moses at the time, "Whoever is for God, come to me!"[3] All the pious Jews assembled immediately, among them the butchers and their "regiment commander" Eliyahu, Yidl's son. Opposite them stood the young people, with the artisans and their "regiment commander" Yechiel Sherer. The two "captains" knew how to give twice as good as they got, if need be.

The atmosphere on Shabbat was very tense. Representatives of both factions watched the entrance to the building where the show was scheduled to take place. Each camp struggled to gauge the mood of its opposer. This continued until after the evening prayer and the Havdalah service that mark the end of Shabbat.[4] After all, we were the children of the generation that was opposing us, and the tradition of Shabbat sanctity was in our blood.

At the end of Shabbat, both groups of men began, as though by order, to march toward the building. They were followed by two groups of women, whose sole purpose was to disrupt and halt the marchers before a hand could be raised and blood spilled. When the two camps met opposite each other, a violent war of words began. However, the watchful women were able to disperse the "gunpowder." This was done

[Page 279]

suddenly, with no advance warning, and the men on both sides halted their attempts and seemed ashamed of themselves. Suddenly, it was still. Everyone stopped in their tracks and raised their hands, as if petrified.

The ticket-holders were escorted into the hall by the organizers, the doors were locked, and the performance finally began. Our "captain," Yechiel Sherer, was paid his wage. He and Gittl Fayl attached ribbons to the clothes of those in the audience, signifying that they had donated to Keren Kayemet.[5] The good people who had remained outside, not comprehending what was happening, slowly began to go home. After all, people really cared about each other and had their good in mind.

One man remained standing outside, facing east, silently praying to God with great devotion. He was probably begging God to have mercy on the boys and girls who had deviated from the true path. This was the rabbi (may his sacred memory be for a blessing), who had believed that he and his followers could disrupt the performance. Who knows how much longer he would have stood praying, if not for the Gentile Baski – wounded in the Polish war – which approached the rabbi, saying, "Mr. Rabbi, there's no one here, everyone has dispersed. You were able to drive them all away. Why do you stay here in the cold?" The rabbi responded, "Thank you, thank you, Mr. Baski. I don't know what happened. Yes, they've all gone home. They're good children after all, just a bit naughty…"

Thus ended the very successful performance. However, the full truth became known the next morning. Here and there, pointless arguments broke out. But the deed had been done. For the first time, we caught a glimpse of the world of culture, and were captivated.

Translator's Footnotes:

1. Another, more dramatic telling of this event can be found on pages 109-111.

2. The source of this popular saying is unknown.

3. Exodus 32:26.

4. Havdalah is a Jewish religious ceremony that marks the symbolic end of Shabbat and ushers in the new week.

5. Keren Kayemet LeYisrael, the Hebrew name for the Jewish National Fund.

[Page 280]

Memories of the Not Too Distant Past

by Yosef Aryeh Herbst, Argentina

There was once a Jewish life full of substance and beauty! I say this not only out of a romantic longing for the past, as often happens with people who start to look closely at bygone days, but in light of life today. An objective comparison with the springtime of our life can elevate the past immensely. Our parents, their everyday lives, their Shabbat and holiday practices, their humbleness and charitable deeds, also become idealized. Then you are captivated by your memories of them and begin to understand the beauty of their way of life, their refinement, and their Jewishness.

Yes, my friends, it is more than a romanticization of bygone days. It is only a sober evaluation of a vanished period, in the perspective of time, with the understanding gained by years of experience and through the lens of current reality.

* * *

My father, Shmuel Herbst (may his memory be for a blessing) was a fine person, an enthusiastic member of Radzin Hasidism, an ecstatic prayer leader, whose prayer melodies were renowned. My mother, Toybe (may her memory be for a blessing), was a righteous woman, who was well known in the town as a very smart person. She was a truly capable and industrious wife, who saw to all our household needs.[1] She was modest, extremely pious, and did not miss a single daily prayer.

As mentioned above, my father was a Radzin Hasid, and one of the rebbe's most eminent followers. Following custom, he would travel to Warsaw to celebrate the High Holidays with the rebbe.

[Page 281]

One year, my father was ailing, the result of an accident that he had suffered. As if that wasn't enough, his income was low as well.

As usual, he traveled to Warsaw to see the rebbe, Rabbi Mordkhe Yosef Eliezer (may his righteous memory be for a blessing). Apparently, the rebbe knew about the condition of his health and poor economic situation. However, my father did not want to disclose this. When the rebbe asked, "Are you making a living?" my father replied, "Living comfortably."[2] He was always careful to paper everything over and present a happy face.

The rebbe then told him to go to Otwock for a rest cure and not to pray, for the sake of his health. However, he could not forgo praying, as he would pour his heart and soul into the practice, and was renowned for this.[3]

When my father stopped travelling to the rebbe because of his deteriorating health, the rebbe would ask his other Horodlo followers how Shmuel of Horodlo was doing, with his "living comfortably," and the phrase became popular in Hasidic circles.

* * *

My father would always chant the Akdamut prayer in a special melody, rather than in the traditional recitation style.[4] The memory of his melody still evokes sweet memories.

When he was sick, and not allowed to chant, his hasidic enthusiasm induced him to pray and chant. He very much wanted to do so, but Shmuel Biderman told him, "Uncle, didn't the rebbe tell you not to pray and chant?" Father was such a fervent hasid that he ignored Shmuel. So Shmuel pressured him more strongly and did not let him pray,

[Page 282]

out of concern for his health. Father was annoyed, but was later appeased by Shmuel, during the Kiddush.[5]

* * *

In the afternoon of Simchat Torah, after the service, the Hasids would visit each other's home, eat and drink, and celebrate.

One year, Father was tired, and lay down for a nap. The Hasids came in and hauled him out in his underwear to Leybl Zavidovich's home. The party lasted until the evening, which would end with a chant of *Chasal Siddur Pesach*, linking two mitzvahs: the High Holidays with Pesach[6], as was customary in our synagogue.

* * *

Our synagogue had a "Throne of Elijah."[7] The custom was that every male Jewish newborn was circumcised in the synagogue, and the sandek would sit on the "throne." During World War I, the custom was canceled out of fear.

When my son Mordkhe was born (the Yiddish translator of this [original printed edition] book), Moyshe Tversky, the Rebbe of Turiisk (may his righteous memory be for a blessing), was visiting Horodlo from Lublin. Rabbi Moyshe-Leyb Ha-Levy Berman (may his righteous memory be for a blessing) who could serve as mohel and sandek, handed the role of sandek over to Rebbe Tversky.[8]

When I went to the rebbe, to invite him to the circumcision and give him the honor of being the sandek, he ordered me to refurbish the synagogue's "Throne of Elijah," as was customary. I followed his order. The traditional town custom was revived on the first day of the Hebrew calendar month of Tammuz.

* * *

Woe is me! I am writing down reminiscences of the lovely bygone days that were so cruelly obliterated, and my Mordkhe is translating a Horodlo memorial book…

Translator's Footnotes:

1. This is a reference to Proverbs 31, which enumerates the qualities of a capable wife, and is chanted by the husband before the Friday night meal.

2. The response is an adaptation of a quote from Psalms 119:45.

3. Otwock was famous as a health resort.

4. The Akdamut is an important liturgical poem (piyyut) of the 11th century, recited on the Jewish holiday of Shavuot by Ashkenazi Jews.

5. Kiddush literally, "sanctification", is a blessing recited over wine or grape juice to sanctify the Shabbat and Jewish holidays.

6. Said at the end of the Seder, the prayer translates as "The Pesach (Passover) service is finished, as it was meant to be performed, in accordance with all its rules and laws."

7. Synagogues designate a special chair for Elijah the Prophet at every circumcision. Some have the custom that the sandek, the one holding the child on his lap during the circumcision, sits on this chair.

8. A mohel is a person who performs the brit milah, the ritual circumcision. The sandek (Hebrew: "companion of child") is a person honored either by holding the baby boy on the knees or thighs while the mohel performs the brit milah, or by handing the baby to the mohel.

[Page 283]

A Memorial Dedicated to My Family

by Rokhl Zuberman Bergman, Argentina

I would like to offer reminiscences of my early childhood, and of my grandfather Yoel-Itshe Zuberman, his sons, daughters, daughters-in-law, sons-in-law, and grandchildren.

I was four years old. My grandfather Yoel-Itshe and grandmother Chane-Reyzl lived in a large, comfortable house in Łuszków. They had granaries. Grandfather owned many fields but did not work in them. He was busy in the nearby forests, and would come home only for Shabbat.

When Grandfather came home, we, all the grandchildren, gathered around him joyfully. He would pinch our cheeks and joke with us. On Shabbat, he studied Torah all day. He was a scholar, as well as a kind person; Grandmother was also a loving mother to everyone. They had ten children, five sons and five daughters. The sound of studies was constantly heard in that home. They hired the best melameds [Hebrew teachers for children] as well as teachers of secular subjects. All the children and the aunts were good students. The home was steeped in scholarship. Grandfather and the boys were Radzin Hasids, except for Uncle Yoske, who was a Turiisk Hasid.

Aunt Chaya was the oldest of the children. She and her family first lived in Wieslowicz, and later in Chelm. She had five children, one of whom is alive, in North America. The rest were killed by the murderers.

Yoske was the second: Uncle Yosef Zuberman. His wife, Rivtshe, was the daughter of Dovid Note, Moyshe's son. They had seven children, of which only

[Page 284]

one, Moyshe, is alive and lives in Israel. One granddaughter, Shoshana, survived and lives in Israel.

Uncle Yoske would sit in the shop and study by candlelight. He seemed to resent it when clients came in and disturbed his studies.

All the children were diligent students of religious topics, and were also familiar with world literature.

Uncle Yankl and his wife Chaya-Sore lived in Horodlo, with their nine children. Uncle Yankl, too, devoted his free time to studying sacred books, but he was actually short of spare time. They had a wide range of business, and were constantly busy, taking care of family members who were needy as well as of strangers. They raised good children, all of whom were scholars. Almost all were murdered in Ludmir; the only survivors were two sons and one daughter.

Next in age was Aunt Maradl. She was married to Yoel; they had five sons, daughters, sons-in-law, and grandchildren. All were murdered in Ludmir by the Nazi butchers.

My parents lived in Horodlo. My memorable father Hershke-Tzvi (may he rest in peace) devoted much of his time to studying Torah. I can still hear his beautiful chant. He was a dear, sincere man, like my unforgettable mother, Beyle. She was a Ludmir native, the daughter of Dovid Shreiber. My two brothers, Henekh and Moyshe, were both very learned. My remarkable, brilliant brother Henekh was also familiar with secular literature. His house was full of bookshelves. His wife, my sister-in-law Chane, was the daughter of a rabbi. They had two young boys, Dovid and Yankele.

My youngest brother, Moyshe, was also a fine, intelligent young man, and a good student. Their tender lives were cut short in Ludmir.

[Page 285]

My aunt, Foygl-Feyge, her husband Shmuel, and their five children – boys and girls – were all murdered.

Aunt Chame, her husband Fishl, and their three children lived in Chelm. All were murdered.

Our aunt Esther was the youngest of this large, beautiful family. She lived in Ustyluh, with her husband and two children. None survived.

Aunt Miriam, Uncle Moyshe's wife, survived, along with her children. They are living in Israel and America.

It was a family of scholars, pious Jews, who fulfilled the phrase "Torah and merchandise."[1]

Translator's Footnote:

1. The phrase is derived from *Midrash Tanchuma*, a 9[h-]century Midrash on the five books of the Torah. One of its verses praises the virtues of Torah over the value of merchandise.

[Page 286]

An Ashkenazi Jewish Family

by Hirsh Zuberman, Argentina

My grandfather (may he rest in peace), Yoel Yitzchok Zuberman, was born sometime around 1855, in the village of Łuszków, four kilometers from Horodlo.

As the only son of my great-grandfather, he was raised as a very pious Hasid. After his marriage to a woman of the Radzin Rebbe's family, from Chelm, he left for two years of religious studies with the 'Orchos Chaim' (may his righteous memory be for a blessing).[1]

Shortly after the death of my great-grandfather, his oldest son was born and named after this ancestor, Dovid Yosef Zuberman (may he rest in peace). He was followed by a daughter, Fradl, my father Yankev (may he rest in peace), a daughter (Chaya), another son, Tzvi (the father of a daughter, Rokhl, who is living in Buenos Aires), a daughter, Nechama (may she rest in peace), son Moyshe Aaron, and daughters Feyge and Esther (may they rest in peace).

The children were raised in the village, completely surrounded by Ukrainian Gentiles, and were busy with studies and prayer. Even Fradl, the daughter, would participate in the discussions on a difficult issue in the Mishna.

The oldest son was married in Horodlo. My father and mother (she was from Grabowiec) continued to live in Łuszków, as did Fradl.

My grandfather, one of the most renowned mohels in the region, circumcised his own grandsons. Two of his daughters were married in Chelm. Feyge, who was born in Horodlo, also continued to live in our village, as did his son, Tzvi, from Ludmir. Moyshe was married in Wieslowic. Incidentally,

[Page 287]

he was the only one to be conscripted into the Russian army, and was taken prisoner by the Hungarians.

All began to have children. Thus, my mother, in the village, gave birth to six sons and two daughters.

Grandfather led the prayers beautifully. He had his own minyan, at the home of his son, Tzvi.[2] They celebrated the High Holidays at the nearby town of Ustyluh.

I was barely four years old then, yet I remember – as though it was today – the joyous Saturday evening gatherings at my grandfather's house. Each son and son-in-law honored Grandfather with a song. We, the grandchildren, played and danced in the dark, until there was a rap at the window. It was the Gentiles, letting us know that stars were visible overhead, so that my father could open up the shop and sell them kerosene.

Grandfather was highly respected by all the Gentiles of the village, and even by the authorities. They valued him so much that he was once able to refuse taking an oath in court, and was relieved of that duty.

And so we lived, near each other, until the disaster of 1914. The retreating Russians set the village on fire. We had to find a new home, and initially moved to another village before settling in the town of Horodlo.

There, we shared in all the misfortunes and joys of the town. We provided the town with prayer-leaders, Torah readers, mohels, Bible experts, and scholars in general. At the end of the war, when my brothers, cousins, and many young people began to leave the benches of religious scholars in the synagogue and the House of Study and devoted themselves to Zionism, Hebrew, and settlement in the Land of Israel, we –

Zubermans, Goldbergs, Lerners, Zavidoviches, Herbsts, Stavs, Bidermans, Bermans – as well as many others, constituted the so-called intellectuals of the town.

Oh, life was truly lovely!

[Page 288]

Thousands of families like ours, Ashkenazis as well as Sefardis, were murdered at the despicable hands of our foes, the Germans. Let our people never forget these martyrs! Their shining memory will illuminate our paths as long as we live! And the enemy will never be forgotten, the subject of mockery, condemnation, and revenge!

Translator's Footnotes:

1. Rabbinical authors were often known by the titles of their books. I was not able to identify the 19th-century author of a book with this title.

2. The minyan is the traditional quorum of ten Jewish men required to recite certain prayers.

[Page 289]

Memorial

In the Holy City of Jerusalem To the Horodlo Jewish Community

[Page 290]

[Blank]

[Page 291]

[Text on image of Memorial]

In Memory of the Horodlo Jewish Community
(Hrubieszow County, Poland)

May God remember the
Horodlo Jewish community
And its members, and may He take revenge for the blood
Of our dear brothers and sisters
Who were exterminated together with their leader, the Rabbi,
Author of *Tiferes-Bonim* and *Chok Moyshe*,
By the Germans and their lackeys, may their memory be blotted out, in the destruction
Of the Jews of Europe during World War Two.
Their precious, pure memory will always be with us,
The memorializers.
Natives of Horodlo in Israel and the Diaspora.

Memorial on Mt. Zion in the Holy City of Jerusalem to the Horodlo Jewish Community

[Page 292]

Memorial to the Horodlo Jewish Community,
on Mount Zion, in the Holy City of Jerusalem

By Yosef Chaim Zavidovich, Israel

In [the Hebrew month of] Iyar, 1957,[1] a delegation of Zionist activists from the United States came to Israel. Among them was Henech Berman, the son of the Rabbi of Horodlo, the great Rabbi Moyshe HaLevi (may his righteous memory be for a blessing). The delegation members visited many historical sites; they also climbed Mount Zion in the holy city of Jerusalem.

The members first walked around the hill, which is rich in historical memories of the great history of the Jewish people. They immersed themselves in the beautiful location and the clear air, and its associations with the reign of King David and the heroism of Jewish leaders in ancient times, as well as the bravery of present-day Jewish fighters in Israel's War of Liberation. Then they went down into the cellar space that houses the Chamber of the Holocaust.[2] In profound sorrow and pain, they inspected documents concerning the catastrophic destruction of the Jews of Poland and other countries of Europe. The document fragments were collected in the death camps of Poland and Germany, and brought to Mt. Zion.

Trembling with emotion, the members of the delegation studied the searing documents and the stone plaques set into the cellar walls. These memorial inscriptions tell the story of the Jewish communities destroyed by the German murderers and their partners, and bear witness to the suffering of the Jews of Europe, who were killed by their foe.

That is when Henech Berman decided to create a memorial to

[Page 293]

the Jewish community of Horodlo, in the sacred location where the Jewish prophets walked, as well as Jewish kings – chief among them King David – and where Jewish heroes defended Jerusalem in ancient times, as they did during Israel's recent War of Liberation.

Henech Berman being greeted by Yitzchak Ben-Zvi, President of Israel

When Henech Berman returned from his trip to Israel, he told me of his desire to create a memorial to the Horodlo Jewish community in the Chamber of the Holocaust. Both of us went to Jerusalem, where we met with representatives of Israel's Ministry of Religions, which oversees Mount Zion; they agreed to our plan to set up a memorial plaque.

That same day, we brought an expert stone engraver to Mount Zion. After the Mount Zion authorities and

[Page 294]

those in charge of the museum identified a location for the projected plaque, and gave us the project instructions, we gave the artisan the text to be engraved on the memorial.

After he had finished his work and set the stone plaque into the wall of the Chamber, near the memorials to other communities, we, a group of Horodlo natives (including Henech Berman), traveled to the holy city of Jerusalem on April 4, 1957. We climbed Mount Zion and went to the Chamber of the Holocaust to pay our respects to the memory of the Jews of Horodlo and all the martyrs of Europe's Jewish communities.

We directed our glance towards King David's Old City, now in enemy hands, towards the Temple Mount, the site of our destroyed Temple, and towards Mount Scopus.[3] We looked at the Old City wall, and were reminded of the ancient Jewish fortresses and the heroes who defended them. Imbued with the sanctity of the site and the memories of our great Jewish history – memories of the period when the kings of Judah reigned, and the bygone days of glory, with the prophets and the visionaries – we made our way to the Chamber of the Holocaust. Overcome by sorrow and pain, we studied the evidence of the tragic destruction, the collection of the remnants of murder and torture: sacred Torah scrolls steeped in the blood of sacred martyrs, scraps of Torah scroll parchment desecrated by the grisly enemy, tear-soaked sacred books, and boxes with the ashes of our martyrs, who were incinerated in the crematoriums of the abominable Nazis.

We stood there in silence, shivering as we read the words engraved on the Horodlo memorial plaque. We became one with the sacred memory of the Horodlo martyrs and the entire Jewish population that was martyred.

* * *

As the cantor led the memorial service for the Jewish martyrs of Horodlo, next to the final resting place of King David of Israel, he began to chant,

[Page 295]

loudly and clearly, the El Malei Rachamim prayer.[4] When he mentioned the martyrs of Horodlo, we felt that his prayer was becoming part of the prayers of Jewish martyrs and heroes throughout history, prayers that were hovering, shrouded in mystery, throughout the holy city of Jerusalem.

[Page 296]

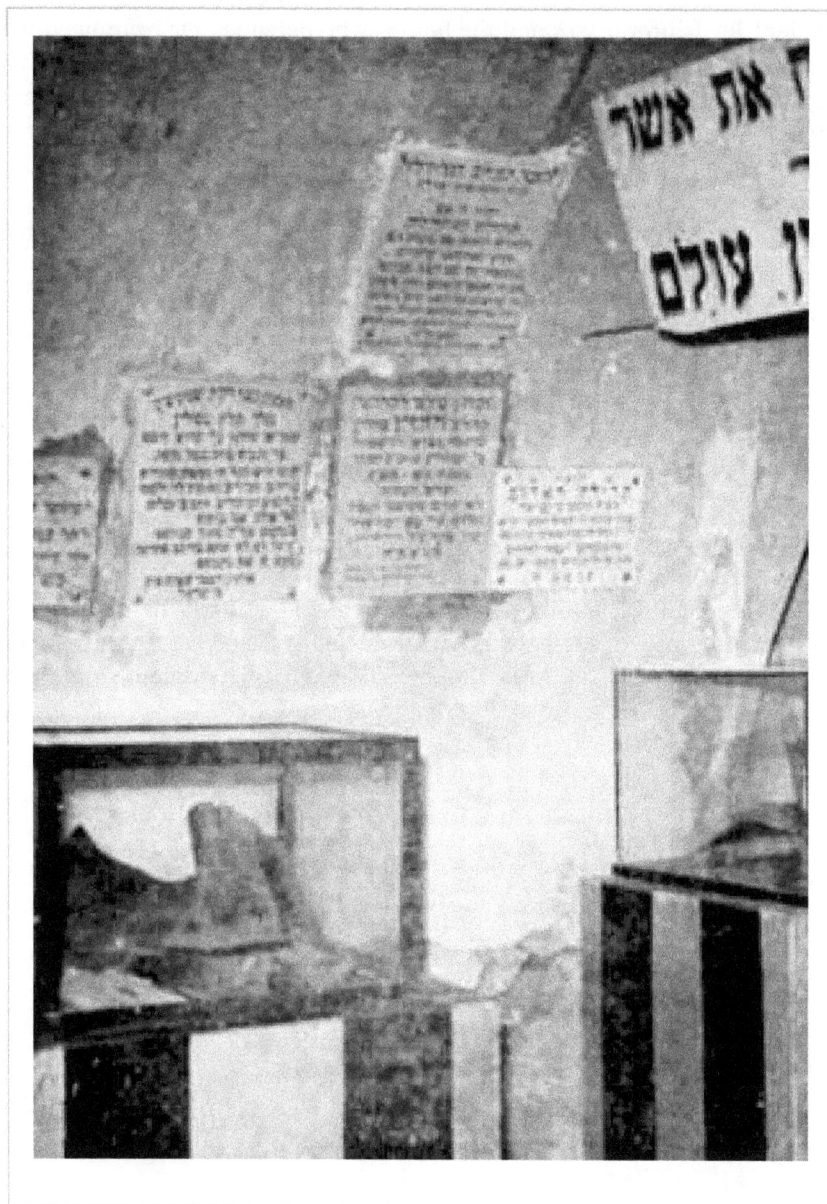

The memorial plaque to the Horodlo martyrs
(top row, left) among the memorials to Jewish communities in the
Chamber of the Holocaust,
on Mount Zion in the holy city of Jerusalem

Translator's Footnotes:

1. The Jewish month of Iyar usually coincides with April-May.

2. The small "Chamber of the Holocaust" (Hebrew "Cellar of the Catastrophe"), Israel's first Holocaust museum, was established in 1949.

3. During the years 1948-1967, all of these sites were held by the Kingdom of Jordan, and entry by Jews was prohibited.

4. Tradition locates the tomb of the biblical King David on Mount Zion, adjoining the Chamber of the Holocaust. The El Malei Rachamim prayer is a plea that the soul of the departed be granted proper rest.

[Page 297]

In Rhyme

[Page 298]

[Blank]

[Page 299]

"A Tragic Story"

by Fradl Shiffer (Perlmutter), Canada[1]

I will sing you a tragic song --
My heart feels like a stone.
Let the whole world ring
With the tale of the murderers who let us die.

When the Germans arrived --
No one could know
How they took our lives
And slaughtered us in the streets for no reason.

They wrapped our hands in white rags,
And our faces burned with shame.
Our mothers and fathers wore these
So that the killers would recognize them.

The killers spent days thinking
About how to deal with the Jews.
They made "ghettos" for us
So we would starve to death.

They imprisoned men in camps,
Tormented them with hunger,
Torture and blows,
Until dark death arrived.

[Page 300]

They did even more to us,
Ordered us to leave our homes,
And took us to *Miączyn*.
Woe is us! Terrible things happened to us there!

They separated us from our parents,
And we saw it all.
As we watched, almost half of us were killed.
We were silent, gnashing our teeth.

A dreadful train soon came.
"Why did this happen to us?"

They loaded mothers and children,
And the train started to move.

Oy, woe is my life!
I remained, forlorn, like a stone.
I couldn't believe
That I would never see Mama again.

Now we are alone, desolate,
No Papa, no Mama, no home;
We were forced into hard labor,
Exhausted until we couldn't move.

A star fell from heaven
And stained the earth…
Gone is the crown of Jewish daughters,
Our beautiful ornament.

And after the hard labor – what?
The murderers ordered us to be shot.

[Page 301]

Their bandits obeyed
And shed that young blood.

God! It's time you accepted our tears.
Our hardship and our suffering!
No one else wants to hear us out.
"When, when will salvation come?"

I wept a river of tears
And God helped me in my need:
Bodniewski, the Gentile, took me in
And saved me from a terrible death.

[Page 302]

A Plea in the Pit

by Fradl Shiffer (Perlmutter), Canada

Oy, wake up, my pious Mama,
And pay close attention.
See the oceans red with Jewish blood
Quick, pray for your only child.

The world is so beautiful,
And I can't enjoy it.
I lie concealed, all alone,
Woe is me.

Take my tears
And run to beg God
Not to lose my suffering,
To accept my plea.

Wake up, my little brothers,
Enough of your silence.
Make great noise,
So that our blood will not rest.

It's time to take up arms
And rush to battle!
Erase all of Germany;
I want to live to see revenge.

[Page 303]

I Long for My Home

by Fradl Shiffer (Perlmutter), Canada

When the Germans arrived
They immediately killed us.
I had to go to Russia
And, so young, leave Mama.

I thought it was a joke,
Abandoned my sweet home,
Not knowing the years would pass
And I would not be able to see Mama.

I received sad letters
Reporting that they were being tortured;
She was lying hidden in the house with the children,
And her life was so hard.

When there was peace in the world
And I lived at home,
Time went by like a dream,
But I cannot forget.

I also remember my little town,
My hometown -- so beautiful!
I long for my Mama.
How can I witness it all?

[Page 304]

And I stand by the water,
The border, the River Bug.

Let me go home to Horodlo.
Let this be enough!

The war made everything so bad.
Our sun has set.
I'm searching so hard for bygone times,
But I can never find them.

Translator's Footnote:

1. Pages 299-304 are tributes written in verse about the catastrophe and its victims. The translation is literal and I have not reproduced the rhymes.

[Page 305]

[Blank]

List of Horodlo Martyrs

[Page 306]

[Page 307]

List of Horodlo Jews

Men, women, and children, who were murdered by the Nazi Germans and their accomplices (may their names be blotted out) in the catastrophe that befell the Jews of Europe during World War II.

A א

Ayzen, Pinches, wife Chana, and two children: Elkanah and Yoysef.
Ayzen, Pesheh.
Ornshteyn, Ayzik, and wife Royzeh.
Ayzik, Leybush, wife Malke, and children: Brocheh, Feygeh, and Meir.
Ornshteyn, Mindl.
Ornshteyn, Yoysef.
Ornshteyn, Rochl.
Ornshteyn, Shmuel.
Ornshteyn, Yitzchok.
Ornshteyn, Mates.
Ayzen, Chana, and two children.
Ayzen, Shloymeh, wife Hindeh, and children.
Ayzen, Toybeh, and three children.

B ב

Blat, Ptachyeh, wife Rachil, and daughters Brocheh and Chana-Tcharneh.
Berger, Pinches, wife Esther, and children Binyomin and Masheh.
Berger, Moysheh, wife Soreh, and six children.
Brenner, Avrom, and wife Sheva.
Bobes, Moysheh, wife Bobeh, their daughter and son-in-law, and his son Shmuel.
Blum, Yitzchok, wife Leya, and children: Malkeh, Rochl, Elimeylech, and Moysheh.
Blay, Fishl, and wife Soreh.

[Page 308]

Blat, Ahron, and wife Bluma.
Bergman, Yoysef, wife Soreh, and four children: Moysheh-Chayim, Shmuel, Chaykeh, and Dina.
Berger, Rochl, and four children.
Berger, Ahron-Asher, wife Tzirl, and son.
Berger, Yehoshua.
Barnholtz, Dina, the daughter of Shloymeh.
Bloch, Yisro'el, wife Rasheh, and three children.
Berman, Shmuel, wife Soreh, and three children: Mordcheh, Yoysef Elozer, Dovid, and Tzvi-

Hirsh.
Rabbi Moysheh-Leyb Berman (town Rabbi), and wife Rivka.
Boymeyl, Moysheh, wife Feygeh, and family, and grandchildren Soreh and Yitzchok.
Berger, Yechiel, wife Sheveh, and children.
Berger, Yechiel, wife Dishkeh, and children.
Berger, Borekh Yankev, wife Bluma, and five children.
Barili, Esther.
Barili, Toybeh.
Blat, Shloymeh, and family.

G ג

Gertel, Mordcheh, and wife Rivka.
Goldberg, Leybush, and wife Nechomeh.
Groysburd, Dov, wife Tehila, and two children.
Groysburd, Moysheh, wife Chana, and two children.
Groysburd Tzvi, wife Chana, and two children.
Goldenberg, Moysheh, wife Reyzl, and six children.
Goldenberg, Eliezer, wife Malkeh, and two children.
Goldberg, Shimen.
Goldberg, Shmuel, and wife Feygeh.
Goldberg, Bluma.
Goldberg, Toybeh.

[Page 309]

Goldberg, Shmuel, wife Feygeh, son Shmuel, and daughters Bluma and Toybeh.
Gruber, Yoel, wife Miriam, and children.
Gruber, Yitzchok, and wife Chaya.
Gruber, Dovid.
Gruber, Yankev.

D ד

Druker, Soreh.
Datelgeld, Freydeh.
Datelgeld, Meir, wife, and two children.
Datelgeld, Rochl.

H ה

Hak, Moysheh, wife Pesheh, and two children.
Hendl, Ben-Tziyon.
Hirsh, Chayim, wife Hinde, and three children.
Herbst, Mendl, wife, and two children: Leyb and her daughter.
Harbst, Toybeh.
Hekht, Gitl Royzeh, and two children: Bluma and Yisro'el.
Halperin, Elozer, wife Sheveh; their son Moysheh, his wife Nechomeh and son Avrom with wife Beyleh, daughter Tcharneh, and grandson Itcheh.
Halperin, Mendl, wife Freydeh.
Hecht, Yoysef, wife Hindeh, and sons Shloymeh and Leyb.
Harfin, Shmuel.
Harfin, Feyeh, and son Moysheh.
Mordechai Sherer, son-in-law of Shmuel Herbst.

V ו

Vayntroyb, Avrom, wife Soreh, and children: Dovid, Mindl, Gedalyahu, and Shulamis.

[Page 310]

Vayntroyb, Dovid, wife Rivka, and two children.
Vogshal, Avrom (son of Moysheh).
Varman, Yisro'el, wife, and child.
Varman, Pintcheh, and wife.
Vaynroyb, Shmuel, wife Feygeh, and three children.
Vayntroyb, Chayim Me'ir, wife Leya, and children: Beyleh, Zlateh, Reuven, Rochl, Yitzchok, Soreh.
Vayntroyb, Shmuel.
Vayntroyb, Moysheh, and wife Chana.
Vinrzh, Tzvi, and family.
Vinrzh, Malkeh.
Vayntroyb, Dovid, wife Rivka.
Vinrzh, Avrom, wife Leya, and three children.
Vayntroyb, Shmuel, wife Chana.
Volach, Moysheh Mendl, and wife Chaya Sheyndl.
Volach, Rochl, husband, and three children.
Volach, Esther, husband, and two children.
Volach, Malkeh, and husband.

Z ז

Zuberman, Yoel Yitzchok, and wife Chana.

Zuberman, Yankev, wife Soreh, and son Yitzchok.

Zuberman, Moysheh, wife Yocheved, and children: Ahron, Rivka, Chaya.

Zuberman, Shmuel, and son Chayim Muni.

Zuberman, Beyleh, and son Moysheh.

Zuberman, Henech, wife Chana, and children Dovid and Yankev.

Zisberg, Yehoshua, wife Feygeh, and two children.

Zayf, Zelik.

Zisberg, Shloymeh, and wife Mirl.

Zaydl, Avrom, wife Reyzl, and daughter Brayne.

Zayf, Avrom Ahron.

Zayf, Yoysef, wife Chaya, and two children.

Zilberberg, Moysheh-Mikhoel, and wife Necheh.

[Page 311]

Zis, Dovid, wife Leya, and children Meyer and Bluma.

Zavidovitch, Perl.

Zavidovitch, Moysheh, wife Broche, and daughter Rivka.

Zavidovitch, Yekutiel.

Zisberg, Moshe, son of Shloymeh and Tzirl.

Zisberg, Chaya, daughter of Shloymeh and Tzirl, husband and baby.

Zaltzman, Etl, and son Tzvi.

Zuberman, Dovid-Yoysef, wife Rivka, and son Shimen.

Zuberman, Ben-Tziyon, wife Chaya, and two children, Dina and Chana.

Zuberman, Tzvi, wife Mechleh, and two children.

Rabbi Zisberg, Shmuel, and wife Bluma.

Zaydl, Rivka, and four children.

Zisberg, Malka, and two children.

Zis, Yankev (Yankl), wife Basha, and son Me'ir.

Zilber, Yechiel, and five children.

Zaydl, Tzvi, wife Gitl, and daughter.

Zaydl, Avrom, wife Henya, and daughter.

Zavidovitch Zisl, wife of Leybl Zavidovitch (daughter of Rabbi Yekutiel).

Zavidovitch, Yekutiel, and wife.

Zavidovitch, Fishl, and family.

Zavidovitch, Mordcheh, wife Malka, and two daughters.

Zavidovitch, Malka,, husband Avner Tzuker, and sons.

Zavidovitch, Yoysef, wife Rochl, and daughter (in Ludmir).

T ט

Trach, Yechezkel.
Tzukerman, Toybeh.
Tenenboym, Etl.
Tchesner, Yankev (the ritual slaughterer) and wife Miriam.
Tenenboym, Moysheh, wife Chana, and three children.
Tenenboym, Dov, and three children.
Tayershteyn, Soreh-Mindl, husband, and three children.

[Page 312]

Y י

Yank, Malkeh.
Yank, Zeldeh.
Yung, Tzvi.

Ch כ

Katzhendl, Chaya, and three children: Sonia, Rochl, and a son.

L ל

Lerner, Mendl, wife Soreh, and five children.
Link, Lipe, wife Esther, and children.
Lerner, Dovid, and wife Feygeh.
Lerner, Yitzchok, wife Sheyndl, and son Eliezer.
Link, Yankev, son of Tzvi.
Link, Rivka, daughter of Tzvi.
Link, Yitzchok.

M מ

Mernshteyn, Chayim-Leyb, daughter Feygeh and son Nosn.
Mernshteyn, Yitzchok, wife Vitl, and children Soreh-Rivka, Eydl, and Yankev.
Massmit, Chayim, wife Hinde, and children.
Massmit, Shmuel, wife Mirl, and two children, Avrom and Rivka.
Mastenboym, Tzaytl, and daughter Dvoyre.

Massmit, Shloymeh Todres, and wife Simeh.
Mastenboym, Chayim, and family.
Mederdrut, Gitl, and her two children.
Maynhaym, Motl, and wife Noneh.
Mlinek, and wife Mindl.

[Page 313]

Mlinek, Dov (the Rabbi's son-in-law), wife Fradl (the Rabbi's daughter), and children.
Mabeh, Tzvi, wife Fradl, and two children.
Mabeh, Pesl.
Mederdrut, Avrom, wife Chana, and three children.

N נ

Nayman, Bluma, and two children.
Rabbi Naftuleh Ebershtark (the Rabbi's son-in-law), wife Rochl, and daughter Feygele.

S ס

Stav, Chana (Eliyohu's daughter), and husband.
Stav, Bluma.
Stav, Dov, and daughter.
Saller, Yitzchok, wife Chasheh, and three children.
Soyfer, Yisro'el, wife Soreh, and six children.
Soyfer, Shloymeh, wife Nechomeh, and two children.
Stav, Yehuda-Aryeh.

E ע

Enk, Tuviya, wife Leya, and two children.
Ehrlich, Rivka.
Ehrlich, Royzeh.
Ehrlich, Pesl.

F פ

Feder, Aaron-Chayim, and wife Soreh.
Fayl, Yitzchok, wife Elkeh, and son Shimshen.
Fayder, Mirl (Kopel's daughter).

[Page 314]

Fayl, Avrom, wife Perl, and daughters Rivka and Toybeh.
Fayl, Soreh, Tzvi's wife.
Fayl, Tzipeh, and two children.
Fayl, Gitl, and two children.
Fayl, Moyshe, wife, and two children.
Flaks, Moysheh, wife Soreh, and three children.
Fraynd, Tzvi, wife Chaya-Feygeh, and four children.
Perlmutter, Chaya, and children: Moysheh-Yitzchok, Mordcheh, Yoysef-Elozer, Yekutiel, and Brocheh-Tsirl.
Fivisheche, Batsheva, and son Gershon Henech.
Flax, Pinches, and family.
Fraynd, Yitzchok, wife Ada, and daughter.
Fraynd, Dovid, wife Chaneh, and two children.
Fayl, Avrom, wife Henya, and two children.
Fayl, Shimshen, wife, and two children.
Fraynd, Tzipeh.
Fraynd, Zlateh.
Flaks, Yitzchok, wife Chaya, and four children.

Tz צ

Tzigl, Yankev, wife Etl, and two children.enya.
Tzigl, Avrom, wife Chaya, and children Soreh and Henya.
Tzigl, Chayim, wife Dina.
Tzung, Efrayim, wife Rochl.
Tzimerman, Mordcheh.
Tzung, Avrom, and wife Malka.
Tzung, Shmuel.
Tzuker, Chayim-Dovid, wife Rasheh, and children.
Tzukerman, Toybeh.

K ק

Klayner, Avrom.
Kremerman, Yehoshua, and wife.

[Page 315]

Krayner, Avrom.
Krayner, Chanina.
Hen
Kupershtok, Yehoshua, and sons Efrayim and Eliyohu.
Keller, Shloymeh, and family.
Kenol, Golda, and family.
Kulish, Chaya.

R ר

Rozenfeld, Shmuel, wife Raysheh, and seven children.
Rayf, Dovid.
Rozenblum, Shmuel, wife Soreh Mindl, and daughters Sheyndl, Chana, and Fradl.
Rozenblum, Yitzchok, and wife Chideh.
Rozenfeld, Eliyohu, wife Soreh, and five children.
Rozenfeld, Zalmen, and five children.
Rozenblum, Yoysef, and family.
Royter, Rochl.
Rozenberg, Yankev, wife Feygeh, and children.
Rozenfeld, Ahron, wife Frumet, and two children.
Rubinshteyn, Simcheh, wife Bluma, and four children: Ruzhka, Zanvl, Esther, and Dina.

Sh ש

Sher, Efroyim, wife Chaykeh.
Shruver, Feygeh-Beyleh.
Shechter, Mendl, wife Itteh, and children.
Shnayder, Yisro'el.
Shek, Itteh-Leya.
Shek, Dov, and wife Feygeh.
Rabbi Shek, Hillel.
Shmidt, Borekh, wife Beyleh-Brocheh, their daughter and son-in-law.
Shmidt, Chava.
Sher, Nosn, wife Pesheh.

[Page 316]

Shek, Yankev, wife Elkeh, and four children.
Shtayn, Yankev-Henech, and wife Rivka.
Shek, Alter, wife Tzipeh, and daughter Babeh.
Shafir, Reyzl.
Shturm, Bluma, and daughter Chana.
Sherer, Mordcheh, wife Miriam, and three children.
Shek, Avrom, wife Gitl, and five children.
Shvartz, Yitzchok, wife Keyleh, and three children.
Shruver, Noteh, wife Perl, their children, and Noteh's sister.
Shek, Fishl, and wife Soreh.
Shek, Henech, wife Matl, and three children.
Shechter, Dovid, wife Mindl, and two children.
Shlachter, Efroyim, wife Malkeh, and children Kalmen and Soreh.
Shek, Yankev (Shabseh's son), wife Elkeh, and four children.
Shek, Yankev (Moyshe's son), wife Chaya, and children.
Shnurmacher, Leybish, wife Chameh, and daughter Rivka.
Shayer, Mordcheh, wife Miriam, and daughter Freydeh.
Shek, Efroyim Eliyohu, and wife Fradl.
Shteyn, Dovid.
Shteyn, Dov.

[Page 317]

List of the Martyrs of Stryszow, Slaughtered by the Nazi Murderers

(Strzyżów, Poland)

50°51' 24°02'

A א

Ornshteyn, Yitzchok (Itche), wife Leya, and children Rivka, Yehudis, Dvoyreh, and Dovid.
Ornshteyn, Soreh (Yitzchok's mother).
Ornshteyn Ze'ev (Velvl).
Ornshteyn, Reyzl.
Ornshteyn, Toybeh, and children Yoysef and Yisro'el.
Urgan, Elozer, and children.
Ayzen, Dovid, wife Chana, and children Yisro'el and Rivka.

B ב

Boyer, Leybish, and wife Feyga.
Boyer, Shloymeh, his wife and child.
Boym, Simche, wife Brayndl, and son.

G ג

Gruber, Yehoshua.
Gontcher, Gitl, and mother.
Gontcher, Bluma.

H ה

Herbst, Leybish, wife Chana, and children Moyshe, Maleh, Ayzik.
Herbst, Itteh, and children Mendl, Krayneh, Feleh, Genendl.
Herbst, Yehoshua, wife Dobeh, and children Ayzik and Yisro'el.

[Page 318]

Y ׳

Yung, Dov (Berish), wife Chana, and child Leybish.
Yuchenzon, Lipeh, wife Brocheh, and children Yisro'el and Esther.

M מ

Milshteyn, Avrom, wife Toybeh, and children Yoysef, Eliezer, Pinches, Zalmen, and daughter.
Milshteyn, Meyer, wife Miriam, and children Toybeh and Yitzchok.
Milshteyn, Yoysef (Meyer's son), and wife.
Mural, Menachem-Mendl, wife Soreh, and children Ze'ev, Dov, and Perl.

F פ

Fuks, Ben-Tziyon, wife Chaya-Rochl, and daughter Toybeh.
Fuks, Zalmen, wife Reyzl, and children Yitzchok, Toybeh, Etl, Leya, and Shmuel.
Frayn, Tzvi Babeh, and children Chana and Sima.

K ק

Kornfeld, Chayim.
Kleynman, Yehoshua, wife Miriam, and children Yitzchok, Tzvi, Beyle, and Berl.

Sh ש

Shnol, Ze'ev (Velvl).
Shafran, Dovid, wife Chana, and two children.

[Page 319]

Supplements

[Page 320]

[Blank]

[Page 321]

Supplements

This section consists of three circular letters that were sent out to natives of Horodlo in Israel and throughout the world. We called on Horodlo natives to write impressions of the town and its residents, and to provide us with the names of Holocaust victims, as well as photos of the victims, for inclusion in this Memorial Book.

The material that the committee received was printed following the required processes of editing and correction, as needed.

The letters served as an urgent call to Horodlo natives to create the Memorial Book, as well as a request to provide us with the necessary help, and join in a common effort to publish the book.

As we completed the Memorial Book, we decided to include these circular letters in the text.

[Signed]
The Editorial Committee

[Page 322]

Committee of Natives of Horodlo (Poland)

Circular No. 1

The committee of Horodlo natives in Israel, and the committee in Buenos Aires (Argentina) have decided to establish memorial projects to commemorate the martyrs of Horodlo: our parents, sisters, and brothers, who were slaughtered by the German murderers (may their names be blotted out). One of these projects is the production of a Memorial Book, to provide a picture of Jewish life in Horodlo in the past, during the years of the recent war and the catastrophe it brought.

However, at the outset of our work we realized that we were facing a shortage of documents describing life in Horodlo, as well as pictures of people and of events, the major sources of material for this type of work. Nor did we have a list of the Jews who lived in Horodlo on the eve of the war, or information about their tragic end.

We therefore turn to all natives of Horodlo and ask them to send materials that can help to create this Memorial Book, such as letters, documents, pictures, and the like. We promise to return everything once the book has been published,

We beg you to write down your memories of the town and its Jews. Send us photos of the Rabbi, the synagogue, the House of Study, social activists, etc.

Dear brethren! Postpone your business for a few hours, and write down your memories, which will help us to create a memorial to the martyrs of Horodlo who were so tragically murdered.

Please send all materials to the following address:

S. Fraynd, Bet Ha-Po'el Ha-Mizrachi, 108 Achad-Ha-am St., Tel Aviv, Israel,

Yours sincerely,
Yoysef Zavidovitch

[Page 323]

Committee of Natives of Horodlo (Poland)

Elul, 1954

Circular No. 2

Dear Sir/Madam,

Further to our circular letter of Nissan 1954, in which we announced the resolution of the Committees of Horodlo Natives in Israel and in Argentina to publish a Memorial Book to commemorate the natives of Horodlo slaughtered by the German murderers and their collaborators (may their names be blotted out), a book that would include – among other material – a list of the Horodlo Jews who were murdered or died during the war, we are enclosing a form in which you are requested to note the names of your family members and relatives who were murdered or died during the war. Obviously, anyone who does not supply us in good time with the names of his relatives will not have these names in the book.

If you know of families that were completely blotted out, with no survivors, please include them in the list. You will be performing the sacred duty of remembering their pure souls.

Please write these details on the form in Hebrew or Yiddish, in clear handwriting, and add details to the Comments section.

Sincerely, and with good wishes for the nearing High Holy Days,

Yoysef Zavidovitch

P.S. Please send replies to Shmuel Fraynd, 108 Achad Ha-am St., Tel Aviv

[Page 324]

Committee of Natives of Horodlo (Poland)

June, 1955

Circular No. 3

Dear Sir/Madam,

In our two previous circular letters, we announced the resolution of the Horodlo Natives Committees in Israel and in Argentina to publish a Memorial Book, and requested you to send materials for inclusion in the book. Circular No. 2 enclosed forms to use for entering the names of your murdered family, friends, and neighbors, so that they can be included in the book, which will constitute a monument dedicated to the martyrs who are so dear to you and to us. However, we have to date received no material from you.

The Horodlo Committee met on May 11 to discuss publication of the book, and resolved to inform those who have not yet sent materials, that the deadline for sending materials is September 1, 1955. We cannot take responsibility for non-inclusion of their relatives' names in the Memorial Book.

We are sending you the forms once again, and ask you to fill them out and send them to us immediately, so that we can print the information in the Memorial Book.

We are also asking you to set down your memories of Horodlo and its residents, and send these to us immediately, as well as group pictures of Horodlo residents. We will return these to you after copying.

Remember! September 1 is the last date for us to received materials. Afterwards, we will not be responsible for any complaints you might have.

Sincerely,

Y. Berg	A. Kulish
M. Zuberman	S. Fraynd
A. Shmid	Y. Zavidovitch

P. S.

Please send materials to:

S. Fraynd, 108 Achad HaAm St., HaPo'el HaMizrachi, Tel-Aviv.

Y. Zavidovitch, Modi'in St., Bnei-Brak.

[Page 325]

Horodlo natives in Israel

[Page 326]

The Horodlo Committee in America

[Page 327]

Horodlo natives in Argentina

INDEX OF SURNAMES

This index contains surnames of the residents of Horodlo referenced in the text, as well as names of historic characters. Rabbis identified by forenames or town are also included in the index, as are selected individuals with unique jobs or positions making the forename identifiable.

www.ingramcontent.com/pod-product-compliance
Lightning Source LLC
Chambersburg PA
CBHW082003150426
42814CB00005BA/213